# The New Global Marketing Reality

# The New Global Marketing Reality

*Richard Brookes*

*and*

*Roger Palmer*

First published 2004 by
PALGRAVE MACMILLAN
Houndmills, Basingstoke, Hampshire RG21 6XS and
175 Fifth Avenue, New York, N.Y. 10010
Companies and representatives throughout the world

PALGRAVE MACMILLAN is the global academic imprint of the Palgrave Macmillan division of St. Martin's Press, LLC and of Palgrave Macmillan Ltd. Macmillan® is a registered trademark in the United States, United Kingdom and other countries. Palgrave is a registered trademark in the European Union and other countries.

ISBN 1–4039–0520–7

This book is printed on paper suitable for recycling and made from fully managed and sustained forest sources.

A catalogue record for this book is available from the British Library.

A catalog record for this book is available from the Library of Congress.

Editing and origination by
Curran Publishing Services, Norwich

10   9   8   7   6   5   4   3   2   1
13   12   11   10   09   08   07   06   05   04

Printed and bound in Great Britain by
Creative Print & Design (Wales), Ebbw Vale

# CONTENTS

# Contents

# LIST OF FIGURES

# LIST OF TABLES

This book is dedicated to Robert Bilton (1941–2002).
He was a colleague, a friend, and a mentor.

R.W.B.

To C.D.H. K.-J.
A truly admirable person.

R.A.P.

# ACKNOWLEDGEMENTS

The authors would like to acknowledge the work and invaluable contribution of their colleagues in the Contemporary Marketing Practice group (cmp.auckland.ac.nz). The group was founded at the University of Auckland in the mid-90s by Professor Rod Brodie, and is led by him and Professor Nicole Coviello, also at Auckland. In addition to the work being conducted at the Cranfield School of Management in the UK, international group members now include Professor Jaqueline Pels at the Universidad Torcuato Di Tella, Buenos Aires, Argentina, and Professor Wesley Johnston of the J Mack Robinson College of Business at Georgia State University, Atlanta, USA.

The work of the group has generated wide interest, with many researchers using research protocols developed by the group to extend their own work and contribute to the growing body of knowledge on contemporary marketing practices. Colleagues include Dr Ing Adam Lindgreen of the TechnischeUniversiteit Eindhoven, Dr Mairead Brady of Trinity College, Dublin and Professor Peter Danaher and Vicki Little in the Marketing Department at the University of Auckland, and many others who we hope we do not offend by not mentioning personally.

We are indebted to all our colleagues for their intellectual input, challenging ideas and suggestions. Their collegial approach makes it a pleasure to work with such an interesting and stimulating group of collaborators. At the same time as acknowledging their contribution, we also make clear our responsibility for interpreting the research in the context of this book, and for any mistakes and anomalies.

Lastly, the authors have each spent time living and working at each other's homes during the course of this work, and would like to thank Susan Brookes, who also prepared the index, and Ginnie Palmer for their good natured tolerance of our sometimes obsessive preoccupation.

Richard Brookes, Auckland
Roger Palmer, Cranfield
September 2003

## THE CHANGING NATURE OF MARKETING

Some time in the early to mid-1980s, in North America especially, the 'classical' approach to marketing management as then taught in business schools, and as practised by marketing powerhouses such as General Motors, Kodak, IBM and Procter & Gamble, began to change. This change process also spread to Europe and Asia, to include the likes of British Airways, Nokia, Philips, Unilever, Sony and Toyota. It is still going on for, just as there was no clear beginning, there appears to be no likely endgame either, where winner takes all. Winning nowadays is but transitory in any case.

For many firms caught up in the transition, recognition of their decline in fortunes has come late and acceptance of the need for change has been slow, as their market shares and financial returns inexorably dissipated in the face of unremitting pressures from without, and their shortcomings in leadership decision-making and implementation from within. What they had in common was a gradual, debilitating malaise indicating that previously successful marketing strategies and practices were no longer working. Another way of marketing – of doing business even – had somehow to be found. Overarching everything there were the unclear and unpredictable impacts of digital convergence, and everywhere the clair-voyants predicting that information technology (IT) was about to 'change everything', including marketing.

What the companies also shared was a realization that few of their stakes for greatness still really mattered: their market capitalization value, corporate growth rate and industry leadership position; their brand portfolio and loyal customer base; their manufacturing, marketing, R&D and other resources and competencies; their structures, systems, processes and controls; their mission, values and culture; and their depth of executive talent and leadership, including celebrity CEOs and Board members out of the corporate world's 'who's who'.

Companies such as GM, IBM and Unilever demonstrate that even those firms which, over the past century, became leaders in their respective industries are neither immune nor immutable. Like any other company they too can be buffeted by changing market forces, and eventually they too have to change if they want to hold on to their position – and even simply survive.

And when indomitable corporations such as GM, IBM and Unilever respond in ways – and sometimes at speeds – that seem quite contrary to previous, and successful, patterns of organizational decision-making and competitive behaviour, then there is a strong possibility that more fundamental changes are taking place in the ways that wealth-creation and market-share battles are being fought in the increasing number of mature and overcrowded markets that now characterize many advanced marketplaces.

Even though their efforts have been extensively reported, the full implications of what may appear to be seemingly isolated events are not readily apparent, probably even to those directly involved.

There has not been a cohesive, concerted movement across the spectrum of companies that make up the world's commercial base. Rather, individual firms of all sizes and from many industries have been in the vanguard. Cumulatively and collectively, they are fashioning a new way of marketing. What characterizes their new marketing is not quick-fix cost-cutting pragmatism or dramatic entrepreneurial risk-taking. Nor is it the adoption of the latest fad in strategic thinking, or following the latest breed of marketing gurus who often blur the distinction between cause and effect, and cannot seem to agree whether marketing is part of the problem or part of the solution. The reality is that there are scant examples of success or of 'rules' that work today. Not surprisingly then, most firms are finding the transition to the new marketing to be slow and painful, and their twin goals of having continuously to increase corporate and customer value metrics to be problematic and elusive. Like General Motors, trapped in the traditional ways of marketing, many appear as though they may simply be stumbling into their future.

Mostly, there has been an incremental, do-it-yourself approach to the breaking down of ingrained rules and practices and starting anew, as firms have grappled with the exigencies of recessions; deregulation; fluctuating exchange rates; waves of new global competition; maintaining output and cash flow in times of overcapacity; accelerating technological change and other discontinuities; the growing countervailing power of large retail chains and new forms of intermediaries; the splintering of mass markets and mass media; the emergence of new communication channels; and the incessant demands of increasingly disloyal customers.

In addition there are the unexpected events and crises that cause uncertainty both in markets and the investment community. These have ranged from the two oil crises in the 1970s, which began much of this transformation in business thinking and practices, to the implosion of the so-called dot-com bubble, the events and uncertainties of post-11 September 2001, and the loss of investor confidence in once-lauded corporations and their front-page executives, advisers and auditors.

There is no single or simple event or explanation to account for the changes that have been taking place. Nor can it be argued that it is only the practice of marketing that is changing. Rather, the whole process of creating and delivering value and wealth, of being more competitive – of 'doing business' – is undergoing transformation. The new marketing is just one manifestation.

## WHY ANOTHER BOOK ON MARKETING, THEN?

Marketing managers and students today will not currently find an in-depth understanding of the changing nature of marketing practices in most of their academic text-books or do-it-yourself manuals. Much of what they are now learning is likely to be irrelevant or misleading, and unlikely to be advantageous to their careers! The main reason for this is that while many of these changes have been examined at an individual incident, situation or company level, they have not been evaluated from the overall perspective and viewpoint that the practice of marketing may have fundamentally changed, though the underlying principles have remained constant.

When examined more closely, the marketing practices of today are substantially different from those practised in what might be termed the golden decades of marketing after the Second World War, when most of the major ideas, concepts, theories, models and frameworks were being defined, developed, tested and popularized. Most are still in use today. Where, then, is the evidence of this new marketing? The answer, as Zaltman (2000) puts it, lies in seeing 'relevance in seemingly distant fields'. Similarly, our argument is that individual firms are looking anywhere for new ways to sense, create and deliver value. As they do so, even if in relatively unstructured, unsystematic and 'unknowing' ways, it is possible for new concepts, theories, models and frameworks in marketing to be revealed. Our goal has been to find a pattern that might show a new way of marketing – in effect, new practical theories. This book is the result of our efforts. In it, we:

- Consider a variety of sources in order to document the changes and their impacts on marketing.
- Examine the results of an ongoing international study into the changing nature of contemporary marketing practice (CMP), and other studies of marketing practice.
- Assess their implications for managers.

- Provide guidance for those executives looking to implement internal changes that will improve their firms' sensing, creation and delivery of value. What they need to consider is whether their efforts are likely to result in the reinforcement, enhancement or transformation of their organizational status quo.
- Illustrate our ideas and comments with examples, short vignettes and longer, in-depth case studies. Some of our longer examples are drawn from the automotive industry, one of the biggest industries in the world and one that will be familiar to many readers. We do this in order to give depth to our analysis, and to avoid the temptation to use shorter vignettes which, while they might be 'interesting stories', do not necessarily constitute anything more substantial than that.

## OUR TARGET AUDIENCE

The book is a distillation of our research and studies. It is written for:

- *The busy marketing executive* trying to find new ways to create value and to be competitive. While there should be few surprises for the astute and attuned marketer, our intention is that the book will provide you with:
  - a better understanding of what is now happening 'out there'
  - a means to consider how these changes might be impacting on your specific situation, and
  - a greater confidence in reconfiguring how your firm might 'do marketing' in the future. Executives in other traditional functional areas should also find this book helpful since – even though marketing and marketers are under pressure to be more performance oriented – marketing is still 'everything' in the firm. As Piercy (1998b) says, '"going to market" is a process owned by everyone in the organization'.
- *The senior marketing student* trying to make sense of the uncertainties, complexities and paradoxes 'out there'. While it challenges many of the assumptions and prescriptions in your current textbooks, our goal is that it will better prepare you for (re)entering a marketing career in this new environment, and making a difference.
- *The marketing academics* trying to interpret and explain the changing nature of marketing theory and practice, and who are frustrated by having to differentiate the business realities of today from the theories and prescriptions of the past that are still found in many textbooks. We hope this book will encourage you to initiate your own research and

thereby add to our growing body of knowledge of contemporary marketing practices (CMP).

## HOW THIS BOOK WAS PUT TOGETHER

This book attempts to synthesize the various ways in which this new marketing is now being interpreted and practised. To understand this, a method known as discourse analysis (Fairclough, 1992, 1995) is employed. Four main sources of information have been used: the academic theory-building discourse; the business press reportage and commentary discourse; the managerial practice discourse of the middle-level executives in our CMP research programme; and finally, the 'action-learning' discourse, where theory, research results, workplace experiences and activities all come together in both our executive classrooms and our 'real-world' consulting activities. The main reason for this multi-method approach is that the changes tend to take their own meaning, relevancy and impact from within each particular discourse. For example, 'purist' academics may argue the necessity of long-term relationships, or for organizations to become more 'market-driven'. On the other hand, 'applied' researchers such as Fournier, Dobscha and Mick (1998) caution that 'managers will need to separate rhetoric from reality', and stressed-out executives complain privately that their firms are becoming so overly short-term results-driven that theory has little relevance. Nevertheless, we believe that the four discourses do provide new insights:

- *The academic discourse.* Writings in the academic press are useful in order to follow the development of concepts, theories, models and frameworks, as academics try to answer Webster's (1988) question: 'What is the nature of "knowledge" in marketing?' An example of an academic discourse is the ongoing one on developments in our understanding of something called 'strategy'. According to Normann and Ramirez (1993): 'Strategy is the art of creating value. It provides the intellectual frameworks, conceptual models, and governing ideas that allow a company's managers to identify opportunities for bringing value to customers and for delivering that value at a profit.' Throughout this book we will be using models and frameworks, such as that in Figure I.1 regarding the delivery of value, as a way of expressing our representation of current marketing knowledge.
- *The business media discourse.* In examining the business media discourse, one is likely to conclude that the adoption of new approaches

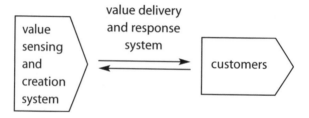

Key questions (not necessarily in order):
- Who are my target customers?
- What do they value?
- What value do I want to deliver to them?
- How will I create it?
- How will I deliver it?
- How will I control it?

**Figure I.1** Elements of a simple business model

Source: Piercy, 1998

to marketing has not been the result of emerging theories promulgated by academics, or of sure-fire solutions promoted by consultants. Rather, it appears to be happening as a result of a series of separate decisions made over time by executives in many firms in a variety of businesses and industries. There are times when it appears these are reported and dramatized in the world's business media almost as a virtual-reality theatre of unfolding fortunes and events that also features an ever-changing cast of leading characters, some of whom may be presented as victors, and some as villains. The headlines provide indications of what story or issue is currently hot: 'A Finnish fable' (*Economist*); 'BA seeks a new chief as Ayling is axed' (*Financial Times*); 'Troubles build for Ahold, the Dutch grocer' (*New York Times*); 'Coca-Cola: the bubbles pop' (*Economist*); 'Can this man save IBM?' (*Fortune*); 'Can Jack Smith fix GM?' (*Business Week*); 'Can Fisher fix Kodak?' (*Fortune*); 'Can McDonald's shape up?' (*Time*); 'Does P&G still matter? '(*Advertising Age*); 'DaimlerChrysler: the reckoning' (*The Economist*); 'Show time for AOL Time Warner' (*Business Week*); 'The wickedness of Wall Street' (*Economist*). While adding to the drama and suspense, an examination of such reportage has helped to expand and reaffirm what our more formal research has been telling us.

- *The Contemporary Marketing Practices (CMP) discourse.* Six years of international research by the Contemporary Marketing Practices (CMP) research group, of which the two authors are members, has shown us

how the practice of marketing has evolved. First, managers from all kinds of industries and from countries all around the world have told us there are up to five underlying changes currently impacting on their marketing practices:
- The increasing emphasis on services and service aspects of product delivery.
- The greater focus on financial accountability, loyalty and value management.
- The transformation of organizational structures and operations.
- The shifts in power and control within industry and marketing systems.
- The increased role of IT-based interactivity.

The changes are likely to be interrelated, depending on the industry context and their possible impacts. For some, the changes signal a time of opportunities and promising starts; for others it is a time of threats and unrequited efforts.

The executives in our studies also tell us there is no longer a common form of marketing, such as the traditional 'transactional' approach based around economic exchange and the '4Ps', of the kind appropriate to the different environments of the 1950s and 1960s. Rather, we have uncovered up to five approaches to marketing practice today, including a greatly revised version of transactional marketing. We label this 'the new pluralism' in marketing practice:

- *Transaction marketing (TM):* managing an updated mix of the 4Ps of Product, Place, Price and Promotions to attract and satisfy customers.
- *Database marketing (DM):* using technology-based tools for data-sharing purposes in order to target and maintain communication links with individual customers.
- *Interaction marketing (IM):* developing long-term interpersonal relationships, such as between individual buyers and sellers.
- *Network marketing (NM):* positioning the firm 'systemically' in a connecting set of inter-firm alliances and relationships.
- *e-marketing (eM):* facilitating information-led customer relationship management via IT-enabled interactivity, to create and mediate dialogue and exchange.

We also identify as a practice in itself an approach that did not emerge as such from the research programme, but was widely acknowledged as vital to implementation:

- *Internal relationship marketing (IRM):* linking all other aspects of marketing practices and building greater intra-organizational knowledge, collaboration and commitment to the firm's purpose of creating, delivering and increasing 'things' of value.

Some researchers have proposed that there has been a paradigm shift from transactional to relational marketing (for example, ranging from Kotler, 1991, to Gummesson, 2002). The work of the CMP group suggests that while a particular style of marketing may be dominant within a sector (for example, the relational style of marketing tends to be associated with business-to-business firms), a complete transition or shift to one approach appears unlikely. In practice, most firms demonstrate a range of approaches, depending on their past and present situations and their future expectations. This is because Levitt's 1983 maxim: 'The purpose of a business is to create and keep a customer', while contextual, remains valid two decades later.

- *The 'action-learning' discourse.* A fourth source is what we term 'action-learning', starting with the classroom. Both authors teach on executive programmes in their respective universities, and we rely heavily on feedback from participants to help in the validation process of discovering practical theory through the interplay of 'Does it hold in theory; does it work in practice; and vice versa? You tell us!' This is followed, in second place, by the sharing and learning that comes from our consulting activities.

## DID YOU FEEL THE EARTH MOVE?

Are we really seeing a fundamental shift in marketing practices, in that firms are now abandoning their old transactional exchange approaches based on the 4Ps of product, price, promotion and place? Are they replacing them with a completely new approach based on the principles of relationship marketing? In other words, has there been a paradigm shift? If so, did you feel the earth move?

Relationship marketing has been presented by numerous eminent thought leaders in the field as a 'paradigm shift' in the field of marketing. Wow! 'Paradigm' is one of those words which many people think they know but cannot actually define. The term paradigm shift is laden with implication, but fuzzy with respect to meaning. But it sounds good, and dramatizes and emphasizes the significance of relationship marketing. In this book we consider whether or not relationship marketing really does represent a seismic change in the way that we might view the field of marketing.

The term paradigm came into popular use after the publication of Kuhn's book, *The Structure of Scientific Revolutions* (1970). This discussed the history and nature of science and developed a philosophy, a way of thinking, which helped to explain the progression and development of scientific thinking.

Chalmers (1982) defined a paradigm as being 'a series of general assumptions, laws and techniques for their application that the members of a particular scientific community adopt'. It therefore constitutes a set of intuitive and inherent assumptions that act to guide the understanding and behaviour of that community, an unwritten but generally accepted law that frames the subject area. The term paradigm shift is more usually used in the natural science sense where observed anomalies to the current paradigm build to a state of extraordinary science, leading to a scientific revolution (Blaikie, 1993).

In discussing what science is, Schon (1983) presents a view of hard and soft sciences. Hard sciences constitute subjects such as astronomy, physics and even agronomy, and are amenable to quantification and scientific investigation. Schon also argued that advances in the hard sciences required the free interchange of problems and ideas between academics and practitioners.

The soft sciences demonstrate fewer of these characteristics and the application of scientific method is less relevant, or indeed irrelevant. We shall leave to one side the debate as to whether marketing is an art or a science, for this has been eloquently discussed elsewhere (Brown, 1996). Suffice to say marketing is a subject or field of study that does not have a separate and distinct existence, as do chemistry or physics for example. It exists only with the presence and involvement of people and their actions. If that explanation is accepted, then marketing is a soft science in Schon's terms, in a similar way that social science may be termed a soft science. It is thus highly questionable whether the term paradigm shift is appropriate to marketing in the way that it might be to the hard sciences. Furthermore, while there may be a 'free interchange of problems and ideas' between marketing academics and practitioners, the nature of the respective discourses appears to be quite distinct, as we shall see.

Hard science involves observation, measurement and explanation, so some of the constituent parts of the new paradigm may be observed and discussed for many years before the new paradigm emerges (Kuhn, 1970). As observations and evidence that are unexplained by the current paradigm continue to mount up, a jolt-like shift then occurs from one paradigm to the next. The new paradigm gives an altogether better explanation of the phenomenon that takes into account all the evidence that has been found. A classic example is the contrast between Ptolemaic and Copernican explanations of the solar system, with the heliocentric explanation eventually changing the paradigm and, quite literally, the way that people saw the world. Needless to say, there may also be strong disagreements and bitter rivalry between the proponents of differing views. Chaos theory, for instance, could be deemed one latter-day example of a scientific paradigm shift (Gleick, 1987).

A fundamental property of scientific theory is that it is capable of prediction. We can predict with a very high degree of accuracy the time at which the sun will rise and set, the phases of the Moon and tidal flows.

Early astronomers dating back to the time of the Greek philosophers sought explanations of such observable events and Ptolemy produced an explanation for the motion of the planets, but one which was based on the assumption that the Earth was at the centre of the universe. With subsequent corrections and additions Ptolemy's original work continued to provide a reasonable, but incomplete, explanation. The variance of 11 days from the spring equinox accumulated by the Julian calendar over several hundred years was evidence of this.

A number of competing explanations, or theories, were put forward to explain the variances observed. Foremost among these was that of Copernicus, and fundamental to his theory was that the Sun was at the centre of the universe. Although Copernicus's information improved the quality of prediction it suffered from one great disadvantage. It did not conform to writings contained in the Bible and was eventually placed on the Index of Forbidden Books by the Catholic Church.

With continued improvements in technology and the development of the telescope Galileo was able to obtain confirmatory evidence that supported the explanation proposed by Copernicus. From that point on the heliocentric explanation gained general acceptance, and thus the paradigm shift from one theory of science to another had occurred, even if Galileo had to recant his own findings in order to escape the gallows, or worse.

As we move into the social world of soft sciences it is questionable whether the term paradigm shift is even appropriate. However, if we seek dramatic examples of social change that might justify the term paradigm shift, then these might include: the change from subsistence to cash agriculture; the invention of the printing press; the industrial revolution; railways;

sanitation; electric light and power; and most recently, the impact of information technologies and its concomitant rallying cry that 'the internet changes everything'. All of these brought about dramatic social change and had a great influence on people's lives. But relationship marketing as a paradigm shift?

With respect to marketing the term has been widely used, and is intended to emphasize the dramatic shift from transaction to relationship marketing. As a paradigm, relationship marketing is a recent phenomenon. Berry (1983) is often credited with first mentioning it. In their review of the evolution of marketing schools of thought Sheth, Gardner and Garrett (1988) barely mention the term, although Sheth is now seen as a leader in the field (Sheth, 1995). While most writers using the term paradigm do so in a way that supports the emergence of the view, there is still discussion as to the nature of the paradigm shift involved: in other words, a shift to what?

The nature of relationship marketing is discussed in more detail later, but on this basis it can be argued that a distinct body of knowledge is emerging, although it is rather more disparate than the all-encompassing term relationship marketing would imply. For example Gronroos (2000), another pioneer, argues that relationship marketing has its roots in at least five research fields: services marketing, business-to-business marketing, total quality management (TQM), marketing channels, and direct and database marketing.

However, while relationship marketing as an emerging body of knowledge may be distinct, it does not represent a paradigm shift with the implications of discontinuity and lack of comparability between transaction and relationship marketing that this suggests. Our examinations and research findings presented here suggest that: some elements of transaction and relationship marketing may be adopted; transaction and relationship marketing may be practised concurrently; and a position somewhere between fully transactional and fully relational marketing emerges. A paradigm shift? We think not, or at least not yet.

## OUR CENTRAL MESSAGE

Our central message is that, from a managerial perspective, contemporary marketing practices are highly contextual and pluralistic. In any given organization there is likely to be a range of marketing practices, with some combination of new relationship marketing approaches carried out in conjunction with some updated form of the more traditional transactional marketing. This combination includes developments in IT-enabled interactivity that will reinforce, enhance or transform their organizational status quo, even though the executives concerned may not have set out to achieve a major change either deliberately or strategically. Rather, their intention is often more prosaic, and based on the imperatives and logic of cost and efficiency. This mixture all adds to the complexity of their management task, and to the importance of finding new guidelines or frameworks for the most effective marketing practices possible.

This new pluralism in marketing thus signals that while the underlying principles of value sensing, creation and delivery may not have shifted, firms are fundamentally changing their marketing practices to integrate the various strands of marketing practice into a more complex coherent whole that is appropriate to their competitive situation and value delivery requirements. To date, this has been happening with varying degrees of understanding and success. Based on our overall research, the nature of these interrelationships is shown in Figure I.2.

With a greater managerial emphasis on value creation (including the market capitalization value of the firm; the value of the firm's tangible and intangible assets, such as its brands; the value of the firm's customer base, and so on) there is also a growing realization that marketing has less to do with the traditional 4Ps and economic exchanges to gain customers. Increasingly, it has more to do with building and maintaining relationships, networks and continuous interactions between players in the entire business value system, including: suppliers, producers, intermediaries, service providers and end-customers. While this expanded approach has been termed 'relationship' marketing, this descriptive term does not adequately capture the complexity and paradoxes that characterize the pluralism that is the new marketing.

Figure I.3 illustrates an overall model or framework of the organization

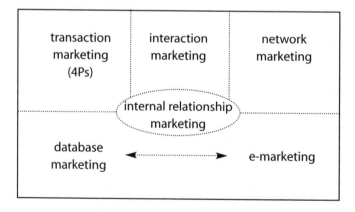

**Figure I.2** The new pluralism in contemporary marketing practices

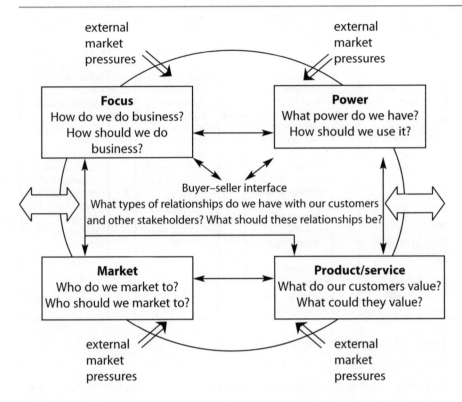

**Figure I.3** The change model and pressures on marketing

that includes within it the framework of the new marketing outlined in Figure I.2. It will also be the main framework that underpins this book and will be used throughout, as we examine the development, characteristics and implications of the new pluralism in marketing. A full description of this model will be given later.

## THE STRUCTURE OF THE BOOK

Figure I.4 shows the structure of the book and the flow of the discussions in the form of a diagram. The book is divided into four sections.

A summary of the content of each chapter in more detail is given below.

### Chapter 1: Understanding Business Today

In this chapter we consider the complex and paradoxical pressures on

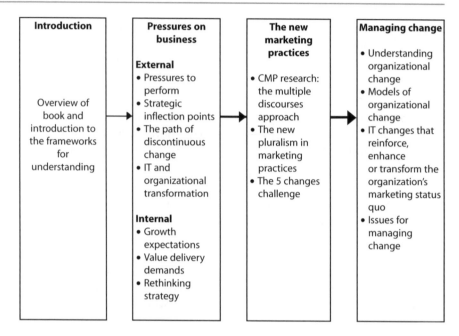

**Figure I.4** The structure of the book

businesses today to deliver many things: more corporate value; more volume; more revenues; more profits; more quality; more cost savings; more technical features; more service; and so on. We ask what are the implications for marketing when companies are currently having to answer to so many differing measurements (hard and soft) of accountability and performance. We explain the conceptual foundations that underpin the changed nature of marketing practices, and hence this book, by examining the constituent parts of the model shown in Figure I.3.

## Chapter 2: Explanations of Marketing: Evolving, Changing or Competing?

In Chapter 2 we consider questions such as: How has marketing evolved these past few decades, and is there a 'maturing' of marketing theory and practice? Why is there an increased interest in what is known as relationship marketing? The factors influencing the emergence of relationship marketing are discussed, together with the main schools of thought and some of the key concepts that are emerging. The resources required to develop and sustain a relational focus are outlined, leading to insight into the elements that constitute the topic. These elements or dimensions have formed the basis of the CMP research programme leading to the derivation of the five marketing practices.

## Chapter 3: The New Business Reality

In this chapter we revisit the issue of pressures on business, by considering questions such as: How is strategy development and implementation shaped by the pressures to grow and create more value? What are the implications for companies opting to grow from within, as opposed to growing from without through, for example, mergers and acquisitions? How is value created and added; at the organization level; at the business unit level; and at the product–market interface level? An in-depth case study is used to explore the complexity of these issues.

## Chapter 4: Growth and Value

This chapter continues the discussion from the previous chapter that examined pressures to grow. External growth by merger or acquisition is illustrated by a further case study, and the requirements for value and strategies to deliver it are discussed. This is explored from several perspectives and presents very real insight into the emerging role of relationship marketing in managing a value system, with all the implications for a network of relationships that this implies. This is heightened by increasing customer demands and the opportunities presented by the knowledge economy.

## Chapter 5: Finding and Creating Advantage

We consider what is meant by marketing advantage and power. For example, what does a company now need to possess to gain and keep customers and relationships, or to build and hold leadership positions in the market? What does a company need in order to sense, create and deliver what customers value, especially when customers may not know what it is they value? And when all of this is within an extended network of relationships where the definition of customers and how to relate to them suggests the answer is also not obvious?

## Chapter 6: Organizational Transformation

The influence of IT is such that it can dramatically change the nature of business by acting as a strategic inflection point. In Chapter 6 we consider questions such as: What is meant by digital convergence? In what ways is there increasing 'pervasiveness' of information technologies in every aspect of running a business? What are the impacts of IT not just on adding value to existing forms of products or services, but also on creating new forms of value? Are IT and the internet really transforming the nature of products, services, structures, functions, processes, communications and even strategic advantage?

## Chapter 7:  Contemporary Marketing Practice and the Five Changes Challenge

This chapter leads us into an explanation of the findings underpinning the contemporary marketing practices (CMP) study. One such set of findings is that there appear to be up to five major changes affecting marketing practice today, based on what executives have told us. We consider how these changes might be interrelated, and how they might impact on organizations overall. A theme developed later is whether their collective impact is likely to be seen as reinforcing, enhancing or transforming the organizational status quo.

## Chapter 8:  Pluralism in Marketing Practice

In this chapter we examine the six different approaches to contemporary marketing practice (Transaction, Database, Interaction, Network, e-Marketing, and, briefly, Internal Relationship Marketing) that our various researches have uncovered. We then attempt to address questions such as: What are the different types of contemporary marketing practices? In what ways might they be context- or industry-specific: that is, do B2B goods firms take a different approach from B2B services firms? How might the various approaches to marketing be interrelated, or are firms tending to emphasize one approach only?

## Chapter 9:  The Future of Marketing

In this chapter we consider the changes in marketing practice from the perspective of change in organizations overall. All firms face change, increasingly on an ongoing basis. It may be on a small, incremental scale designed continuously to cut costs out of a particular process, or it may involve a transformation of the entire organization as it struggles to survive. We also examine the impacts of information technologies on change, and, as first proposed in Chapter 6, with special emphasis on when a firm's IT goals, in particular, may be intended to reinforce, enhance or transform their organizational status quo.

In our book we attempt to present the latest findings on contemporary marketing practices by considering four sources of information, or discourses: the academic debate; the business media; contemporary marketing practices research; and the executive dialogue developed through our teaching and consulting. We have also considered in-depth the issues or pressures behind these changes in marketing practice. We have tried to present all this in a rigorous fashion, but not to the point that it is seen as 'just another boring academic text-book'. Rather, our goal has been to provide a blend of the theoretical and the 'real world' that is complete, readable, interesting, challenging and, above all, useful. The emphasis is on useful because we especially want you, the busy executive – or you who are about to become the busy executive – to find this book useful when you set out to effect change in your organization's current marketing practices. And if you think they don't need changing, or that they can't be changed, then perhaps you're stuck in the wrong firm or the wrong job!

## CHAPTER 1

# Understanding Business Today

## CHAPTER OBJECTIVES

In this chapter we consider the question of what are the complex and paradoxical pressures on businesses today to deliver, for example, more corporate value; more sales volume; more gross revenues; more profits; more quality; more cost savings; more technical advantages; more customer service; and so on. We consider the implications for marketing when companies are currently having to comply with so many differing measures (hard and soft) of accountability and performance? We attempt to make sense of their efforts to absorb and reconcile these pressures by first examining what they are actually doing. We use the example of McDonald's to illustrate the struggles of one of the world's great marketing corporations to hold its leadership position in a changing business, and consider whether or not it seems able to create a new business 'model' in response to these changes. We then explain the conceptual foundations that underpin the changes in marketing practices – and hence this book. We do this by examining the constituent parts of our 'model' of contemporary marketing practices that has been developed from our research and studies of the various discourses. This in turn will provide a framework for the remainder of the book.

## THE PRESSURE OF PRESSURE

What do customers most value? Increasingly it seems, more of everything! As Treacy and Wiersema (1995b) said:

> Customers today want more of those things they value. If they value low cost, they want it lower. If they value convenience or speed when they buy, they want it easier and faster. If they look for state-of-the-art design, they want to see the art pushed forward. If they need expert advice, they

want companies to give them more depth, more time, and more of a feeling that they're the only customer.

In this chapter we are especially interested in how pressures from outside create pressures within to conceive, create and deliver more value. Pressures can come in many forms, and the result for many companies is a mix of complexity and paradox:

- Consumers', customers' and clients' needs and values continually shift, and this places pressure on companies to track these shifts, anticipate future directions, and craft strategies to position themselves accordingly.
- New competitors enter the market and challenge how business is to be carried out; new technologies force companies to redefine existing products, services, processes and industries.
- Market and technology dynamics mean that there is a relentless internal pressure to speed up the process of researching, developing and introducing new products and services.
- While their most important, and possibly most powerful, customers say what they really require now are continuous improvements (in quality and delivery, servicing, transparent costings, trading terms and competitive pricing), suppliers still promote something called trust and relationship marketing.
- New regulations (and de-regulations) redefine existing competitive practices and even entire businesses; mergers and acquisitions mean companies quickly have to achieve synergies and cost reductions in order to placate nervous shareholders and maintain their momentum in the marketplace.
- Strategic alliances require cooperation where previously there was implacable competitive warfare.
- Impatient shareholders insist that next year's financial results must be an improvement on this year's, so that companies always have to redouble their efforts to squeeze more costs out of their businesses; and so on.

Not surprisingly, perhaps, Sheth and Sisodia (1999) proposed that marketing's context as we entered the new millennium was changing dramatically in terms of physical distance, time, markets and competition. This in turn was leading to fundamental changes in the way marketing was practised. A challenge for corporations may have been to make fundamental changes in the ways they do marketing – and do business, even. A challenge for marketing academics has been to understand the nature of the changing context and practices of marketing, and to translate this new knowledge into their research and teaching. Just ian (2000) argued for consumer researchers 'learning to see relevance ingly distant fields', we agree that marketing academics need to look their particular discourse for a more complete understanding of the which marketing practices and theories are changing.

In this book we consider how organizations have changed their marketing practices in the face of pressures from their external environments, and we present these changes in the form of a model, or framework, of marketing practices, as shown in Figure 1.1. As we developed this model we were reminded time and again of Webster's (1988) question: 'What is the nature of 'knowledge' in marketing?'

Rossiter (2001) argued that marketing knowledge can take several 'forms':

- *Marketing concepts*, which are sets of marketing terms, each defined by its main attributes, such as segmentation, life cycles, and marketing strategy.
- *Structural frameworks* help 'frame' a marketing problem, and therefore help marketers to think about concepts in some ordered or structured fashion, such as that provided by the 4Ps and the BCG grid. The risk is that they become prescriptive for actions: 'Milk the cash cows and sell all the dogs.'
- *Strategic principles*, which are prescriptions for managerial action based on a dynamic, causal framework format, and are often conditional and normative: 'If the market does this (X), then do that (Y).' The argument that all principles are conditional means that there are unlikely to be any universal principles in marketing (Rossiter, 2001). This argument has many implications for our research findings presented in Chapter 8, when we examine the nature of pluralism in marketing practices.
- *Research principles* are also conditional, but are applicable not to strategic action but to when managers commission or use a particular market research technique: 'If in situation (X) then use technique (Y).' Here the risk is the principles may be overly prescriptive when, for example, the reality is that there are times when consumers simply cannot tell researchers what they really think, or prefer, or will do.

To obtain this knowledge, we embarked on a process of uncovering what we might term 'practical theory'.

## UNCOVERING PRACTICAL THEORY

In *What Management Is*, Magretta (2002) explained her approach to book writing by means of a metaphor: 'Start digging and you will pass through many layers of the earth's surface, each one generally different from the others. At some point however, you will hit bedrock – the common layer underneath it all – the solid foundation.' For her, the concept of value creation was in the bedrock of contemporary management thinking, as it will be in this book. The geological sciences might provide a useful metaphor for how the new marketing thinking is being unearthed and considered. In a recent book, Winchester (2002) examined how it was that the field known as geological sciences began some 200 years ago.

---

In the late 1790s William Smith, an orphaned son of a blacksmith in a village near Oxford, began work as a surveyor for the Somerset Coal Canal Company. Early in his life he had become interested in rocks and rock formations, and while down in the coal mines of northern Somerset and in the excavations of the land for the canal, he began to notice and query a phenomenon that had largely gone ignored or unquestioned previously, namely that: 'Every single one of the specimens of one kind of fossil found in one bed of rock may be the same throughout one bed, but would be subtly different from those of the same kind of fossil found in another bed. A period of time would have elapsed between the deposition of the two beds, and thus a period of time between the existence of the two kinds of animals it embraced. Evolution – we can say this today but Smith had not even the vaguest conception of it back then – would have occurred.'

Smith's realisation, based on his ability to perceive a pattern that had gone unnoticed before, and the resulting geological map he eventually produced in 1815, heralded the beginnings of a new kind of science; the development of new kinds of industries based on coal, oil, iron ore, and so on; and laid the foundations for a field of study later popularised by the work of Charles Darwin. As Winchester said, it was 'the map that changed the world'.

---

One of our main arguments is that firms are looking anywhere and everywhere for new ways to sense, create and deliver more value. It appears – as revealed in the various discourses that were discussed in the Introduction – they are doing this in relatively unstructured, unsystematic and 'unknowing' ways. Through a layer by layer examination of their efforts, our goal has been to find a pattern of behaviours and practices that we might then present as a 'map' of marketing with its corresponding concepts, frameworks and principles – in effect, a map based on practical theories.

While we accept that the results of our diggings – and our map – are unlikely to be as profound as Smith's, we nevertheless trust that they will go some way towards adding to our knowledge base of how marketing is practised today, and why. Perhaps equally telling, our findings and map will provide us with more insights into how companies are creating their own maps of how their marketing is done, and possibly should be done. As we examine some of the world's great marketing corporations, it appears many are in need of new maps.

## The Failure of McDonald's Old Map

As it approaches 50, McDonald's is a US$75 billion food-service company renowned for its global marketing prowess and increasingly ubiquitous golden arches. *Time* (1998) noted that McDonald's success was based on two key characteristics of its owner, Ray Kroc. One was his innate perceptiveness in identifying popular trends and tastes:

> He sensed that America was a nation of people who ate out, as opposed to the Old World tradition of eating at home. He also knew that people here wanted something different. Instead of a structured, ritualistic restaurant with codes and routine, he gave them a simple, casual and identifiable restaurant with friendly service, low prices, no waiting and no reservations.... One goes to McDonald's to eat, not to dine.

His other characteristic was, in an era before mission statements, an obsession with the company's four pillars of excellence: Quality, Service, Cleanliness and Value.

McDonald's success was largely on the basis of an internally-driven growth strategy and international geographic expansion. For decades it has been a quintessential growth stock. It was also a company that thrived on the seemingly insatiable eating habits of its two key market groups: young families and Hoo-Foos (Heavy Fast-Food Users – typically young, single males). It was so consistently successful that the *Economist* regularly published a foreign exchange league table based on the prices of Big Macs in each country in which it was located.

However, as Stires (2002) recently noted, this success may be coming to an end:

> With 30,000 worldwide restaurants serving 46 million customers a day, the burger chain is the largest in the world. And with that universality, it seemed, came a universal truth: just as you could count on a Big Mac

tasting the same in Connecticut as in Columbia, so could you rely on the company to deliver 12 per cent to 15 per cent earnings growth year after year.... Now that good feeling has been Hamburglared in a big way.

The reason for that last comment is that McDonald's has belatedly begun to discover the limitations of its strategy: its share of the fast food market shrunk marginally to 15.2 per cent in 2002, a decline of 3 per cent from 1997, and late in 2002 it announced that only about 600 new outlets would be opened worldwide in 2003, compared with 2000 in 1996. As a couple of industry watchers noted: 'McDonald's is suddenly reaching the boundaries of growth' (Ghazvinian and Miller, 2002). For example, from the beginning of 2001 to mid-2002 it reported 'earnings disappointments' in all six quarters. For its last quarter of 2002 McDonald's posted its first quarterly loss since it became a publicly listed company in 1965, and finished the year with its share price some 40 per cent down.

According to, for example, the *Economist* (2002a), and Day (2003), there are several reasons for McDonald's struggling to achieve its once-vaunted growth targets, and thereby losing the confidence of both customers and investors:

- First, over the 1990s it expanded so far so fast, with new store openings throughout the USA in particular, that it ran out of room to add more at the same pace without cannibalizing sales from existing outlets. Same-store sales declined in the USA especially, and this in turn has caused revenue growth to stall, since some 50–55 per cent of its operating income comes from its domestic market. As one long-term franchisee told Day (2003): 'I don't think that McDonald's has the waiting list (of future franchise owners) it used to, and part of that reason is that the return on investment isn't what it used to be.'
- Second, despite having more stores overseas than in the USA, its international expansion has not produced the expected results, for a number of reasons: difficulties in enforcing quality controls standards worldwide; greater than expected local competition in key markets such as Japan; and possibly some anti-'corporate America' sentiment in a number of countries.
- Third, despite some local adaptations, such as the 'Kiwiburger' in New Zealand, Chicken Maharaja in India and a chicken flatbread sandwich in the USA, McDonald's has not had a global new product success since Chicken McNuggets, which were launched in 1983. Its major burger competitors, such as Burger King and Wendy's, are now bringing out more appealing offerings. For example, Wendy's offer a line of

premium salads and this has helped give them a better reputation for freshness.

- Fourth, McDonald's has been slow in responding to health complaints about the high fat content in its products, and missed its deadline when changing to a healthier cooking oil early in 2003. Further, its efforts to extend its product line to appeal to those concerned with healthy eating have not been successful. As a result, other more health-conscious fast-food restaurants are claiming success. For example, there are now more Subway sandwich outlets in the USA than there are McDonald's.

- Fifth, the company's response to its burger competitors' threats, by introducing a food-preparation system designed to improve food quality, was poorly executed and caused an increase in meal delivery time, thereby adding to customer complaints. This is from the company that had written the operating manual on fast-food standardization, including its fries and hamburgers, its decor, its uniforms: in effect, everything from its golden arches to the cleanliness of its toilets.

- Sixth, its Happy Meals sales to children were no longer so appealing since its ten-year licensing arrangement with Walt Disney had not yielded any new toy premiums from movie hits since *Toy Story 2*.

- Seventh, to regain market share and win back lunchtime customers from its rivals, late in 2002 it introduced Dollar Meals in the USA, a $1 value menu that included some of its premium sandwiches. The move drew more customers into stores but failed to generate a sufficient lift in sales revenue. It also stimulated a general price war, thereby creating depressed earnings throughout the fast-food industry.

- Eighth, it may have become a tired icon of a way of life that no longer existed. Leonhardt (1998) said: 'McDonald's has lost some of its relevance to American culture – a culture that it, as much as any modern corporation, helped to shape.' Day (2003) observed that the company that once 'symbolized to some people the American way of eating the way that General Motors once represented the open road.... In an era of obesity lawsuits and $5 lattes, McDonald's seems downmarket. Last year, in a survey in *Restaurants and Institutions Magazine*, respondents ranked McDonald's 15th in food quality at hamburger chains.'

- Finally, despite making many changes to its menu; despite testing healthier items; despite introducing many menu items tailored to local tastes; despite closing hundreds of unprofitable outlets; and despite the departure in 2002 of its CEO, the company was suffering from one of the same afflictions of many other great companies slowly being worn down by the intense pressure: an unwavering belief in the business 'model' that had worked in the past, and that somehow it would still prevail.

As the previous CEO said to *Business Week* (Leonhardt, 1998): 'Do we have to change? No, we don't have to change. We have the most successful brand in the world.' Or, as the new CEO, a 28-year veteran of McDonald's who was brought out of retirement in 2002 to rebuild the company, said to the *New York Times* (Day, 2002): 'We remain focused on growing our existing restaurants' sales, and we're committed to making the changes necessary to succeed in the challenging worldwide economic and competitive environments in which we operate.' Another senior executive said to Ghazvinian and Miller (2002): 'We have issues that we're addressing. But nobody has the marketing we have, the brand power we have, the franchises we have. That news gets lost.'

A piece of news McDonald's may have lost is that, by focusing on its internal growth strategy and the threats from its traditional fast-food competitors, it perhaps underestimated both the threats and the opportunities offered by other categories. For example, Starbucks, which one newspaper labelled as 'caffein-fuelled' (*Sunday Star-Times*, 2003) is now the most expansionist food chain in the USA, 'pulling in an aspirational, high-spending crowd McDonald's would kill for'. However, McDonald's is only slowly expanding its McCafe concept, where patrons are able to purchase pastries and premium coffee.

One of the fastest growth categories in the food service industry overall is what is known as 'fast-casual' restaurants. While this category accounted for only about 4–5 per cent of the $150+ billion fast-food sector in the USA in 2002, it grew by 12 per cent in that year while the restaurant industry overall shrank marginally. The category's appeal was that it combined 'the convenience of a fast-food joint with a more sophisticated fare, atmosphere and price of a sit-down restaurant' (Eisenberg, 2002).

To be fair, under its previous CEO McDonald's had purchased a number of players in this sector, such as Chipotle Mexican Grill, Donatos Pizzeria and Boston Market. These restaurant chains were placed under a separate umbrella group called Partner Brands. The company had also tested a McDiner concept, a 1950s style sit-down diner serving made-to-order meals such as steaks. However, in terms of the strategic thinking behind these moves, the executive in charge of acquisitions acknowledged (Eisenberg, 2002): 'No matter what we do we won't be able to attract those people (who prefer fast-casual restaurants) to the Golden Arches.'

By the end of 2002, five years after its first acquisition, the Partner Brands group's turnover was approximately US$1 billion, and it was operating at a loss of about US$66 million. Early in 2003 McDonald's announced it was seeking to sell a controlling interest in its non-McDonald's group of restaurants. According to Sorkin (2003): 'Strategically, Partner Brands was set up as a growth vehicle and an experimental lab of sorts for McDonald's management to study emerging fast-food businesses, while lending their own expertise.' While commenting that McDonald's new CEO had 'begun an aggressive campaign to undo much of Mr Greenberg's expansion strategy', Sorkin added that another top executive said the move was being done 'in an effort to focus more tightly on its namesake business'.

However, given McDonald's share price slide over 2002, its efforts to reduce costs by closing unprofitable outlets, its development of new formats, and its foray into and out of acquisitions could all be seen in hindsight as 'too little, too late'. Another industry observer was more incisive: 'The company is in trouble because its business model is out of date' (Ghazvinian and Miller, 2002).

## The Lessons of McDonald's

McDonald's in recent times suffered from what Day (1999) terms 'market blindness', and it therefore exhibited 'many of the worse features of a self-centred organization'. He listed three main symptoms:

1. *Weak ability to capture market signals:* for example, that food-consumption attitudes and patterns had begun to shift and that direct and indirect competitors were reacting faster to these changes.
2. *Product-focused organization:* for example, it saw its future as determined by controlling its own assets and competencies.
3. *Short-run, cost concerns dominate:* for example, its recent efforts to improve efficiencies and quality by introducing a new food-preparation system, and the fact that in introducing Dollar Meals it was prepared to trade short-term share gains against longer-term profit growth.

Two other symptoms may also be appropriate:

4. *Creeping marketing myopia:* for example, the unwavering belief by top executives, in particular, in the traditional market or business the company is in, and the customers it is best able to serve. In McDonald's case this was shown by their pulling back from moving into new formats, including by acquisition.
5. *Leadership paralysis:* for example, even if it still is the industry leader in terms of size, it may have lost the will – or capacity – to change the 'model' of industry behaviour to its advantage as its

circumstances change. Rather, it either becomes passive and accepts that its destiny depends on the changing fortunes of the industry, or it retreats into denial and attempts to preserve the old 'model', seen in its traditional ways of marketing and its inviolable brands. This is exemplified by the 'no we don't have to change. We have the most successful brand in the world' type of comment from McDonald's previous CEO.

How is it that one of the world's great marketing corporations allowed its supposedly unshakable 'business model' to become out of date? McDonald's is not alone. Over the past couple of decades the business models of traditional leaders in many businesses have passed their use-by dates. As with McDonald's, this has been shown in their weakened marketing and their deteriorating results, in industries as diverse as air travel, airplanes, automobiles, computers, financial services, retailing, steel and telecommunications.

## A MODEL OF CONTEMPORARY MARKETING PRACTICES

Figure 1.1 shows a model of contemporary marketing practices that is derived from the various discourses noted in the Introduction, including an extensive individual research project (Palmer, 2001). Our view of what is a 'model' is similar to what Rossiter (2001) earlier termed a 'framework', and it is composed of a series of constructs that will be discussed later in this chapter.

In one sense a model represents a theory, and is analogous to and indistinguishable from that theory (Whetten, 1989). However it is important to note that Figure 1.1 is not a cause-and-effect model in the scientific sense. Rather, we attempt to explain the underlying mechanisms that loosely govern the relationships between the constructs from which the model is developed. Our goal is to provide a more generalized understanding and explanation, rather than a mechanistic analysis.

Figure 1.1 has been developed by taking an understanding of relationship marketing and then 'testing' that against a combination of what has been said in the various discourses and in our observations of actual marketing practice. This is a theory-building technique sometimes referred to as 'analytic induction' (Bryman, 1988). It is in contrast to theory testing or deductive types of models which are, in a sense, more 'hard-wired' and which explicitly show the relationships between each

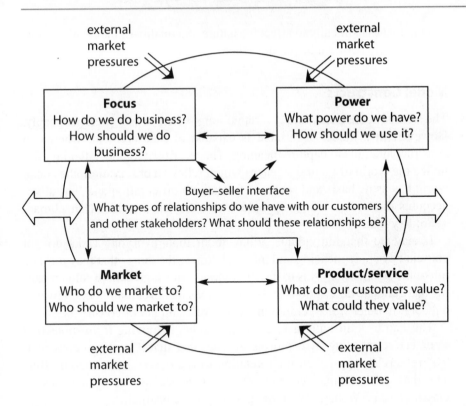

external
market
pressures

external
market
pressures

**Focus**
How do we do business?
How should we do
business?

**Power**
What power do we have?
How should we use it?

Buyer–seller interface
What types of relationships do we have with our customers
and other stakeholders? What should these relationships be?

**Market**
Who do we market to?
Who should we market to?

**Product/service**
What do our customers value?
What could they value?

external
market
pressures

external
market
pressures

**Figure 1.1** Model of contemporary marketing

element of the model in order to establish causality and the direction of causality. The model presented here has been developed in order to give an overall sense to, and understanding of, the processes at work. We term this approach 'interpretative' research.

There are a number of important points to note with respect to the model:

- *It is contextual.* That is to say, it takes account of the stresses and strains imposed on a firm by its external business environment. These will be discussed in more detail in Chapter 6. This means that it is likely to give a better explanation of company events in the circumstances or situation it is in.
- *It is dynamic.* It is designed to allow for continuous action and interaction between players. Central to the model is the nature of the relationship between buyer and seller represented by what we term the 'constructs' of power, interface and focus, as will be seen later. Rossiter uses the term 'concepts' to mean much the same thing. In our model the constructs

interact dynamically to affect the nature and quality of the relationships, especially between buyer and seller.

## Model Constructs

The terms 'construct' and 'variable' are often used interchangeably. However, in a model a variable is capable of measurement, whereas a construct attempts to capture meaning. This is critical to understanding for, unlike the world of natural sciences which relies on observation, the social world has as its basis and sources of data both observation and 'narrative' accounts that social actors – people – give to their activities (Hirschman, 1986; Bryman, 1988).

It may be that individuals going about their everyday tasks do not consciously apply meaning and interpretation to the things that they do. The job of the social scientist is to interpret these actions, give them some meaning and generate descriptions and explanations that eventually build towards a theory: in other words, craft a model out of a number of constructs.

This can be a difficult task, as the researcher is moving from subjective to objective meaning by capturing the meaning that is within a construct. The researcher applies an interpretation to the observation in doing this. The data are systematized and organized, hence producing a series of classifications (Weber, 1964) that make up the construct.

The implication is that, in effect, a series of 'labels' is given to a set of actions and behaviours. They identify each of the constructs which are classified and then arranged into a final model configuration, as in Figure 1.1. It is this model that summarizes and represents the meeting of theory with practice.

## Derivation of the Data

Do executives consciously get out of bed in the morning and 'do' relationship marketing? Almost certainly not. The individual who has been interviewed or observed may not consciously be aware that what they are saying or doing constitutes what might be later termed 'relationship marketing' or 'contemporary marketing practice'.

By obtaining and analyzing data from observations and from 'listening to the voice of the respondent'; by analyzing other source material in detail; and by comparing and contrasting this data with existing or emerging theory, it is possible to devise further or more complete explanations of the findings by reducing the data from these various sources to a series of constructs. In this way we attempt to say with more certainty what relationship marketing now is, and what contemporary marketing practices now are. This is the rationalization provided through the process.

Throughout the iterative, comparative process, the source data were examined to determine if there were sufficient similarities for a number of common constructs to be allocated across the various sources of data. Concurrently, definitions were developed for each construct in order to give meaning to the field data that had been abstracted. Each emerging construct was supported by various elements of the different data in order to provide what is termed 'triangulation' (Jick, 1979), or an additional check on the process.

The output is a series of constructs. These capture an abstracted or higher level meaning and objectives, as shown in Table 1.1 This table explains marketing practice as ranging from what is termed transactional to relational. It also provides a touchstone against which the field data could be compared and classified. This is a two-way process: the data help to validate the constructs, which in turn help to classify and reduce the data. As the research process continued the relationships between constructs were also considered in order that they could be arranged into the model (Figure 1.1), finally resulting in an interpretation of the underlying marketing processes.

## How Do We Know What We Know?

The question naturally arises: How do we know that this is 'true'? That the person developing these explanations has taken into account all the information and applied appropriate research techniques to arrive at this understanding? That the model 'holds': in other words, that it works in practice? With this type of research there is no way of determining actual proof, in the sense that a statistical test, for example, can be applied to the data to show that the results are true or otherwise. In fact, there is an interesting debate as to the nature of truth, for what we have achieved with a model is an interpretation of a wide range of actions and behaviours.

As noted earlier in this section, a model is composed of a series of constructs. These constructs are abstractions that provide a higher-level summary of the data accumulated. While they are approximations, since each construct contains within it a range of thoughts and ideas, this does not mean that they are remote and removed from the 'real' world. Although abstract, they must be open to commonsense interpretation and understanding. Blaikie (1993) nicely summarizes this point: 'In short, if social actors cannot identify with the types which have been constructed to represent their actions or situations, then the researcher has either got it wrong or has strayed too far from the concepts of everyday life.'

**Table 1.1**  Constructs with transactional and relational definitions

| Construct | Transactional pole | Relational pole |
|---|---|---|
| *Focus* <br> The basis underlying the marketing activity of the organization. Primarily transactional, relationship, services or value driven. | • Completion of the sale <br> • Maintain/improve volume | • Improve volume <br> • Customer satisfaction achieved <br> • Value created |
| *Targets* <br> What are the markets identified or addressed through the actions of the firm? This would include the customer market, perhaps also suppliers, internal market, influence groups etc. or maintenance of the relationship and network itself. | • Primarily or exclusively customer market orientated | • Identify a number of markets <br> • Commit resources to these markets |
| *Criteria* <br> Information concerning customers that is used to make strategic decisions. | • Previous sales history <br> • Assessment of likelihood of repurchase potential <br> • New customer focus | • Customer information system <br> • Key customer value identified and monitored <br> • Customer plans known |
| *Intangibles* <br> Activities and commitments made to improve intangible and time-related aspects of the product offering. | • No complaints handling procedure <br> • Delivery and other service standards not monitored | • Service recovery procedures <br> • Complaints and inquiry review process <br> • Service standard measures |

**Table 1.1**  continued

| Construct | Transactional pole | Relational pole |
|---|---|---|
| *Customization* The extent to which the product offering is different or unique for individual customers. | • One standard product offering • Little customization to specific requirements | • Product and service flexible to meet individual customer requirements |
| *DIU (Decision Involvement Unit)* The parties or firms involved in the relationships between, and perhaps beyond, the supplying firm and the buyer. | • Few people involved • Little senior management contact • Mainly sales/ purchasing contact | • Multiple contacts • Senior management involvement • Cross-functional contact |
| *Interface* The extent to which the relationship is discrete or continuous and extended over a short or long time period. | • Infrequent contact • Formal meetings • Product/technical focused discussions | • High level of informal contact • Frequent contact • Extensive sharing of information |
| *Power* The degree to which power is recognized and used in the relationship | • Win/lose style • Highly competitive | • Mutually seeking to generate value and satisfaction |
| *Exchange* The actual basis of exchange, to include physical product, services, warranties, reputation and other intangibles. That which the firm considers to be present and necessary for the relationship. | • Physical product or discrete service • Formal contracts • Written specifications | • Product and service integrated • No formal agreement • Trust and openness |

The constructs are arranged into a model to give an overall understanding of the phenomenon being studied, such as the nature of contemporary marketing practices. The test of the model that is derived is not one of statistical proof, but of plausibility (Harre, 1970). Hence, the academic process that is followed provides for various checks and balances to assess the credibility of the findings. As Hirschman (1986) says: 'ultimately in all scientific endeavours, one is either believed or not believed; assigning a number will not make the research "better".'

In this world of interpretive research we therefore seek to provide better explanations of what is happening 'out there'. Of course, there will always be those who have an innate scepticism with regard to subjective data. However, even apparently objective data now have their drawbacks. The shareholders of Ahold, Enron and WorldCom may not have the same faith in other company accounts in the future, even those that have been independently audited by large, international and, at one time, highly respected, firms of accountants.

## THE DYNAMIC NATURE OF RELATIONSHIPS

### The Relationship Continuum

The model in Figure 1.1 demonstrates the actions, reactions and interactions that occur and the elements that drive the process of marketing. The relationship between two organizations is represented by the triangle formed by the focus, power and interface constructs. Different styles of relationships are often presented as a continuum with the transactional/competitive style at one pole and relational/cooperative at the other, as shown in Figure 1.2. With the many changes that are taking place in the business environment, the concept of relationship marketing would suggest that a change in the style of relationship is also appropriate.

For example, a business-to-business company working within its industry supply chain may find that participants are becoming fewer and larger, as a process of attrition continues. Buyers no longer have the choice of suppliers that they once had. Nor may they wish to incur the significant transaction costs that are involved in managing a portfolio of suppliers. There is more to be gained by reducing the number of suppliers, offering each more volume business, and then working more closely with them to reduce costs further. As their interdependency increases, and the drive for lower costs continues, there is a case to be made for a change in the style of relationship.

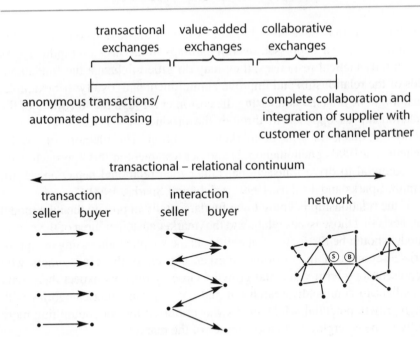

**Figure 1.2** The relationship continuum

Source: based on Day, 1999a

The model (Figure 1.1) suggests that this change can occur in a number of ways. Suppliers can make tactical changes to their product offering by addressing the constructs within the 'product' box. The product may be enhanced in some way, perhaps by adding additional features. Its costs may be reduced by greater automation or outsourcing non-core activities. Service competitiveness may be increased by improved just-in-time delivery and continuous stock availability. The product or service could be customized to meet the individual requirements of the buyer. All of these address the need to build relationships largely through the medium of the product or service offering. This might also be termed the 'marketing mix' response to relationship requirements, such as the imperative to prevent customers switching to competitors. They are characterized by firms manipulating their '4, 5 or 7Ps', or however many are regarded as relevant for that company and its context (7Ps = Product, Price, Promotion, Place + People + Processes + Proactive Customer Service: the acronym of the Ps is a way of describing the main components that constitute what the customer actually purchases).

These are likely to provide short-term benefits, but potentially longer-term downsides, as critics of McDonald's claim. As we saw, McDonald's

Dollar Meals may have brought more customer traffic to its outlets, but the ensuing price war depressed overall earnings in the fast-food industry. As essentially tactical responses, they may do little to change the fundamentals of the relationship and improve commitment and loyalty: for example, that might be done by addressing the customer through the 'medium' of the relationship as opposed to through the product or service. It is more a spray-on, quick-fix type of marketing solution. The plethora of loyalty schemes, a 1990s phenomenon, is another testament to this approach, with its potential to drive transactional rather than relational behaviour (Hart, Smith, Sparks and Tzokas, 1999; Wright and Sparks, 1999).

If the relationship is going to be fundamentally improved then the model suggests that those issues relating to the 'market/customer' area of the matrix model should be the focus of attention. Is the supplier addressing an appropriate segment of the customer market, especially those customers who represent long-term value and growth? Grocery retailers expect their main suppliers to continually search out and develop emerging categories with high growth potential. McDonald's was criticized for not committing more fully to the emerging fast-casual sector of the market.

Other stakeholders will also be important in the process of managing the network of relationships. This includes a firm's employees, for it is hardly novel to think that it makes good business sense to engage staff by informing them of what the company is trying to achieve, and involving them in developing appropriate solutions. Some previous work demonstrates quite clearly the important and fundamental role of internal marketing (Millier and Palmer, 2000; Gummesson, 2003). Other stakeholders might include trade associations, legislators, environmental groups and so on. Monsanto found that their failure to win the battle for hearts and minds with respect to genetically-modified food products in the European market was in part due to their failure to develop a meaningful dialogue with a wider group of stakeholders.

Having identified the customers and stakeholders that are relevant, then developing a full understanding of the key information for decision-making purposes is a notable feature of companies that successfully manage their relationships. For example, a multinational pharmaceutical company working with the medical profession has built a comprehensive database of medical practitioners. Each time a practitioner is contacted details are recorded electronically into the database and shared via an intranet system, so that detailed and accurate information can be accessed regularly by the sales team. Sales calls by various members of the field force are coordinated to maximize their time in front of doctors and the impact deriving from the consistency of their message and offerings.

## The Relationship Spiral

The marriage analogy is sometimes used, perhaps a little uncomfortably, to describe relationships (Tynan, 1999). In commerce, relationships have considerably more focus on the commercial realities, as perhaps some marriages also do, but without the intensity of emotional engagement. However, one area in which the analogy may be helpful is in understanding that relationships are not consistent in terms of their quality over time. While there may be fluctuations, relationships in which power is shared and commitment, trust and transparency are apparent will probably endure for the foreseeable future. In Chapter 5 we will examine in more detail the various dimensions of the power construct. Suffice it to say here that the actions of both parties can influence the direction and intensity of the level of competition or cooperation, and we refer to this as the relationship 'spiral', as shown in Figure 1.3.

The model reflects this in the dynamic that exists between the three constructs: interface, focus and power. The interface construct describes whether the relationship is discrete or continuous. If a supplier wishes to move from a series of discrete transactions and develop longer-term relationships with its customer, the model helps to understand how this might take place, always assuming that the buyer also seeks to build long-term relationships. If the relationship was initially based on transactions the focus, on behalf of the seller at least, was on gaining the sale. In order to develop a relationship basis the seller must undergo an attitudinal or even cultural change, demonstrate this to the buyer and seek a reciprocal indication of intent, based on some form of sharing.

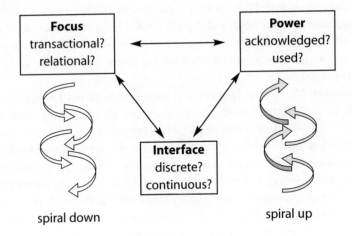

**Figure 1.3** The relationship spiral

In 1997 Marks and Spencer won the MORI/PA Consulting 'Quality of Management Award'. Gavin Barrett, a director of PA, commented that 'the awards ... were designed to focus on those management actions and priorities most likely to influence the performance of a company in the longer term for shareholder value'. His colleague, MORI Chairman Roger Stubbs, said that 'it is encouraging that the right formula, if there is one, for company success four years ago is very much the same as it is today'.

Prophetic words indeed, as four years later Marks and Spencer had spectacularly fallen from grace. With the benefit of hindsight such words can be classed alongside corporate flagpoles, personalized number plates and fish tanks in the reception area as a predictor of impending doom, as proved to be the case with Marks and Spencer. The management actions for long-term shareholder value and an apparent formula for company success had resulted in profits more than halving and Marks and Spencer's traditional ways of working, relationships and reputation changing dramatically.

The company was renowned for its insistence on quality. To be a supplier to Marks and Spencer was regarded as a seal of approval to its suppliers. The company had considerable involvement with its suppliers in all aspects of their production processes and raw material sourcing. There was little that the company did not consider it appropriate to be involved in. While there was no question that the company was a demanding customer, the supplier enjoyed the cachet of working with a blue-chip customer, which in some sectors, such as the food industry, was regarded as the highest of accolades. Suppliers also enjoyed the benefits of consistent volumes, mutual planning, the assurance of payment, and the personal relationships that developed over time. Some suppliers had enjoyed relationships stretching over many decades and the involvement between customer and supplier was deep and complex.

However, Marks and Spencer lost touch with its marketplace in the 1990s. Its core clothing products became somewhat less fashionable than those of its high street competitors, and competition eroded their value-for-money image. When asked to describe Marks and Spencer at this time one shopper noted that it seemed to centre around 'green, beige and tartan', green being the trademark house colour, beige referring to the blandness of its store environment, and tartan the unfashionable nature of its products. In 1999 alone profits more than halved compared with the previous year, and the share price plummeted.

Drastic action was required. Among other things the overseas businesses were disposed of, and issues such as branding, store layout and the design of its core clothing products were rapidly addressed. The company also needed to drive costs down in order to improve profitability, yet still meet the increasingly demanding price expectations of its own customers. Traditionally most of its products were manufactured in the UK, but the business review resulted in new suppliers being sourced from cheaper countries, such as Morocco and Israel. Some UK suppliers to Marks and Spencer found that their long-standing relationships were unceremoniously broken. Many of them supplied a significant proportion of their output to the company and while a written contract may not have existed, they had nonetheless planned forward and made commitments in anticipation of orders. Relationships rapidly soured to the extent that one of the previous suppliers, a clothing manufacturer by the name of William Baird, attempted to sue the company for £53.6 million after trading for over 30 years.

This story is a dramatic illustration of how power can be ruthlessly exercised, and the effect that it can have on transforming long-standing relationships.

Oh, and the company that came second in that 1997 survey? British Airways!

www.mori.com/polls/1997/awards.shtml,
wwws.marksandspencer.com,
Johnson and Scholes (2002)

The third element constituting the relationship is that of power, which will be examined in more detail in Chapter 5. Porter (1980) helps us to understand that while both buyers and suppliers have power, the use of that power is discretionary. If mutually committed to a relationship then both suppliers and buyers may restrain themselves from the overt use of their power, which would otherwise cause the relationship to become more competitive and transactional. The reality is that while power is always present in a relationship it is used less coercively than it could be. In that way the relationship is based on cooperation and trust, but with the knowledge of both parties that their power can be used as a last resort. As Kumar (1996) cautioned, after examining the power of trust in retailer–manufacturer relationships: 'Exploiting power may work in the short run, but it is self-defeating in the long run.'

## The Striped Leopard?

As mentioned previously, the idea that relationships can be seen as a continuum, as shown in Figure 1.2, with transactional styles at one pole and relational styles at the other, is a common one. This is referred to and accepted throughout the business-to-business marketing literature (Anderson and Narus, 1999; Hutt and Speh, 2001), as well as with respect to relationship marketing (Gronroos, 1990a).

Variations on this concept are common throughout the marketing literature. In discussing these ideas with managers, our personal experience suggests that a number of conclusions might be drawn:

- That a more advanced or progressive style of relationship is in some way 'better' than a lower order relationship based more on transactional thinking.
- That the length of the relationship is an indicator of the type of relationship, in that having traded for a considerable period of time might suggest strong, positive and continuous relationships.
- That by implementing good relationship practices it is possible to move from one position on a continuum – however that may be expressed – to another, and as a consequence to 'improve' the quality of the relationship.

These conclusions, however attractive they may appear, are open to questioning. For example, the length of the trading history may have little correlation with the extent to which a relational approach has developed. Second, they do not take into account the attitudes or needs of the customer for whom only one specific style of relationship may be appropriate. Third, while relationships may be expressed as being at some point on a continuum, this does not mean to say that an existing relationship style can be changed, or moved closer to some implied 'ideal' position.

When considering the nature of individual relationships, these are likely to be less flexible than the concept of a continuum would suggest. Taking these factors into account we can accept that leopards may try to change their spots, and cosmetic improvements can occur, but adopting stripes is likely to be altogether too demanding!

## The Relationship Triangle

How individual buyers and suppliers can understand their approach to relationships can be explained in Figure 1.4. Here, the interface between the two organizations is represented by a triangle. A line, as in Figure 1.2, implies a continuous and incremental approach to relationships. What Figure 1.4 suggests is that changing an individual style of relationship is difficult and demanding, since it requires a shift in the values, attitudes and culture of an organization for the transition to be successful. While a transition from one angle of the triangle to another may be difficult, it may also be necessary for companies such as McDonald's. Nor is it an impossible task, as an examination of the literature on the management of change theory will attest.

The triangle demonstrates that there may be little linkage between the length of the relationship and its quality, in terms of the extent to which mutual trust and commitment may exist. On the other hand, the stability of the relationship, that is the extent to which repeat and incremental business is likely to be obtained, is more likely to be closely related to the relationship quality. The diagram shows the positioning of a highly transactional relationship as being short-term, unstable and primarily driven by price. One example of this is local grocery retailers purchasing fresh produce regularly at auction.

The length of the relationship can often cause suppliers, in particular, to overestimate the quality of the relationship. In this circumstance, what might be termed 'sustained transactions' are assumed to be more akin to a cooperative and continuous relationship. However, buyers who are questioned about this often rate the quality of the relationship lower than their suppliers might, and couch their comments in terms of their subsumed

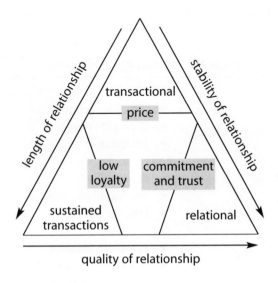

**Figure 1.4** The relationship triangle

power. As the sales director of a multinational company said to one author: 'I mean, we have long-standing relationships with many of our customers but they are pretty much ad hoc. Any single aspect could break that relationship. Short term, medium-term or long term or indeed forever!'

The marketing director of the European business unit of an American multinational described relationships in the following way:

> We have just signed a five-year agreement with one of our customers on a joint brand which is also taking some cost out of the chain, so we are trying to leverage our brand and enable ourselves to go down the chain and take them through our strategy.

These various types of relationships can be characterized in more detail, as in Table 1.2.

## Marketing Practice Typologies

The concept of a continuum is generally acknowledged to apply to all relationships, but, as has been argued, it does not necessarily apply to specific and individual supplier/buyer relationships. In the circumstances, modification of the type of relationship is feasible, but can be influenced by a wide range of factors. These could include: the type of industry and business; the culture attitudes and values of the respective buyer and supplier; and individuals within organizations who perceive that changes to the relationship could affect their status or power. In many cases there will be a

**Table 1.2** Relationship characteristics

| | |
|---|---|
| *Transactional* | • Minimize time to gain order |
| | • Low transaction costs |
| | • Low costs to serve |
| | • Importance of price |
| *Sustained transactional* | • Adversarial |
| | • Few supply alternatives |
| | • Frequent price check behaviour |
| *Relational* | • Extensive personal relationships |
| | • Collaborative activities |
| | • Mutual objectives |

limited discretion as to the types of relationships that are possible and indeed appropriate. The type of relationship will also affect the style of marketing practice that is adopted, and these marketing styles can be characterized into the typologies described in Table 1.3.

**Table 1.3** Typologies of marketing practice

| Typology | 'Relational' | 'Transactional' | 'Transactional Plus' |
|---|---|---|---|
| Focus: Transactional or relational? | Relational | Transactional | Transactional |
| Use of Power: Acknowledged? Asked? | Low | High | High |
| Interface | Relational | Transactional Sustained transactional | Transactional |
| Market/customer understanding | High | Low | Low |
| Marketing mix enhancement | High | Low | High |

These typologies provide a theoretical basis to our research findings, and will be discussed in Chapter 2 as we examine the nature of relationship marketing.

## CHAPTER 2

# Explanations of Marketing: Evolving, Changing or Competing?

## CHAPTER OBJECTIVES

This chapter seeks briefly to show how and why marketing has become an important business discipline. Towards the end of the twentieth century marketing experienced something of a reversal in popularity and esteem as a business function, with questions being asked as to the value of the contribution that marketing could make to business success. The classically successful approach to marketing, that which initially established it as a vital and perhaps even fashionable strategic tool, seemed to lose focus and application.

Various other explanations, theories even, of marketing emerged. Relationship marketing gained prominence, but did this represent a development of current marketing ideas? Was it a completely new way of thinking or perhaps just a confusing, unhelpful, contradictory and clever but impractical collection of ideas, serving only to divert time and resources from things that would really help the business. Managers nowadays are cynical about quick-fix solutions, yet the pressures they are under drive them constantly to seek out ways of meeting their objectives. Better to be seen to be doing something, anything, that has the potential to deliver, but how many such initiatives ultimately disappoint? Does marketing fall into that category now, and is relationship marketing the promise for the future?

This chapter will help to explain why this may or may not be the case by analyzing the background to relationship marketing, and discussing some of the issues that arise from that analysis, before then putting in place the background to the current research work and the findings it is generating.

## THE EVOLUTION OF MARKETING

The life cycle is a concept well known to marketers, and it can be used in a number of different contexts. Primarily we think of it as a tool for understanding how products perform over time. Michael Porter (1980), for example, used it in the context of analyzing industries. If the emergence of marketing as a business and management phenomenon is considered, then it is possible to propose a life cycle for marketing to illustrate how the discipline has developed (Figure 2.1). Marketing first emerged as a distinct business function in the period between the First and Second World Wars. This is when the classic consumer goods companies, such as Unilever and Procter & Gamble, started to develop the concepts of product and brand management (Shaw, 1998). There was a huge growth and interest in the subject of marketing in the postwar period through the 1950s and 1960s as the concepts of transaction marketing were developed (Borden, 1964) as embodied in the '4Ps' – namely, Product, Price, Promotion and Place (distribution) – which have served as a basic framework for marketing ever since.

As the life cycle illustrates, the rise in consumer demand and disposable income in the 1950s, together with new means of mass communication, notably television, stimulated growth. Of course such early television advertisements viewed now seem quaint and naïve, but the persuasive power of advertising heralded a golden age for manufacturers. Rapid technological development and innovation in the post-war period, often a by-product of military efforts, produced a continuing stream of new and innovative products.

With hindsight, the challenge for businesses during this period can now largely be seen as putting in place the means of production to satisfy growing demand, using the new and powerful techniques of marketing to

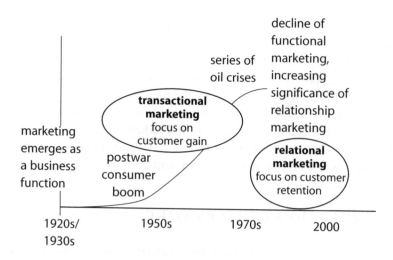

**Figure 2.1** The evolution of marketing

capture consumers as they enter the market. The focus was transactional: that is to say, on gaining these new customers, with the primary intention of selling products against a backdrop of apparently ever expanding demand as the disposable income of consumers increased in line with economic growth. By expanding and developing the product range new features and benefits help to sustain demand. Micro-economics – the relationship between price, quantity, supply and demand – offer an underlying explanation of this type of marketing practice, as product ranges expanded to offer more features delivering more benefits at enhanced prices. It was said of this time 'American manufacturing industry could not go wrong even if it tried' (Heskett, 1994). This concept then was largely a North American one exported to other developed and developing economies.

The series of oil crises in the 1970s reverberated throughout the global economic system. The continual rise in consumer demand was halted due to the economic problems that arose. The high inflation that followed acted to alter customers' perceptions. Within society there was a growth of interest in consumer and wider environmental issues. For example, Rachel Carson's book *Silent Spring* (1962) is widely acknowledged to have kick-started the environmental movement, and consumers increasingly appreciated the power they had to influence manufacturers. Consumers were no longer passive recipients of persuasive marketing messages designed to extract their disposable income. Chapter 7 discusses these drivers of change in more detail.

The decline of manufacturing industries saw a rise in service industries. Increased emphasis was placed on the development of services, and how these can be incorporated into products. This was one of the bases for the concept of relationship marketing which will be discussed later in this chapter. Nowadays manufacturers of products find themselves competing in a very different environment from that of the 1950s and 1960s, the golden age of transactional marketing. Markets are saturated: consumers are more aware and questioning of the products and services they purchase, and more than ever able and willing to use their purchasing power to tame marketers who are perceived to abuse their trust. The title of a book by Robert Rodin, *Free, Perfect and Now* (1999), seems to summarize quite nicely the attitude and needs of the smart, information-empowered, e-enabled consumer of the twenty-first century. Anything less than free, perfect and now results in disappointment; the task now is not to raise and meet customer expectations as a way of competing, but to manage them in such a way that they can be sensibly achieved. Marketers may beat their breasts in frustration at the way the market has evolved, but perhaps the way we have treated our customers has influenced the way they now treat us.

The UK financial services industry was deregulated in the mid-1980s. This allowed consumers greater freedom of choice as to how they manage their own affairs, and companies rushed to develop products and services to attract their savings and pension fund investments. However, some consumers were not sufficiently astute or aware of all the issues surrounding the purchase of the various financial products available. The sales methods that the companies used in selling such products, and in particular the attractive upfront commissions offered to sales staff and agents, led to the widespread misselling of investment and pension products. Those selling them benefited greatly in the short term from the high levels of commission that such sales generated but the long-term consequences for their clients, and indeed for their suppliers, were appalling.

It later became apparent that many thousands of investors were sold products that were not suited to their needs. The regulatory authorities intervened and companies then became mired in complex and expensive compensation procedures. Once-great brand names developed over decades, even centuries, had been substantially degraded. The reputation of an industry had been ruined and trust and confidence eroded. Customers had been abused on such a wide scale that Nick Gardner, a respected commentator at the time, writing in *The Sunday Times* (2000) under the headline 'Financial Services can be Trusted to Play Dirty', began his article: 'I would trust financial institutions with my money for as long as I trust my cat in the kitchen with the Christmas turkey.' Continuing in a similar vein, he concluded: 'Imagine the most cynical businessman you can, then add a respectable name and you have captured the essence of the British financial services industry.'

Has the industry learnt from this lesson? Apparently not. A loan scam in Australia resulted in investors buying property valued above market rates with loans provided by a bank. The bank subsequently recompensed some investors under the terms of a strict non-disclosure agreement. It took a 63-year-old grandmother, troubled by her moral duty to other investors, to make her settlement public despite concerns that she might be sued. Sources close to the bank said it would be a 'PR catastrophe considering it was Westpac's involvement in the marketeering that caused her so much grief in the first place'. The bank refused to comment as to why it was paying off some customers but invited customers to contact their Complaints Review Committee (*Courier-Mail*, Brisbane, 15 March 2003).

> Is it any surprise that consumers have generally become much more aware of their rights, more demanding of the value that is delivered in the products that they purchase, and generally more cynical and battle-hardened?
> It's called learning – and who taught them?

The automotive industry is often taken as a bellwether for manufacturing and the economy generally. In Western Europe currently one-third of manufacturing capacity is not utilized. The automotive market is, like so many others, mature. Capacity exceeds demand; corporate and individual purchasers know how to use their buying power, and are happy to exercise it. Combine this with greater access to information from consumer groups, the Internet and so on. Add in more open markets and transparency between markets, then not surprisingly manufacturers find their volumes and margins squeezed despite their efforts to manage markets and maintain their price and position in them (Wootten, 2003).

Or consider the comparison between television ownership in the 1950s and 1960s and today. Then a grainy black-and-white television was regarded as an aspirational consumer luxury. Now, most of our homes have several television sets, perhaps in different rooms and for use by different members of the family. In addition reliability has improved, and replacement due to irreparable failure only occurs after an average of around 14 years; frequently replacement takes place for other reasons, such as an upgrade to take advantage of a new feature.

The question therefore arises for providers of goods and services as to whether the concepts of the 4Ps or transactional marketing developed in the very different environment of the 1950s and 1960s are still relevant and appropriate in the twenty-first century. These concepts were developed with particular application to consumer markets some way removed from the highly competitive, saturated markets that we now experience. Of course we should also remember that behind every consumer is a supply chain, with the inference that most marketing is actually between members of that supply chain. In fact, due to this, marketing is practised more in the context of one business and another, but is less visible. In these circumstances different criteria are important and the conventional view of marketing from a consumer perspective, with its focus on brands, the range of products, and communication in its various forms is less relevant.

Many commentators have expressed these ideas by suggesting that marketing has passed through a series of stages or eras (for example

Webster, 1992); underlying this is a change in emphasis from transaction to relationship marketing. This has led to a discussion as to whether or not the magnitude of change is such as to justify it being described as a paradigm shift, a point which was discussed in the Introduction. As an alternative to the paradigm shift argument, the transactionally based view of marketing may simply be supplemented with more 'Ps' in addition to the conventional 4Ps. This represents the 'marketing mix plus' perspective, whereby change is understood as incremental rather than stepwise. While there are arguments for and against these development routes, which will be considered shortly, there is widespread agreement that relationship marketing is a new phenomenon.


## NO NEW CUSTOMERS

Businesses today find themselves in circumstances where markets are largely mature. Few if any new customers are emerging; in fact, mergers and acquisitions actually reduce customer numbers and increase the commercial significance of those that remain. Hence those customers that remain are larger and more significant. They are also something else – smarter. They have to be to have survived in the challenging business environment of today. This is happening on a global scale as industries rationalise and individual companies seek more effective ways of managing their customers and beating their competitors. The automobile industry provides an example of this as competitors have left or been taken over to leave just a few major, global players, who themselves are predicted to rationalize still further (Figure 2.2).

The consequences of this are felt both upstream and downstream within the supply chain. For example, there are now only five major global suppliers of glass to the automotive industry, the largest single customer being General Motors. This type of analysis can be repeated with other industries – pharmaceuticals, airlines, brewing, consulting services, banking, and so on. With the growth in buying power and the increased reach of such companies there are clearly implications for the way that they work with their suppliers. Some of the other implications of maturity are noted in Table 2.1. Arguably transaction marketing is likely to be less effective; no new customers are entering the market, products are broadly similar and there is a high degree of customer knowledge and understanding of the products being purchased.

Relationship marketing emphasizes the financial value of the retained customer (Reichheld and Sasser, 1990). What is more, in mature

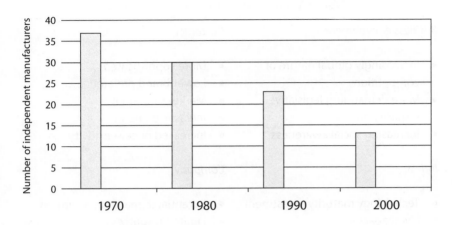

**Figure 2.2** Global automotive industry – rationalization over time

markets such customers have a different and more important strategic value to the firm. The emphasis is at least as much on retaining current customers, and therefore depriving competitors of the benefit of having them, as it is on attracting new customers with all the costs of acquisition that this entails. This would argue that relationship marketing is a contextual response to a changing, largely adverse, mature business environment.

## THE MOMENTUM FOR RELATIONSHIP MARKETING

As Wensley (1995) states: 'the basic micro-economic framework...should not be seen as an adequate description of the analytical and processual complexities in specific situations'.

The reason for this has been ascribed to changes in the pattern of demand as the postwar boom in consumer and industrial products, particularly in the affluent markets of the west, has declined (Sheth and Parvatiyar, 2000b). In tandem there has been a rise in service-based industries, and an overall increase in the importance of service as an integral part of the product offering (Gummesson, 1987). The reasons for this relate to fundamental changes in the business environment and the nature of customers and demand (Buttle, 1996). The dramatic increase in the development and application of technology makes more information more available in more places, and at costs that are orders of magnitude lower than before (Table 2.2).

**Table 2.1** Implications for marketing practice

| Business environment | Customer |
|---|---|
| • Increasingly global nature of competition<br>• More demanding legislative requirements<br>• Increasing social awareness | • More sophisticated<br>• Lower brand preference<br>• Market saturation<br>• Inelastic demand<br>• Increased price sensitivity |
| Industry | Company |
| • Technology maturity investment<br>• Overcapacity<br>• Stabilization of production methods<br>• Technology and cumulative experience common<br>• Stabilization and concentration of market shares | • Potential to maintain return on<br>• Limited resources<br>• Little opportunity for differentiation<br>• Increase in private label<br>• Product modification rather than innovation |

The factors that presage relationship marketing can be summarized as:

- the decline of traditional mass marketing techniques as customers become more discriminating and demanding
- the saturation of markets as they mature
- the consequent focus on price
- technological developments providing new solutions and products
- the changing nature of markets, particularly the increase in competition and development of fragmented/regional/global markets and companies.

Another factor that cannot be summarized quite so explicitly is the search for new solutions, as managers address increasingly intractable problems. Relationship marketing also tapped into this vein of enquiry, and with promulgation of the concept by academics, consultants and others relationship marketing became, in a word, fashionable.

All of this would imply that relationship marketing is a consistent concept that leads on incrementally from transaction marketing, and all that a manager has to do is pick up on the techniques and await the results. Of course the reality is substantially different. The genesis is by no means

Table 2.2 Price of computing power and speed

|  | 1970 | 1999 |
|---|---|---|
| Cost of 1MHz processing power | $7 601 | 17 ¢ |
| Cost of 1MB storage | $5 257 | 17 ¢ |
| Cost of transmitting 1 trillion bits | $150 000 | 12 ¢ |

Source: *Economist*, Federal Reserve Bank of Dallas

straightforward, and there are a number of streams of thought that contribute to the understanding of the subject area.

To define relationship marketing is to distinguish it from the microeconomic paradigm. Central to relationship marketing lies the concept that customers have continuing value over and above that of individual and discrete transactions. The focus is therefore on the relationship rather than the transaction. An early definition of relationship marketing is provided by Gronroos (1990a):

> The role of relationship marketing is to identify, establish, maintain and enhance relationships with customers and other stakeholders, at a profit, so that the objectives of all other parties involved are met; and that this is done by a mutual exchange and fulfilment of promises.

Further objectives of relationship marketing include the satisfaction of customers through the delivery of sustained or increasing levels of satisfaction, and the retention of those customers by the maintenance and promotion of the relationship.

These are appealing objectives, particularly for sellers seeking to secure their business. The reality, however, is that not all customers want or require a relationship with their supplier (Blois, 1996). Thus the contrast between transactional or traditional marketing and relationship marketing may be indistinct; furthermore, it has yet to acquire 'uncontested status or meaning' (Buttle, 1996). In addition the research work in the area suffers from a lack of co-ordination between the research areas and different streams of work, to the extent that one prominent academic described this as 'scientific myopia' (Mattson, 1997). The next section attempts to explain some of the perspectives that have contributed to the current understanding of relationship marketing.

## A SYNTHESIS OF RELATIONSHIP MARKETING

If relationship marketing is not quite as discrete and all-encompassing as a cursory insight into the subject might suggest, then there is a need to explain the subject so that the nuances can be understood. In principle the analysis could be conducted in two main ways. First, by looking horizontally, as it were, across the various clusters of research. In this way the concepts involved can be compared and contrasted. For example, the concept of a relationship could be examined from a number of different perspectives.

Alternatively, a vertical approach can be used whereby the various research 'streams' are analyzed; these are often referred to as 'schools of thought'. However, these are not 'schools' in the accepted sense of an establishment on which the research focuses, but more a recognition of, and mutual commitment to, a discipline through research, academic publications and practice.

The schools of thought approach is actually more commonly used in the academic world to analyze relationship marketing, and also formed the basis of the work of the Contemporary Marketing Practice group.

## THE NORDIC SCHOOL OF SERVICES

The Nordic area is strongly associated with relationship marketing. This school of thought originated from the field of services marketing: the Nordic school of services. The Nordic school originated in the late 1970s in response to perceived shortcomings in the conventional transaction marketing approach. Its central core of researchers and practitioners developed the concept of service as a means of improving the quality of the relationship, stimulating customer loyalty and extending the customer life cycle.

SAS, formerly Scandinavian Airline Systems, is an example of this approach in practice. The then Chief Executive, Jan Carlzon, practised the idea of the 'moment of truth' (Carlzon, 1989). This suggests that in a service encounter there are certain critical elements that define the customers' perception of the service they have received. There can be few of us who have not been told by a pre-recorded voice that 'your call is important to us' when telephoning a company – so we will waste your time because we cannot be bothered to put a human being on the phone. An immediate negative moment of truth in many cases!

This illustrates that people are actually important in providing service. It is people, not faceless companies, that provide empathy and concern for the customer. This is an early clue that our own employees have a critical role to play in the context of relationship marketing, to the extent that we could regard our own staff as a market in themselves. This idea is enlarged upon elsewhere in this book.

## THE IMP TRADITION

Another research group with links to Scandinavia is the IMP (Industrial Marketing and Purchasing) tradition. This is associated with business to business markets and the understanding of organizational relationships. It is one of the largest research groups of its type, and has made a major contribution to understanding in the area, although it is sometimes criticized for being unduly academic and lacking application in the context of business. As with the Nordic school, this group of researchers, formed in the 1970s, identified the distinctive characteristics of business to business relationships and the factors that caused these relationships to evolve. They could be forgiven for questioning the latterday focus on relationships in marketing; their work has illustrated that relationships have always been important, particularly in the context of business to business marketing.

The IMP group focuses on the interaction between companies on the basis that transactions are not isolated events but part of a continual stream of engagement. This is an important point to note: most business to business relationships are not transactional – discrete and independent of each other – but ongoing. Companies can and do have a long tradition of trading together, of forming complex interdependencies, while their respective workforces form business and personal relationships.

The individual interactions takes place within the context of a relationship, and this in turn is part of a network of relationships within which companies are positioned (Wensley, 1995). A network therefore consists of a complex web of interdependencies. There is an incentive for all members of the network to work together to their mutual benefit and to compete against other networks. A company's failure to establish its position in a network can seriously detract from performance or even affect survival. The lesson to be learnt is that managers should actively identify and manage their position in a network. A good example is that of airline alliances.

There are two major airline alliances in operation: One World and Star Alliance.

| **One World** | **Star Alliance** |
|---|---|
| British Airways | Air Canada |
| American Airlines | Air New Zealand |
| Qantas | ANA |
| Aer Lingus | Austrian Airlines |
| Iberia | BMI British Midland |
| Finnair | Asiana Airlines |
| Lan Chile | Lufthansa |
| Cathay Pacific | Mexicana Airlines |
| | SAS |
| | Singapore Airlines |
| | Thai Airways |
| | United Airlines |
| | Varig |

As can be seen, each alliance is an interesting mix of major international carriers and lesser-known airlines. By working together each airline benefits. The larger airlines have the opportunity to extend their reach and allow their major international routes to feed into local destinations. This enables them to offer enhanced service and capture more revenue but with minimal additional expense, while smaller airlines have the opportunity to gain incremental business from those passengers wishing to connect with international flights. However, once the alliance has been initiated each member will be looking to benefit their own business further while excluding competitors. As alliances form and develop the opportunities for airlines not involved in the network progressively diminish. Unless an airline controls or can give access to a strategic destination then it has little to offer other alliance members. The chronic lack of profitability in the airline industry means that membership of an alliance is a powerful factor in competition and survival.

Sabena, the financially distressed national airline of Belgium, was not a member of an alliance, nor was Swissair. Swissair was under pressure from a number of factors: some questionable management decisions together with the recent entry of low-cost carrier EasyJet into the Swiss market through the acquisition of a local airline. Increasingly desperate to join or develop an alliance, Swissair decided to acquire Sabena; this proved to be a catastrophic move. There was little synergy between the two airlines to generate additional traffic. Swissair itself was hardly enjoying good financial health. Its poor management decisions, the drain on capital caused by the acquisition, and poor outcome from the acquisition combined to bring the company down.

Swissair's failure to recognize and manage its position in an industry increasingly dominated by larger strategic groups proved fatal. However, the loss of the national airline was too great a blow to Swiss pride and powerful financial interests worked to re-establish a new national carrier. It is also interesting to note that shortly after this a member of each of the major alliances also ran into grave financial problems, with both American Airlines and Air New Zealand effectively becoming bankrupt. Qantas plan to acquire Air New Zealand, subject to regulatory approval, and it will be interesting to see how the various alliances adapt and respond to changes in the competitive environment.

The two schools of thought discussed here are acknowledged by many authors in so far as they follow this method of analysis for their contribution to the field of relationship marketing. From this point on views diverge, and a number of other schools of thought are discussed as potential contributors to this analysis. Arguably, the most prominent amongst these other schools is one which has become known as the Anglo-Australian school (Sheth and Parvatiyar, 2000).

## THE ANGLO-AUSTRALIAN APPROACH

This perspective sees traditional marketing as being built upon and enhanced by quality and service, to form a comprehensive approach to delivering increasing levels of value to customers in enduring relationships with the company (Christopher, Payne and Ballantyne, 1991). As with the other traditions this is regarded as a holistic or integrative approach to business, operating in a cross-functional way to provide customer satisfaction and increasing levels of value. A prominent feature is the definition of six markets or stakeholder groups that the firm should address in varying degrees to achieve its objectives (Figure 2.3). Relationships with each of these markets, as appropriate, should be built and maintained.

Quality initiatives were a common feature of businesses through the 1980s, as Japanese management techniques in particular became more widely adopted. This was usually associated with the manufacturing function as a way of improving the physical quality of products. Similarly, customer service achieved heightened levels of popularity, particularly in the financial services sector, as companies with largely similar products sought a means of differentiation.

These developments met with mixed success. Total quality management was mainly seen as the domain of manufacturing and operations (Ballantyne, 1994). Product quality improved and costs were consequently lowered as quality techniques became more universal, whereby competitive advantage and differentiation on the basis of quality, and indirectly lower price, began to diminish (Porter, 1996).

In practice customer service strategies can encounter a number of problems in implementation, such as the functional separation of marketing from logistics since marketing constitutes the service promise maker on the one hand, while the rest of the company acts as the service promise provider on the other. The personal commitment of individuals to provide service is also important. This may be variable due to misalignment of strategic intent, confusing communications and ill-trained and poorly committed staff. Ballantyne (1994) refers to these as 'lost clusters' that are laudable in intent but vulnerable to failure in practice due to the lack of an overarching orientation.

These three 'schools of thought' are identified as the best developed of the conceptualizations of relationship marketing. They are summarized in terms of their main points of difference in Table 2.3.

**Figure 2.3** The six market model

**Table 2.3** Comparison of main components of major schools of relationship marketing versus transaction marketing

| Key variable | Transaction marketing | IMP group | Nordic School | Anglo-Australian approach |
|---|---|---|---|---|
| Basis | Exchange 4Ps | Relationship between firms | Service | Service/ quality/ marketing |
| Timeframe | Short term | Short and long term | Long term | Long term |
| Market | Single, customer | Multiple, network | 30 with 4 categories | 6 |
| Organization | Hierarchical, functional | | Functional and cross functional | Cross functional, process based |
| Basis of exchange | Price | Product/ service, information, financial, social | Less sensitive to price | Perceived value |
| (Product)/ quality dimension | Product/ technical/ output quality | Technological | Interaction quality | Function of value and cost of ownership |
| Measurement | Revenue market share | Customer profitability | Quality, value, customer satisfaction | Customer satisfaction |
| Customer information | Ad hoc | Varies by relationship stage | Individual | Customer value and retention |
| Internal marketing | | | Substantial strategic importance | Integral to the concept |
| Service | Augmentation to core product | Close seller/ buyer relations | Integral to product | Basis for differentiation |

Source: Palmer, 2001

## MID-RANGE PERSPECTIVES

The 'schools of thought' analysis allows us to see that there are a number of alternative explanations of relationship marketing, as briefly discussed, but there are also many other possible explanations competing for attention. This is a diverse field with no single best explanation, and relationship marketing, however appealing as a concept, poses many challenges when subjected to more detailed scrutiny.

The nature of paradigm shift was discussed in Chapter 1, and there are proponents who suggest that this has happened in the field of marketing in response to the overwhelming forces of change that are affecting businesses. However, as these theoretical ideas move closer to the marketplace so the process of matching the explanation with the evidence becomes more difficult. Attempts continue in order to develop a comprehensive understanding. The debate has proliferated and there have been many attempts to post-rationalize the body of research work in order to provide a more unified and coherent explanation of the new realities of marketing. In contrast to the paradigm shift argument – that we move in a binary way from darkness on the one hand to light on the other – there are additional views put forward that suggest various types of marketing can coexist, and that is not the case of either transactional or relational marketing (for example Aijo, 1996; Palmer, 1996; Mattsson, 1997; Eggert and Stieff, 1999; Pels, Coviello and Brodie, 1999). This is the 'marketing mix plus' argument mentioned earlier.

Mattsson (1997) has proposed that there are various types of relationship marketing; these he refers to as limited and extended. The limited view, he proposes, is essentially an elaboration of the conventional marketing model or transactional approach. In his discussion of the extended view of relationship marketing he proposes that this is more aligned with a network or relationship perspective of marketing. Palmer (1996) largely aligns with this view, but also introduces and supports the notion that there is a philosophical element underlying the adoption of relationship marketing practices.

In other words, relationship marketing is not simply a matter of objective analysis and rational decision making, together with a plan of action to switch actively from one approach to another. Rather it is a reflection of the culture, values and attitudes of the organization: the organizational culture, sustained by the belief and commitment of the people working for it. In this case relationship marketing is not an objective concept to be adopted consciously, but the style of marketing is simply a reflection of 'the way we do things around here'.

Eggert and Stieff (1999) have built on this by introducing the idea that relationship marketing can be seen as behavioural or attitudinal. The behavioural approach involves a series of transactions on behalf of the seller designed to achieve repeat transactions through a process of interaction with the buyer, typically driven by economic goals rather than including some of the wider aspects of the exchange such as customer satisfaction.

---

### 'Have a nice day'

How many times have we, as consumers, experienced an insincere greeting such as this? The 'have a nice day' syndrome typifies a routinized approach to customer service where, by establishing procedures, service levels can be consistently maintained and efficiently managed. The downside of this behavioural approach is that it simply becomes meaningless and empty as the perhaps underpaid, undervalued, poorly trained frontline member of staff asks for the thousandth time – 'you want fries with that?'

Those organizations that successfully adopt this managed approach to service can consistently achieve their objectives. First Direct, a telephone banking service established by HSBC in the UK, was said by George Day, Professor of Marketing at the Wharton Business School, Pennsylvania, to be the best telephone banking service in the world. In this case, the staff are engaged and involved, and demonstrate their own commitment to the customer to achieve outstanding levels of customer satisfaction.

Heaven forbid that we have to suffer the truly gruesome experience of one of the authors when checking out of a hotel in Mahwah, New Jersey. When heading for the door and the waiting taxi, the receptionist called out 'Missing you already!'

---

This behavioural style aligns with the tactical or marketing mix plus approach suggested by Palmer and Mattsson. As a contrast to this Eggert and Stieff suggest the alternative is the attitudinal perspective. The relationship is not characterized by the desire of the seller to achieve a transaction or series of transactions, but the motivation is to achieve a state of mutual acknowledgement that the relationship exists.

Pels et al. (2003) introduce the view that transactional and relational marketing can coexist within the organization, and that the styles of marketing discussed are not mutually exclusive but concurrent. Intuitively this has appeal; we can understand that there are different types of customer who need to be treated and managed in different ways. There are ever more opportunities to consider this from a range of perspectives, and these various finer forms of analysis are demonstrated in Table 2.4. The headings used relate to the terminology used by the authors themselves.

As this analysis suggests, transactional or relationship styles of marketing do not necessarily involve a binary decision – it is not a case of either one or the other. In fact, it may not involve a decision at all. The culture of the organization may be such that the approach to customers is inherent within the firm, and that the cultural values of the organization are simply so strong that it is not possible to consider the magnitude of change that would be necessary.

It seems that it is only when a severe and sustained downturn in performance is experienced that organizations are prepared, or perhaps forced, to address the issues of cultural change. Examples would include the turn-around experienced by Marks and Spencer in the UK, under the leadership of the Belgian chief executive Luc Vandevelde. Japanese car manufacturer Nissan saw a dramatic and positive change in its fortunes following the appointment of Carlos Ghosn. The importance of leadership as a catalyst for change in such circumstances has been well researched (Grinyer, Mayes and McKiernan, 1979).

## RELATIONSHIP MARKETING IN PRACTICE

All of this suggests that a company does not necessarily undergo a religious-style transformation from transaction marketing heathen to relationship marketing high priest, but can adopt a position somewhere in between. Rather than making a long term, strategic commitment to relationship

**Table 2.4** Relational exchange perspectives

|                      | Tactical | Strategic | Philosophical | Categorization |
|----------------------|----------|-----------|---------------|----------------|
| Berry, 1995          | √        | √         | √             |                |
| Palmer, 1996         | √        | √         | √             |                |
| Mattsson, 1997       | √        | √         |               |                |
| Eggert & Stieff, 1999| √        |           | √             |                |
| Pels et al., 1999    | √        | √         |               | √              |

marketing it may be appropriate to develop a more tactical approach: for example, by allocating some resources to managing and maintaining ongoing relationships with key clients, or by putting in place a low-cost route to market for those who require the cheapest price. In this way the company can optimize its reach within the marketplace. To restrict the approach to customers and the marketplace may reduce the opportunities for the company. This once again asserts the fundamental necessity to understand the nature of the marketplace, and the role of segmentation of customers as the basis for sound marketing strategy.

The relationship marketing area is, surprisingly, notable for the lack of empirical work to underpin the considerable conceptual development that has taken place (Buttle, 1996; Mattsson, 1997). Hence these tentative conclusions at this stage. However some of the early work by the CMP group supported this pluralistic view of relational exchanges. For example the work of Brodie, Coviello, Brookes and Little (1997) is one of the few empirical studies conducted in this area, and it illustrates a range of transactional and relational marketing approaches exhibited by the companies they studied. Other work by the CMP group noted that 'neither relational nor transactional marketing fully capture the essence of current marketing practice' (Coviello, Brodie, Brookes and Collins, 1997), and also identified that firms can exhibit a range of marketing styles in the same market. Morris, Brunyee and Page (1998) also reported mid-range relationship marketing practice in their survey-based research. All of this suggests that further work is desirable in order to understand and characterize the phenomenon of relationship marketing in more detail. The more recent work of the CMP group designed to investigate this in greater detail is discussed in Chapter 7.

If it is possible, and indeed feasible, to adopt a mid-range position with both relational and transactional practices implemented concurrently, then it could be argued that this would be the ideal solution for most companies. We could expect to see that most would adopt mid-range practices. This is perhaps too simplistic a view, however, and is based upon a widely held but perhaps imperfect assumption.

Barbara Jackson (1985) was one of the first to suggest that relationships could be described along a continuum, with transactional and relational practices at the opposing poles. Somewhere in the middle is the 'always a share buyer' who maintains a small portfolio of suppliers that are constantly traded one off against the other. The concept of the continuum has been widely promulgated, and is a recurring theme in the relationship marketing literature. The assumption that can be drawn from this is that the contrast between transactional and relational styles of marketing is therefore a continuous one, and capable of incremental adaptation and variation. A later chapter discusses a triangular model of relationships that suggests that the transition between styles is somewhat more challenging than a continuous model would suppose. The changes and adaptations to organizational culture are such that it is difficult to be all things to all people, and that some compromise is needed between what the organization is capable of doing and the expectations of the marketplace.

One factor that may affect the organization's approach to the market is the relationship between fixed and variable costs as a proportion of overall selling price (Table 2.5). Some initial research work concerned the relationship between the capital intensity of the business and the propensity to adopt relationship marketing techniques (Palmer, 2001). In this case a high fixed cost business – 70 per cent of selling price constituted fixed costs – was compared to a lower fixed cost business, where the equivalent figure was around 40 per cent and declining as the management team worked to improve efficiency. Both businesses were large, multinational corporations and the research work was carried out in Europe and the USA.

What these findings suggest is that with the low margin, high fixed cost business the primary concern is to generate sufficient revenue to achieve at least a break-even level of return. The emphasis of the business is volume driven, and there is little opportunity to differentiate the

**Table 2.5** Capital intensity and marketing practice

|  | Capital intensity | |
|---|---|---|
|  | *High* | *Low* |
| Service level | Low, supply driven | High, demand driven |
| Product differentiation | Low | High |
| Customer knowledge | Low | High |
| Propensity to add value | Low | High |
| Importance of price | High | Low |
| Add value by | Reducing costs | Product/service/relationship development |

product. In filling the capacity every order becomes a good order, and while the company has long-standing relationships with its customers there is considerable focus on price. By contrast, the low fixed cost business has manufacturing sites around the USA and Europe. The relatively low barriers to entry have encouraged low cost producers in India and China to enter the market, with the capability to produce similar products at prices some 40 per cent lower. To maintain position in the market this company has little option other than to seek points of differentiation; simply lowering the cost base is highly unlikely to achieve comparability with competitors who migrate manufacturing to lower-cost economies.

While these findings are tentative they raise the interesting question of whether industries, particularly mature ones that share common features such as lack of growth, product parity and common technology, also adopt similar styles of marketing. Are there ways in which companies within an industry can change the rules of the game by means of a stepwise change in the cost base? An example would be in the airline industry, where low-cost operators such as Ryanair (Ireland), EasyJet (UK) and Virgin Blue (Australia) have mimicked the low-cost model first developed by Southwest Airlines (US) to compete effectively, and profitably, against the national flag carriers.

So, of course, there is not yet a comprehensive explanation of marketing practice and further work is needed to determine the circumstances and conditions that are appropriate for particular styles of marketing, and what it is that drives change. We need a more detailed contextual understanding to avoid 'tablets of stone'-type prescriptions of what it is good for companies to do, as well as a more detailed understanding of the context that places boundaries around the various marketing practices. This also helps to answer not just the 'what' but the all-important 'why' questions.

## RESEARCHING RELATIONSHIP MARKETING

As is probably apparent from the foregoing discussion, there is a considerable need to develop greater insight into the practice of marketing through the relationship lens. While the field is conceptually well developed, there is insufficient empirical evidence to support and extend the assertions that are made in the name of relationship marketing. Saren and Tzokas (1997) note their concern in this respect and comment that there is a need to 'more carefully define and understand some of the key concepts with which managers practising relationship marketing have to deal'.

The CMP group present two potential solutions to this problem. Both have their basis in a rigorous analysis of the diverse strands of relationship marketing presented by the schools of thought. The benefit of the solutions is that they present researchers with a framework within which the practice of relationship marketing can be further investigated. The results derived from these frameworks represent the basis for this book, and a significant step in bringing this large body of academic research into the practitioner and managerial domain.

## RELATIONSHIP AND MANAGERIAL DIMENSIONS

The original founders of the CMP group developed a series of dimensions that represented an analysis and then synthesis of some of the rather disparate and profound, but not really researchable, academic ideas that prevailed at the time. Brodie, Coviello, Brookes and Little (1997) expanded the work of Coviello, Brodie, Brookes and Collins (1997) and reconciled and focused the various views of relationship marketing from European, North American and other perspectives. This was based on empirical testing and content analysis of how previous researchers had used and defined terms. This elicited twelve dimensions that were divided into two categories:

Relational exchange category:

- the focus of the relational exchange
- parties involved in relational exchange
- communication patterns between parties
- type of contact between parties
- duration of the relational exchange
- formality of the relational exchange
- balance of power in the relational exchange.

Management activities and processes category:

- managerial intent regarding customers and other parties
- managerial decision-making focus
- types of marketing investment made by firm
- organizational level at which marketing decisions are implemented
- managerial planning time frame.

These are described in further detail by each of the relational and management dimensions in Tables 2.6 and 2.7.

The unique benefit of these dimensions – at the time – was that they enabled the diverse field of relationship marketing to be summarized as the basis for further work. This further work took the form of a questionnaire which was then used to investigate marketing practice. This was conceived in the form of a series of typologies that described different types of practice. The initial work identified four typologies, and subsequently a fifth was added that described e-marketing:

Transactional:

1. Transaction marketing (TM) – managing the marketing mix to attract and satisfy customers.

Relational:

2. Database marketing (DM) – using technology-based tools to target and retain customers.
3. Interaction marketing (IM) – developing interpersonal relationships between individual customers and sellers.
4. Network marketing (NM) – positioning the firm in a connected set of inter-firm relationships.
5. E-marketing (EM) – the use of interactive technologies to create and mediate dialogues between the firm and identified customers.

It is unrealistic to think that this is the end point of the research. Good research should not only provide some answers but also stimulate further questions. IT is now ubiquitous within many firms, and we should continue to challenge the findings and ask whether it is realistic to identify database marketing and e-marketing as distinct marketing practices (Brady, Saren and Tzokas, 2002a). Is it not the case that all marketing is facilitated by, and involves, IT tools at some stage? How do we characterize each of these styles of marketing and identify them in practice, and what represents good and bad practice? It is also evident that some firms are attempting to change their style of marketing practice in response to the environmental changes that they perceive: how easy is it to make the transition from one style of practice to another, and what are the critical success factors involved?

All of these are issues that are being addressed by research that is currently in place. However, the dimensions of relationship marketing and

**Table 2.6** Types of marketing classified by managerial dimensions

| | Transactional perspective | | Relational perspective | |
| --- | --- | --- | --- | --- |
| | Type: Transaction marketing | Type: Database marketing | Type: Interaction marketing | Type: Network marketing |
| Managerial intent | Customer attraction (to satisfy the customer at a profit) | Customer retention (to satisfy the customer, increase profit, and attain other objectives such as increased loyalty, decreased customer risk) | Interaction (to establish, develop and facilitate a cooperative relationship for mutual benefit) | Coordination (interaction between sellers, buyers, and other parties across multiple firms for mutual benefit, resource exchange, market access) |
| Decision focus | Product or brand | Product/brand and customers (in a targeted market) | Relationships between individuals | Connected relationships between firms (in a network) |
| Managerial investment | Internal marketing assets (focusing on product/service, price, distribution, promotion capabilities) | Internal marketing assets (emphasizing communication, information and technology capabilities) | External market assets (focusing on establishing and developing a relationship with another individual) | External market assets (focusing on developing the firm's position in a network of firms) |
| Managerial level | Functional marketers (e.g. sales manager, product development manager) | Specialist marketers (e.g. customer service manager, loyalty manager) | Managers from across functions and levels in the firm | General manager |
| Time frame | Short term | Longer term | Short or long term | Short or long term |

Source: Coviello et al, 1997

**Table 2.7** Types of marketing classified by relational dimensions

| | Transactional perspective | | Relational perspective | |
|---|---|---|---|---|
| | Type: Transaction marketing | Type: Database marketing | Type: Interaction marketing | Type: Network marketing |
| Focus | Economic transaction | Information and economic transaction | Interactive relationships between a buyer and seller | Connected relationships between firms |
| Parties involved | A firm and buyers in the general market | A firm and buyers in a specific target market | Individual sellers and buyers (a dyad) | Sellers, buyers and other firms |
| Communication pattern | Firm 'to' market | Firm 'to' individual | Individuals 'with' individuals (across organizations) | Firms 'with' firms (involving individuals) |
| Type of contact | Arms-length, impersonal | Personalised (yet distant) | Face-to-face, interpersonal (close, based on commitment, trust and cooperation) | Impersonal – interpersonal (ranging from distant to close) |
| Duration | Discrete (yet perhaps over time) | Discrete and over time | Continuous (ongoing and mutually adaptive, may be short or long term) | Continuous (stable yet dynamic, may be short or long term) |
| Formality | Formal | Formal (yet personalised via technology) | Formal and informal (i.e. at both a business and social level) | Formal and informal (i.e. at both a business and social level) |
| Balance of power | Active seller – passive buyers | Active seller – less passive buyers | Seller and buyer mutually active and adaptive, inter-dependent and reciprocal | All firms active and adaptive |

Source: Coviello et al., 1997

the questionnaire upon which it is based have been very widely used to test and develop the emerging ideas. In addition, the questionnaire has been used for several consecutive years to give longitudinal data that will add immeasurably to the value of the findings. This work has been carried out in Australasia, North and South America and around Europe, and is now being initiated in Africa and the Far East. The research findings are discussed in detail in Chapter 8.

## CHAPTER 3

# The New Business Reality

## CHAPTER OBJECTIVES

In this chapter we revisit the issue of pressures on business, by considering questions such as the following. How is strategy development and implementation shaped as a result of changing external pressures to grow the business and create more corporate value? What are the implications for companies opting to grow from within – as opposed to without – by, for example, mergers and acquisitions? And, in particular, how relevant nowadays are the marketing principles and practices that may have been instrumental in their glory days?

To understand how marketing has changed – how organizations have changed – we need to understand the context in which such changes might have occurred. In order to do this we examine the business media discourse concerning General Motors, another of the world's greatest marketing companies. We attempt to deduce some lessons from their changing fortunes and misfortunes, especially the destruction of their value. In particular, we are interested in knowing whether, as with McDonald's, their 'model' for creating value and sustaining past success is still relevant. And if not, why not?

## THE PRESSURES TO GROW

Executives – especially those in publicly listed companies – face a relentless kind of pressure. We saw how McDonald's was struggling with this in Chapter 1. As one business commentator said (Rich, 1999): 'The economics of corporate life and death lead to one inescapable conclusion: in the long run, it's grow or die.'

Another commentator (Loomis, 2001) has called this:

The 15 per cent delusion.... Of all the goals articulated, the most common one among good-sized companies is annual growth in earnings per share of 15 per cent ... with 15 per cent growth, a company will roughly double its earnings in five years. It will almost inevitably star in the stock market, and its CEO will be given, so to speak, ticker-tape parades.

In the USA, especially, they would also expect to become fabulously wealthy. Now however, if their pursuit of growth has meant they have destroyed their company's wealth, and they have not been sufficiently judicious in their accounting procedures, at best they could be forced to resign and still be given a golden parachute; at worst, they could go to jail.

When companies are faced with the need to grow, they normally have two choices (Rich, 1999): one, internal growth, by exploiting their own 'capabilities, dynamics or opportunities'; or, two, external growth through mergers, acquisitions or strategic alliances.

A problem with a high growth target is its inbuilt contradiction: the pressure to meet ambitious short term revenue growth targets expected by investors may cause the firm to compromise in its investment in long-term business growth. However, as Peters and Austin (1985) said some 20 years ago, the pursuit of excellence meant that the principles for competing could not be violated:

> There are only two ways to create and sustain superior performance over the long haul. First, take exceptional care of your customers ... via superior service and superior quality. Secondly, constantly innovate. That's it. There are no alternatives in achieving ... or sustaining strategic competitive advantage.

In today's high-speed, high-tech, high-touch environment, many companies are coming to realise there is no such thing as 'sustaining strategic competitive advantage'. Ironically, one of the reasons for this has to do with the combination of a company's own legacy of success and the current pressures on it to be restored to its previous state. As the *Economist* (1998b) noted, when examining what it termed 'the decline and fall' of General Motors in the late 1990s:

> All empires contain the seeds of their own destruction. The ideas on which they were founded cannot adapt to changing times. Their wealth creates bureaucracy and complacency. Meritocracy gives way to an introverted oligarchy that wastes its talent vying for position within the imperial court, rather than expanding the empire's borders. Even as the empire shrinks, an air of unreality persists – right up to the moment when the Goths break into the imperial city.... Nowadays, General Motors' sole claim to imperial status is its size.

## HOW THE GOTHS GOT TO THE GATES OF THE GENERAL MOTORS EMPIRE

How General Motors came to this point in its history is a lesson in both the changing fortunes of organizations and in marketing's preceptory state. As Porter (1996) said: 'A company's history can be instructive.... Looking backward, one can reexamine the original strategy to see if it is still valid. Can the historical positioning be implemented in a modern way, one consistent with today's technologies and practices?'

In a presentation to chief executives of the automotive industry, Lapidus and Cuttler (2003) of Goldman Sachs Global Equity Research summed up the current automotive industry as follows:

- Low equity valuations are the results of low returns on capital, not investor misunderstandings.
- Too much capital, too much capacity, too much supply forcing prices to fall.
- Slow unit growth, perhaps 2–3 per cent worldwide, lagging available supply.
- Inexorably increasing regulatory burdens.
- High exit barriers include labour agreements and government regulations.
- This is NOT the bread business ... it's more like the movie business.
- There are only two groups of value creators in the auto industry: low-cost providers and premium-priced brands.

With respect to the last finding, Lapidus and Cuttler (2003) said that all three US automobile manufacturers fell into a 'stuck in the middle' category. They were neither low-cost producers nor premium-priced brands, as shown in Figure 3.1. How have once-great marketing companies like General Motors become value destroyers, not value creators?

### How General Motors First Redefined Value

General Motors Corporation is one of the world's greatest industrial complexes. With revenue of US$187 billion in 2002 it is second only to Wal-Mart on the Fortune 500 list of companies. Some 20 years ago – facing relentless pressure from its Japanese, Korean and European competitors, and in order to reduce costs, improve efficiencies and quality, and speed up the process of developing and marketing its cars and trucks – it began its most radical internal restructuring since Alfred P.

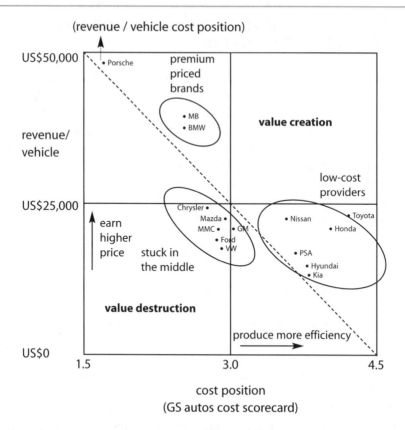

**Figure 3.1** Automobile company value propositions

*Source:* Goldman Sachs Research estimates, 2003

Sloan Jr was appointed CEO in 1923. This restructuring is still going on, as modern-day GM tries to recreate a new dynasty with the lasting power of the original.

Sloan crafted a structure and strategy based on: centralized policy and planning; decentralized executive responsibility and operations that included five competing car divisions (Chevrolet, Pontiac, Oldsmobile, Buick and Cadillac); and vertical integration in which the company made nearly all the parts that went into its cars. Since each division was responsible for most of its own design and manufacturing, they were also relatively free to create their distinct identities.

This approach introduced the world both to the modern corporation and to the marketing logic of product/market segmentation on a grand scale, based on what Sloan (1963) termed 'a car for every purse and purpose'. Starting with an entry-level Chevrolet and moving up through Pontiac,

Oldsmobile, Buick and finishing with the luxury-end Cadillac, each of the five divisions continually altered and improved their models 'to keep pace with changes in demand and the tendency towards increasing prosperity and social status amongst their customers'.

It was a business model that revolutionized the industry long dominated by Henry Ford. Said the *Economist* (1998b): 'The management system pioneered by Alfred Sloan at GM in the 1920s became the basis for the multidivisional modern corporation. Haunted by Henry Ford, Sloan built a company that could run itself, independent of the whims of one man.'

When matched against Henry Ford's reluctance to move away from simplification and permanence of design, it is not surprising that GM quickly overtook Ford, and not only dominated the US automobile market for the next half century but also influenced the theory and practice of marketing over the same extended period.

In his seminal book *My Years with General Motors*, Sloan (1963) divided the history of the automotive industry into three periods:

- The period before 1908 was that of a class market characterized by craft production.
- The period from 1908 to the mid-1920s was mainly that of a mass market, ruled by Henry Ford and his concept of basic transportation ('any car so long as it is black').
- The long period afterwards, lasting through until the mid-1970s, was that of the mass-class market. Especially after the Second World War, this third period was characterized by increasing model diversity, as companies pursued product-market segmentation strategies and adopted the practice of annual model changes. Sloan termed this 'the General Motors' approach.

The main feature of the General Motors approach was that it overthrew the Ford conviction that mass production of a standard product on a grand scale was the only way to achieve cost competitiveness. Its genesis started in 1926, when the company introduced a lower-priced version of the Oldsmobile that was largely developed, tested and assembled within the Chevrolet division. In doing so, GM also introduced a new manufacturing–marketing principle, and one that it was to maintain for some 50 years. According to Sloan (1963):

The Pontiac, coordinated in part with a car in another price class, was to demonstrate that mass production of automobiles could be reconciled with variety in product. This was again the opposite of the old Ford concept, which we persistently met and opposed at every turn. For General Motors, with its five basic price classes by car makes and several subclasses of models, the implication of the Pontiac idea was very great for the whole line. If the cars in the higher-price classes could benefit from the volume economies of the lower-price classes, the advantages of mass production could be extended to the whole car line.

An additional feature of the Sloan approach was his solution to the problem of how to capitalize on the market opportunities presented by mass production, while measuring, monitoring, and controlling the various complexities that became inherent in the new system. His solution was to introduce the staff functions of marketing and finance to complement engineering and manufacturing. Thus began the hierarchical career management structure of line and staff specialists that was to remain relatively unchanged for nearly 50 years, and which served as an organizational model for the rest of the industrial world.

While the way it used to produce cars may help to explain GM's domination of the US auto market during this third period, it also gives us clues about its later vulnerability, and the vulnerability of other car makers following a similar strategy. Charles Burck (1981) explained:

> The genius of the old GM lay in manufacturing: it stretched the lifetime of its machinery and tooling over great unit volumes, and drove down costs through constant improvements in production processes. It did a superb job of making cars better by honing conventional technologies, and it made a lot of money for a long time.... But it was neither a big spender nor much of an innovator. Whether for fear of antitrust action or because there was no market for innovation, the company took few risks.

Sloan (1963) explained GM's fiscal prudence: 'While the completely automatic factory is an interesting possibility, there continues to be a good deal of immediate practical work to be done in reducing production costs, building better machines, improving factory layouts, and designing better factories.'

The system of mass manufacturing was to work for a long time, as explained by Womack, Jones and Roos (1990):

> Take Ford's factory practices, add Sloan's marketing and management techniques, and mix in organized labor's new role in controlling job

assignments and work tasks, and you have mass production in its mass form. For decades this system marched from victory to victory. The US car companies dominated the world automotive industry, and the US market accounted for the largest percentage of the world's auto sales.

Eventually, this dominance came to be challenged by outsiders, and 1955 marked a watershed year in the US automotive industry. Not only was it the first year that more than 7 million new cars were sold; it was also the year the big three car makers (GM, Ford and Chrysler) began to lose market share to imports from Europe, including Volkswagen's Beetle with its trendsetting advertising. And Alfred Sloan retired from GM after 34 years as either president or chair.

## The Waning of GM's Dominance

Since the early 1970s especially, GM's dominance has been constantly eroded by Japanese and European competitors and, more recently, by the resurgence of its two domestic rivals. A key factor may have been that by the end of Sloan's era the role of manufacturing to its marketplace success had waned in strategic importance. Cusumano (1988) said that US auto managers at that time considered automobile manufacturing as a 'mature' technology that had reached 'certain limits to productivity, minimum efficient scales of production, unit costs, quality, and the ability of workers and suppliers to cooperate (or be coerced) and to contribute to improving production operations'.

Abernathy, Clark and Kantrow (1981) cited the auto industry as an example of US manufacturing that had become 'competitively neutral'. They said that while manufacturing was not seen as unimportant, US car makers were no longer seeking to improve their competitiveness through innovative manufacturing. Rather, 'except perhaps for their reliance on economies of scale, they tended to compete by means of styling, marketing, and dealership networks'.

Bennett and Cooper (1981) agreed, and questioned the emerging role of marketing. For example, they noted that between 1960 and 1977 the USA had spent a relatively constant percentage of its GDP on advertising, while the proportion allocated to R&D had fallen: 'We have decided it is easier to talk about our new products than actually to develop them.... In the world of new products we have become a society of tinkerers and cosmeticians rather than true product innovators.'

Sloan (1963) recognized the double-sided impact of styling, and admitted that, during the late 1940s and 1950s: 'New styling features were introduced that were far removed from utility, yet they seemed demonstrably effective in capturing public taste.'

## GM Runs Low on Gas

The 1980s opened with an air of gloom and despondency in the US auto industry following the second oil crisis. The once-mighty US industrial base seemed unable to stem a flood of more fuel-efficient imports that were less expensive and better made, particularly from Japan. In its 1980 cover story, *Time Magazine* concluded: 'A generation of neglect had sapped Detroit's competitive strength.'

In the ensuing debate over whether or not the US auto industry had lost the capacity for competing, Bennett and Cooper (1981) said:

> Pundits claim that the auto industry is in trouble because of cheaper imports that get better fuel economy. This is too simple an answer. A more incisive diagnosis reveals the hard truths. The European and Japanese car makers have simply been better competitors. While domestic automakers regarded small cars as low-technology, cheaply designed products aimed mainly at buyers unable or not willing to purchase a larger vehicle, the foreign manufacturers produced high-quality small cars that were recognized as better by the American consumer.

The authors claimed that between 1955 and the late 1970s, Detroit's car makers had pursued a 'non-product' strategy on the premise that, in an increasingly wealthy society, annual cosmetic changes and style updates, backed by intensive advertising and promotion, and by aggressive selling, would keep their products moving and customers satisfied: 'After all, how can one go wrong simply doing what the customers say they want?'

The inimitable Lee Iaccoca, who is credited with saving Chrysler from bankruptcy in the early 1980s, having first been fired from Ford, had another view. This was that the US auto industry had become too finance-driven, and consequently was unable, or unwilling, to adjust to the new market realities following the two oil crises of the 1970s:

> That's what happened at Ford during the 1970s. The financial managers came to see themselves as the only prudent people in the company.... What they forgot was how quickly things can change in the car business. While their company was dying in the marketplace, they didn't want to make a move until next year's budget meeting.
>
> (Iaccoca, 1984)

## Pressures on the Auto Industry

As is usual, the reality is more complex. In *The Future of the Automobile*, Roos and Altshuler (1984) identified three factors impacting on the automobile industry:

- *A dramatic change in the operating environment*, including government-legislated mandates for safety, lower emissions, and improved fuel economy, particularly in the wake of the two oil crises in the 1970s.

- *Intense competition in the marketplace*, as Japanese competitors, in particular, began to expand from their overcrowded home market by first entering the American market. They did this both by directly importing high-value models from Japan and by establishing greenfield manufacturing facilities to produce mainstream models in areas far away from Detroit's high-cost labour, and in order to circumvent the voluntarily agreed import volume restraints that had been imposed when the American manufacturers eventually recognized the full extent of the threat, and their own inability to counter it initially.

- *Exogenous development of new technologies with applications in the automobile industry*, such as the microprocessor, developed originally for defence and space-travel applications, but with recognized possibilities for improvements in safety, comfort, control, communications and entertainment.

While these three a priori conditions did not necessarily reflect market or consumer demand factors, a fourth one did:

- *Significant demographic and socio-economic shifts*, such as the baby boom cohort hitting the labour market, including females entering in record numbers. To some extent GM and the American auto industry was caught unawares. As one top auto industry executive admitted to *Business Week* (1980): 'We are dealing, or about to deal, with a generation that is inherently anti-big. We still don't know what compromises in vehicle size this younger generation will accept.'

Nor did the three conditions reflect the full extent of the Japanese intent, in that it was not just what the Japanese auto manufacturers produced that threatened companies such as General Motors: it was also how they produced them.

- *Fundamental shifts in manufacturing technologies and techniques.* As *Time* said in 1984: 'Long US industry's neglected stepchild, subordinated to finance and marketing, the process of making products is suddenly coming into its own, commanding more and more attention from company executives.' Ten years later, Bylinsky (1994) was hinting at the marketing implications of this manufacturing change: 'Call it the digital factory, for its dependence on information technology, or the soft factory, for its mix of the human and the mechanical ... soft manufacturing brings unheard-of agility to the plant. Companies can customize products literally in quantities of one while churning them out at mass-production speeds. Soft manufacturing also blurs the boundaries of the traditional factory by tying production ever closer to both suppliers and customers.'

All five shifts are applicable today, though their manifestations may be different. For example, the baby boom generation is now entering middle age. The issue for the likes of GM is not, will they reject American companies in order to buy an entry-level compact hatchback from Japan complete with free floor mats and a radio, but will they now ignore American companies in order to move up to a European-branded luxury SUV made-in-America and fully equipped with the latest in electronic controls. Unfortunately for GM, it missed the first wave and was late in catching the second. And therein lies a message for the unwary marketer.

## Restarting GM

In its own labyrinthine way, GM did begin to install a more coherent new car programme. For example, in the early 1970s, as part of a design centralization policy, it set up 'project centres' – teams of product and production engineers drawn from different divisions and other specialists such as stylists, market researchers, finance staffers and materials management specialists, all brought together to coordinate each new car design and engineering. It was a mammoth task: completely redesigning GM's product line over a decade by bringing out a series of 'down-sized' cars based on what became known as the X, J and A bodies, then 'handing' their work over to manufacturing divisions, and then marketing.

This sequential process, and its inherent problems, was described by Mitchell (1986): 'First, product planners come up with a general concept. Next, a design team gives it form. Their work is then handed over to engineering which develops the specifications that are passed on to manufacturing and suppliers. Each unit works in isolation, there is little communication, and no one has overall project responsibility.'

One problem was that car makers prefer to introduce new technologies to one area at a time, in order to build on the experience gained. For example, microprocessors were introduced first in engines, then incorporated into transmissions, followed by suspensions, and so on. Likewise, new advances tend to enter the market from the fringes before becoming mainstream. For example, the four-wheel drive vehicles now bought mainly by urban dwellers began as work-related niche-market vehicles, such as Land Rover and Jeep. With a cabin that was more car-like, the new compact four-door 1984 Jeep Cherokee was one of the catalysts in creating what became the sport-utility vehicle (SUV) sector. The Toyota RAV4 took the change one stage further. It was the first SUV to use what is known as a car-like 'unibody' construction with fully independent suspension, as opposed to using a conventional truck platform with 'body on frame' construction and live rear axle. Its greater comfort and car-like driving characteristics were quickly recognized and the RAV4 has spawned the fastest growing segment in the USA. It now includes models right up to the European luxury end, such as the BMW X5, and the Mercedes-Benz ML Class (Porretto, 2003). Unfortunately GM was unable or unwilling to shift quite as quickly, as we shall see.

One reason was that the start-up problems proved so enormous. Smaller cars meant switching to unitary body construction, front-wheel drive, more fuel-efficient engines, new transmissions and, most important, stylish designs that looked smaller from the outside, but inside gave a feeling of roominess, comfort and value. Producing small cars from scratch thus demanded development and manufacturing processes radically different from the traditional large cars that companies like GM had been pumping out for decades, but which their Japanese competitors, in particular, had become so proficient at, and American manufacturers in general became so fixated with (Schonberger, 1982; Roos and Altshuler, 1984; Womack, Jones and Roos, 1990).

## GM Stalls, Again

Not surprisingly, the conflicting demands of such a transformation led to delays, cost overruns, mistakes and compromises. For example, while the project centres could cut across divisional and staff boundaries, weaknesses of this approach soon became apparent (Burck, 1983):

> Besides separating designing and manufacturing still further, the project centres badly blurred responsibilities. A centre might, say, choose Chevrolet to design an engine; if the design came up short, neither the

centre nor the division could be held accountable, particularly since a centre disbanded the moment it handed a car over for production.

Given such problems, *Business Week* (1984) claimed that:

> GM's old structure began to break down. Approval for even minor changes in a part ended up requiring huddles between hosts of manufacturing, parts, marketing, and body engineering executives. New-car introduction dates began to slip, quality suffered, costs rose. And when cars finally came to market, GM discovered that customers had a tough time telling one division's model from another.

Eventually, GM's 'non-product' strategy reached a stage where the most visually distinguishing characteristics of a succession of its new models were their bland physical similarities. Critics were most vocal about the styling of the J-cars which, despite costing some US$5 billion to develop, required all five GM divisions to share nearly identical bodies. The differences were to come from 'badge engineering' – separate names, cosmetic exterior and interior differences, individual ride and drive characteristics, and a range of prices. However, when asked to explain the main difference between the premium-priced Cadillac Cimarron and the base-level Chevrolet Cavalier, a top Cadillac engineer told *Time* (1984a): 'Oh, about $5000.'

Inevitably, these problems ensured a continuation of GM's erosion. Nevertheless, when discussing a mid-1980s restructuring with *Time* (1985), Roger Smith, GM's Chair – who had a finance background – optimistically explained how the company was actually helped by its earlier setbacks: 'The worse years made it more acceptable to understand that something had to be done. But once we sold that, it was then our turn to say, "Let's not just go two steps, let's go into the 21st Century." You don't just stumble into the future. You create your own future.'

Later, Smith said in an interview with *Advertising Age* (Snyder, 1985) that the key to the company's success was that it had been guided by two main principles: one, use your weight to your advantage; two, always set the rules.

Despite its weight, and the 1985 restructuring and any new rules it might have set, GM's market share continued slowly ebbing away from a high of 60 per cent in the early 1960s. And as it entered the twenty-first century the restructurings were still going on, as evidenced by the recent dismantling of a failed brand management system that had been controversially set up in the mid-1990s. In 2002, however, GM remained the market leader of an industry that had become much more competitive than in the mid-1980s. And although GM's market share was fractionally under 29 per cent, it was the second year in a row that its share had improved marginally. Had GM finally figured out a way of marketing that leveraged its weight, set new rules and created its own future?

Immediately after 11 September 2001, automobile companies in the USA faced the grim prospect of a major drop in new car sales. To arrest the possible downturn GM began offering zero per cent financing (namely, interest-free loans for three years) to qualified buyers. Other US companies, in particular, quickly followed, by offering everything from discounts, no deposits, and delayed repayments. Partly as a result the US auto industry rose to 17.2 million units in 2001, the second best year on record. However, the *Economist* (2002b) said it was a time of 'profitless prosperity' for the likes of GM for, as one auto executive observed, 'incentives are addictive'. At the end of 2002 incentives were still firmly in place, and costing GM some US$2400 per vehicle, double the US$1200 being offered during the downturn of a decade earlier. In comparison, Toyota was spending about US$525 per vehicle on incentives at the end of 2002.

Despite the incentives, in 2002 industry sales fell by 2 per cent from 2001. Thus, while GM's market share rose slightly, its actual sales fell by nearly 1 per cent in 2002, whereas Toyota's sales rose by the same amount. In other words, according to the *Economist* (2002), GM had sunk so much capital into plants that they were

> strongly tempted to use the capacity to build extra cars that fetch enough revenue to cover marginal costs in the short run, but not total costs in the long run. Keeping cash flowing in and grabbing a bit more market share, as GM is doing now, makes sense for a while. But eventually, if sales dip, it will become clear that the producers have dug themselves a collective hole.

## Has GM Driven into a Big Pothole?

Some critics argued that GM had driven into a pothole and did not have the power to drive back out. For one thing, the company that once exemplified the power and prestige concerned with creating and delivering value and wealth started doing what many other weak marketers do when they have eventually run out of ideas and time: they began throwing incentive money at their customers, but with no clear plan of how or when to stop. For example, at the beginning of September 2002 GM suspended the zero per cent financing offer, and sales immediately fell; by the end of the month the deal was reinstated, for five-year terms.

The long-term difficulty for GM was that it could find it increasingly difficult for consumers to pay more for new models when, as one analyst told *Fortune* (Revell, 2002), companies such as GM are 'getting the consumer to the point where unless they're offering a zero per cent five-year deal, they're not going to sell anything'. However as another analyst said: 'This is a scale industry. These guys just have to sell a certain number of vehicles to cover their fixed costs or they're going to lose their shirts.'

Another concern was that if GM required incentives to lift sales when the new car market was buoyant, what would it do when the market turned down? By the end of the first quarter in 2003 and the war in Iraq, that is exactly what happened. GM continued offering zero per cent financing on five-year loans or US$3000 rebates on nearly all its models, including top-end Cadillacs and Saabs.

Critics also questioned whether a short-term solution to a long-term capacity issue really reflected the sum of some 80 years of learning from history for one of the world's top marketing corporations. If so, then it may be time for GM's business model once again to be overhauled and restarted for it to use its weight and set the rules to create its new future.

### Restarting GM, Again?

Which is what GM is undertaking. In 2002 it made an operating profit of US$3.9 billion, nearly double its 2001 results, despite the discounting. How had it managed to achieve this? By a mixture of old-fashioned and not-so-old-fashioned ways. The old-fashioned way was by slashing costs, cutting payrolls, overhauling aging plants, and making dramatic efficiency gains. GM is now the most productive US auto manufacturer: for example, taking 26 hours, on average, to build a car (compared with 27 and 31 hours respectively for Ford and Daimler-Chrysler, although still more than Toyota (22.5) or Nissan (18)). GM argued that it was this kind of leverage that allowed it to offer the discounts.

GM has made many improvements in its performance, especially in the USA. For example, it has imposed tough new performance standards. As GM's North American President said: 'Everything can be measured' (Welch, 2003). Even the top executive responsible for new product development is judged on 12 criteria, from how well he uses existing parts to save money in new vehicles to how many engineering hours he cuts from the product development process.

It has increased plant flexibility so that, for example, in any pickup or SUV plant it can make any vehicle model designed for a given platform (the components – such as the floor-plan, drive-train and suspension – upon which a vehicle is built, and the common set of 'hard', or locating, points for body assembly purposes). And it has increased build quality to the point that GM, while once ranked below the industry average on virtually every model, is now only behind Honda and Toyota in terms of faults per vehicle after 30 days of ownership, as measured by independent surveys.

It now takes GM 20 months to develop a new car, down from about four years a decade ago, and thus very close to the best of the Japanese at 18 months. Initiatives and results such as these suggest that GM has begun to make fundamental improvements that go beyond the obvious ones to do with cutting costs.

In order to learn how to design desirable cars, GM has tried a new approach. As Park (2003) said, harking back to comments of nearly 20 years ago:

The most dramatic gains (will come) in the way GM selects new car designs and then shepherds them through production. In the past, even if a bold design made it off a drawing board, it had little chance of surviving to the showroom. A concept would go from a designer to the marketing staff, which would try to tailor it to consumers. Then it would go to engineers, who would try to figure out how to build it, and so on. Separate teams worked with suppliers, factories, and parts suppliers on their individual slice of the process, with little interaction.... It was a recipe for mediocrity – and often disaster.

One reason for this situation is that one side often did not understand what the other was saying, and no more so than when GM introduced a brand management system in the mid-1990s, principally to rectify the problem of overlapping look-alike models. The goal was to have the new car-design process driven more at the early stages by consumer input via focus groups, and then creating separate positioning strategies for each model, all the while maintaining economies of scale that come from common engineering and manufacturing.

Many of the brand managers were hired from fast-moving consumer goods companies. As part of their task to bring in the voice of the customer, GM adopted a process of defining and targeting discrete groups of customers through needs segmentation research. Based on surveys of tens of thousands of car buyers the company came up with about 30 needs segments, based on characteristics such as age, income, family size, attitudes to cars and driving, and driving habits.

Taylor (1997) said that GM did not make full use of its market research in the past 'because its engineers thought they knew best ... now information is king, carefully collected and analyzed in a single department'. The head of research agreed:

> Our job is to get engineers and designers to pay attention to the research. GM stopped listening to the customer in the 1980s...it also neutered the brands. We can commonize our cars where customers don't see the differences, and differentiate them where they do.

However, Taylor noted that other US car makers 'view GM research-driven design with everything from polite amusement to jaw-dropping disbelief. Research is fine they say but it produces boring cars.' This view was shared by many in the business. One of the most respected, Maryann Keller (2002), said: 'Using focus groups in which consumers are polled for their reactions to new car designs has its hazards. If everyone says it's beautiful, it's going to look old by the time it gets to market.' Taylor (1997) added that executives needed to rely on their 'own experience and judge-ment' when interpreting market research, and yet: 'Asking questions is a science; interpreting the answers is an art.'

Part of that art included the designers and engineers understanding what the marketers were feeding back to them. McWhirter (1997) observed that inside GM's main design studio were hung with:

> Brave New World banners exhorting them to remember what their 2000-era cars and trucks are supposed to represent. Flying above one such future vehicle is its own set of May Day credos: BOLD! PURPOSEFUL! ATHLETIC! PERSONAL! SPORT SEDAN PERFORMANCE WITH INTERIOR VERSATILITY TO HAUL THEIR 'STUFF' TO COMPLEMENT THEIR ACTIVE LIFE-STYLES.

And on the walls were 'a marketspeak mural of arrows, block charts, one-word product descriptions and macro boxes of jargon like "needs target", "needs profile", "benefit focus", and "reasons for being".' Taylor (1997) summed up the difficulties the brand marketers were creating for auto designers and engineers: 'GM has selected four adjectives to describe the new Oldsmobile: thoughtful, precise, international, and rewarding. Try translating that into sheet metal.'

Agreeing on a new car design is an emotional art that cannot be reduced to a science, let alone a wall of marketing buzzwords. When, early in 1997, GM unveiled its fifth generation Corvette, several factors kept it separate from the rest of the GM fleet, including the research process. For one, the car that introduced Americans to 'red-blooded American sports cars' in the mid-1950s was originally condemned to deletion in the mid-1990s, owing to the lack of capital within GM and its poor sales at the time (Kerwin, 1996). Some 14 years had elapsed between the fourth and fifth generation, given GM's reluctance to commit funds to it, despite its iconic brand status within the Chevrolet division. That sales declined was not surprising.

The new model reached the market only because of the dedication and efforts of a core of designers, engineers and petrol-head executives who brought it through the development process within an unheard-of budget (US$250 million), and at a competitive price (starting at US$38,000) that yielded margins of some US$8000. This was achieved largely by sharing components and systems with other GM cars, by using some 34 per cent fewer parts than the previous model, and thereby cutting assembly time from 64 hours to 45. The result was a better engineered, better built, less expensive and potentially more profitable car than its predecessor. As told in *All Corvettes Are Red*, Schefter (1996) revealed that at one stage, when funding was frozen, to keep the project alive the team even had to hide work done on the new vehicle in the current model's overall budget, knowing that if the internal auditors discovered the subterfuge their heads would roll.

It also had minimal input from the marketers, given the mix and experience of the team and their innate understanding of, and belief in, what the 'Vette' represented to its target group of driving enthusiasts. Schefter (1996) was struck by the passion involved:

> creating a new car was not what I thought. It didn't happen on a computer screen, with techies connecting dots with curved lines. It didn't happen in boardrooms, with the suits voting on Proposition A versus proposition B.... Creating a car, I began to see, was a wonderful, frustrating, gut-wrenching, soaring, and terrible process. It mixed artists with engineers, financiers with bureaucrats, regulators with environmentalists. It threw people with opposing views into the pit where they fought it out until a (design) winner climbed into the light.

How GM failed to take advantage of the burgeoning SUV market is an example of its organizational failings. Chrysler opened up the family minivan in the early 1980s. GM followed shortly after but its models never caught the imagination of the buying public. The same thing occurred with the SUV market, and during the 1990s the biggest shift in the market was the rise in the light-truck market, from family minivans to sport-utility vehicles (SUVs). Although GM had been traditionally very strong in the pickup sector, it entered the SUV market late. 'While it had increasing sales', said Taylor (1997), 'GM never caught up to the truck boom because of faulty market research and stubborn leadership'. For example, in 1998 pickups, vans and SUVs accounted for only 47 per cent of GM's sales, compared with 61 per cent at Ford and 71 per cent at Chrysler. GM's CEO admitted (Kerwin, 1999) that 'the truck trend went much faster than our people ever expected'. A problem was that only three divisions – Chevrolet, Pontiac and Oldsmobile – had SUVs, but not its newest division, Saturn, nor its two up-scale divisions, Buick and Cadillac. This was despite the fact that by 2000 pickups and SUVs accounted for some 90 per cent of US automakers' profits. This was mainly because an increasing number of buyers were moving to luxury versions, as opposed to the more basic versions in the original off-road category.

The situation with Cadillac is illustrative. Renowned as a leader in extravagant style and technology in its heydays of the 1950s, eight out of ten luxury cars sold in the US were 'Caddies'. Its downward slide began in the early 1970s, when it became associated with all that was wrong with large, gas-guzzling made-in-the-USA cars. It could never shake this image, and as quality and style slipped, by the late 1990s it was being outsold by BMW, Lexus and Mercedes, and the average age of a Cadillac owner had risen to 66.

A problem was that GM's research, segmentation and positioning strategies still defined Cadillac purely as a luxury automaker, not as a full-line manufacturer. What is more, the company was not convinced in any case that the SUV sector was more than a passing fad (Simison and Blumenstein, 1997). Thus, when a Cadillac SUV model was proposed to NAO in 1995, it was not accepted since the company was focused on developing luxury car versions to compete particularly with the above three competitors. An uninspiringly designed SUV was finally introduced in 1998. It was not popular and it was not until 2001 that a more acceptable version was launched. By then it was too little too late, given that there were some 56 SUVs on the market. Most importantly, GM's three main competitors, plus the Lincoln division of Ford, had by then entered the still-growing sector with models that were earning profits of up to US$15,000 per vehicle (Welch, 2001).

## GM Brings in a Change Agent to Move the Metal, Faster

In order to get more design winners climbing 'into the light', in mid-2001 GM went outside the company to bring back in Robert Lutz as Vice-Chair for product development. Having worked for BMW and all of the 'Big 3' US car companies over a 40-year career, Lutz was known as a classic 'car guy'. He was also credited with developing some of the 'hottest' vehicles to come onto the US market, particularly when he was at Chrysler, such as the Dodge Viper sports car, the Dodge Ram pickup and the PT Cruiser.

In noting that GM's US market share had shrunk from just under 36 per cent in 1990 to just over 28 per cent a decade later, the *Economist* (2002a) suggested why GM had rehired Lutz:

> After years of thinking that success depended on lean manufacturing and reliable quality, they are coming to realize that these are necessary but not sufficient conditions. They have noticed that it is no good making cars efficiently if they are so dull that it takes discounts and cheap loans to move them.

Lutz's views on how cars should be designed and built are well known, given his long experience in the auto industry and his success in developing new products at Chrysler in the early 1990s. So too are his views on the role of the consumer in the process. For example, to Taylor (1997) he said: 'The customer is usually just a rear-view mirror. Why should we expect him to be the expert in clairvoyance?'

Lutz was brought in as a 'change agent' (Hakim, 2001), and one of his first tasks was to reduce the influence of the brand management system, including that of the head of marketing, who left shortly afterwards. Lutz's view was that GM 'does have a tendency to want to over-define, over-categorize, over-analyze. You can't reduce everything to a formula.' Another opinion was that within GM's bureaucratic system, where it was often safer to say 'no' than 'yes', his main task was to get 'great-looking, low-cost investment-efficient products into our system quickly' (*Just-auto.com*, 2002).

For example, in order to resurrect the Pontiac GTO, a rear-wheel drive 1960s 'muscle car', Lutz tapped into GM's Australian subsidiary, Holden, where an appropriate vehicle, the Monaro sports car, has been developed for Australian driving enthusiasts. The original, known as the Pontiac Le Mans Tempest GTO, was launched at the end of 1963 as an experimental 'muscle car' – a 6.5 litre V8 packed into an intermediate-sized chassis – to give the Pontiac division more visibility with the rapidly expanding youth market. It was expected to sell only about 5000 units in 1994. Instead, nearly 33,000 were sold that year. It gained cult status among America's youth and helped change the image of Pontiac. It also defined an entirely new market sector and, at its peak, was selling close to 100,000 units per year, despite a host of challengers. By 1974 the sector was virtually dead, however: the victim of spiralling fuel prices and insurance costs, and tightening emission control laws (Simpson, 2003).

From Lutz's perspective, there is still a part of America out there with fond memories and sufficient income. Bringing a 340-horsepower American version of the Monaro to the USA from Australia would be a relatively quick (18 months) and low-cost, low-risk solution. It would also give the Australian subsidiary a production fillip and an opportunity to prove itself on the home turf of its parent company. Park (2003) said that before Lutz arrived, 'the idea to bring it to the US never made it out of committee. GM execs simply didn't want to spend what little money it would take to alter the Monaro to meet US safety standards and American styling.' Lutz told Park, 'I just asked "Why not?"'

Under the prodding of change agents like Lutz, GM has again restructured its design and development process. Previously, it had different studios for each division working on car designs that would get passed onto marketing, then onto to engineering, then to manufacturing, and so on. Lutz created one committee, a product leadership team, to oversee the entire process, with two key groups working together and reporting to it (Advanced Vehicle Design and Advanced Vehicle Development). Under the process, design goals for a new product are established by an advanced vehicle development team, such as the team responsible for premium mid-sized and luxury cars. Once these are agreed to by the product leadership team, who meet weekly, design teams develop up to nine proposals, and the product leadership team select three. These models are then produced and tested in consumer clinics representing potential buyers. The winners of this process are approved by the product leadership team and taken to GM's Automotive Strategy Board, which meets monthly, for funding consent. If and when this occurs, vehicle line teams then execute the programme through to manufacturing. There are some 11 vehicle line teams; they mirror and work closely with the development teams. While it may appear overly cumbersome for an organization described by the *Economist* (2002a) as 'the world's most monolithic corporate bureaucracy', the process is expected to reduce development time by several months, and ensure that the best designs are approved and produced (Guilford, 2001; Park, 2003).

Vehicle line executives are now the product development chiefs. They are responsible for a specific vehicle or family of vehicles and will have the final say over vehicle content. In particular they will be responsible for their vehicle's contribution margin, defined as the difference between the cost of making the vehicle and the wholesale price.

The basic brand management structure will stay in place but its role will be subordinated in product development. As with engineering, manufacturing, suppliers and other disciplines represented in the advanced vehicle development teams, input from marketing will come mainly before a product is designed. The marketing role will also include assessment of competition and developing marketing plans rather than focusing on product creation. While one top executive told Guilford (2001) that 'the brand focus is the key to the market', under GM's new system the brand is the division rather than a model, which will henceforth 'live under the umbrella of the brand'. Lutz commented (*Automotive News*, 2001): 'If you look at our competitor across town, they did an excellent job of nurturing and maintaining the Jeep brand, without ever having an overly-formalized brand management structure.'

GM will seek to drive out features that add costs but do not necessarily affect or appeal to customers, and at the same time more effort will be spent improving perceived quality, such as the fit, finish and feel of interior materials and controls. Lutz said that marketers have a tendency to add costs (Guilford, 2001):

> You have a lot of so-called brand-marketing people who are helping to specify the next great new vehicle and they realize that at some point they're going to be responsible for selling the thing, so they want as high a feature count as they possibly can. It's just natural for one side of the organization to drive all these features in, and the side of the organization that's in charge of making sure we have margins has to fight that.

With respect to fighting, recently GM has begun the difficult task of rebuilding relationships with key suppliers and other external partners. Unfortunately, its efforts have been sporadic and its success patchy.

## GM Tries Building Relationships With Suppliers

GM has recently been criticized for its dealings with suppliers, particularly as it now has become so dependent on incentives to 'move the metal'. For example, through what the automakers term 'shared savings' programmes', suppliers were complaining of breakdowns in trust and relationships, reductions in quality, and more financial losses, consolidations and bankruptcies. In a report on the 2002 Automotive News World Congress, one representative of the supply sector said about US manufacturers, such as GM (Wilson and Sherefkin, 2002): 'The OEMs have to recognize that they cannot continue to download responsibility and capital intensity to their suppliers, without also developing long-term relationships.' Another industry participant said (Wilson, 2002): 'Ultimately, survival may depend on long-term collaboration between automakers and suppliers.... If such partnerships result in innovative products for which consumers will pay higher prices, profit margins will improve for everyone.' This is the 'value-adding' view of business and marketing strategy that has held in the automobile and many other industries for nearly 100 years.

However, firms such as GM are seen as still following their traditional one-sided approach, such as in requiring price cuts by suppliers as a condition for awarding contracts. The difference with the Japanese, one industry expert said to the *New York Times* (Warner, 2003), was that they 'balance performance, quality and then price.... Price is usually at the bottom of the list.' While companies such as Toyota expect cost reductions, it is their approach to their relationships with their suppliers that traditionally has differed. As a major supplier told the *New York Times* (Warner 2003), Toyota tells its suppliers: 'On the next future design let's take 20 per cent cost out, but let's work together to get there.'

Warner (2003) noted that at last 'American companies have noticed this, and are starting to rely on suppliers to tell them what customers want, not to just give them the lowest price.' For example, with a turnover of over US$14 billion in 2002, Lear Corporation is one of the largest groups. Late in 2002, for the first time, GM awarded Lear the contract to design and build the full interior systems for two of its top-line models from Buick and Cadillac.

GM almost did not get to this point, largely because of its preparedness to compromise on its relationships with suppliers, as happened during its lean years in the early 1990s, and more recently as noted above. The saga of its relationship with suppliers a decade ago is a case study of what not to do. In mid-1992 GM promoted its European head of purchasing to head of purchasing wordwide and brought him across to Detroit. His job was clear: he had to cut the cost of building cars. He stayed at GM for a year. His leaving, for a similar job at Volkswagen, caused a sensation and an acrimonious lawsuit over the poaching of key staff and the alleged stealing of sensitive GM documents. However, as the leader of a small team that was as much committed to saving costs as he was, during his tenure he saved GM billions of dollars. Within the company – and in the business media – he became a cult figure as the leader of a loyal team known as GM's 'Warriors'; to GM's suppliers, he was a 'Visigoth'.

Elkind (1997) described his approach:

He cared not a whit about long-standing relationships with GM suppliers, even when those suppliers were GM subsidiaries. He put those wanting to do business with GM through relentless rounds of bidding, then demanded that the survivors hit even lower marks. When they squawked that they couldn't meet his impossible targets, he sent teams of efficiency experts to their plants to teach them how to save steps in the manufacturing process.

The result was massive and immediate cost savings for GM, but at the expense of longer-term relationships with suppliers, and quality for customers.

As an example, early in 2003 GM became embroiled in a legal dispute with a major steel supplier. Under the terms of a long-term contract, the price paid by GM declines over time. However the steel firm contended in court filings that GM requested new inspection, testing and quality control systems which increased its costs but, though stipulated in the contract, GM refused to compensate the firm. A spokesperson for GM replied: 'We're expecting them to meet the quality requirements that are part of the contract and we expect them to deliver the steel in accordance with our contract. Whether they've had to incur new processes or additional costs to meet the quality requirements, that's their issue to manage' (Hakim, 2003a).

GM is thus trying to redress this kind of breakdown in supplier relations. To some extent this is because over the past 15 years the whole parts supplier industry has been changing. For example, in the USA, as a result of consolidations, the number of firms selling directly to automakers shrank from around 4000 in 1988 to about 100 'megasuppliers' in 2002. These main supplier groups have become closer collaborators with their OEM (original equipment manufacturer) clients, largely because this has been an approach successfully used by Japanese competitors. Chrysler was one of the first US companies to adopt this system (Mapleston, 1993) since it had by then become the least integrated US auto company, with suppliers providing some 70 per cent of its components – similar to its Japanese competitors – as opposed to 50 per cent at Ford and only 30 per cent at GM.

As OEM companies like Chrysler move toward greater single-sourcing arrangements, they become not so much manufacturers as assemblers of pre-manufactured sub-assemblies, a manufacturing process known as 'modularisation'. This requires a high-degree of inter-firm collaboration and relationship building. Under the system, a small number of firms designated 'Tier 1 suppliers' become fully involved with an OEM from the early concept stage of new car development. The total number of Tier 1 suppliers worldwide was about 800 in 1999 and is expected to decrease to less than 100 as they evolve into what is known as integrated, or 'programme', suppliers for the total fit-out of sections of interiors or exteriors, or 'underbonnet' components. As they are expected to do complete design projects, they will also coordinate the efforts of their respective Tier 2 or 3 suppliers.

Their rewards are the promise of long-term business, the achievement of scale production efficiencies, and greater control over design and quality. For example, when designing and developing a new model, rather than carrying out its own surveys into customer seating preferences, such as width, firmness, colours and fabrics, an OEM may transfer the responsibility of providing the best 'solution' to its preferred supplier in that specialty area. GM's challenge is to overcome its recent supplier-relationship legacy in order to tap into this expertise at the design and development stages of its new process for bringing more desirable cars to the market faster.

## GM Tries Building Relationships With Other Partners

GM has also attempted to build marketing leverage through mergers and alliances with a number of other auto companies. It began this move defensively in the 1980s by taking equity stakes in some of its Asian competitors in order to import and sell cars that it could not make in the USA. These included minicars from Suzuki (now owned 10 per cent by GM) and subcompacts from Isuzu (now owned 49 per cent by GM), plus an early 1980s joint venture in manufacturing with Toyota in California that not only ensured delivery of more subcompacts, but also gave it direct access to Japanese manufacturing methods. GM now owns 100 per cent of Saab of Sweden and it recently bought a controlling interest in the Korean firm Daewoo Auto. It has a 20 per cent share in Fuji Heavy Industries, which makes Subarus, and the same stake in Fiat.

There appears to be much potential for collaborative arrangements. For example, in 2003 GM announced it would use Subaru's four-wheel-drive Impreza platform to create an all-wheel drive Saab 9-2, a smaller hatchback version of the mid-sized 9-3 series. The 9-2 would be built in Japan, and Saab's president was reported as saying the new venture was 'a collaboration between two like-minded brands. We both have a special aircraft heritage and a successful history in rallying, and our cars are known as dynamic, safe and fun to drive. It makes a lot of sense for us to combine our strengths in creating the next Saab and bring it to the market quickly' (*New Zealand Herald*, 2003). The 9-3 shares the same platform as GM's Chevrolet Malibu and Opel's Vectra. As a result of this arrangement, the engineering costs for the three models were cut by one-third. One French interior supplier makes the seats for all three as well, in order to ensure more comfortable, durable, cheaper – and presumably more stylish – seats overall (Welch, 2003).

What lessons can we therefore take from the GM story so far?

## Lessons from General Motors

Like McDonald's discussed earlier, General Motors suffered from what Day (1999a) terms 'market blindness', and therefore exhibited 'many of the worse features of a self-centred organization'. Based on Day, these include:

- *Weak ability to capture market signals:* for example, that over the past 20 years new car buyers were moving toward cross-over vehicles (family minivans and SUVs) and away from traditional sedans and station wagons, and that competitors were reacting faster to these changes.
- *Product-focused organization:* for example, it had focused on issues of improving quality and production cost efficiencies, at times at the expense of innovative designs. In the mid-1980s it (and Ford) had followed Chrysler into the family minivan market with a vehicle that was based on a truck – not a car – chassis platform, one reason being that the car divisions did not want a car-based vehicle that might compete directly with their existing station wagons. The vehicle, which was more of a commercial van size, was criticized for being too big for domestic use, for not driving like a car, for having an engine upfront that impeded visibility, and because its rear-wheel drive shaft meant it had a higher floor and was harder to climb into. It thus disappointed the two key markets that minivans were designed for: baby-boomers with active families who liked all-round practicality, and retirees who liked easy access, roominess and good driver visibility. According to Chrysler's president (Flax, 1985), because of their short-sightedness Ford and GM 'have literally given us a ten-year cash cow'.
- *Short-run, cost concerns dominate:* for example, in the early to mid-1990s its attempts to wrest cost savings from suppliers threatened long-term relationships. Its continuous run of incentive schemes to 'move the metal' meant customers bought on transactional terms, not ones that encouraged their long-term loyalty. Sending US executives to Opel with minimal German language abilities and placing Saab vehicles in Opel dealerships suggested a lack of international–local competitive understanding.
- *Creeping marketing myopia:* for example, the unwavering belief by top executives, in particular, in the traditional market or business GM is in and the customers it is best able to serve. In the 1990s it still defined its product line-up according to traditional categories and characteristics, despite the introduction of a brand management system. In echoes of the family minivan situation of a decade earlier, it saw the emerging SUV market as a fad, and was therefore slow to allow its technology

leader, Cadillac, to introduce a luxury SUV where the highest margins could be achieved.

- *Leadership paralysis:* unlike McDonald's, GM does not appear to be reluctant to change its 'model' of industry behaviour as its circumstances have changed. Neither is it passive and accepting that its destiny depends on the changing fortunes of the industry, nor has it retreated into denial in an attempt to preserve the old 'model', such as its traditional ways of marketing and its inviolable brands. Rather, the problems faced by its leadership may be that their transformation task is now too big; their structure too unwieldy; their competitors too competitive; their shareholders too impatient; and their customers either too old or too fickle for the company to have a real chance of success in the long term. Time is not on its side.

- *A focus on structure and procedures that ensure control and conformity as opposed to processes that encourage innovation, speed and risk-taking:* for example, as Lutz commented (*Autoweek*, 2001), people in GM 'have been held back a lot by a set of internal procedures and rules that carried over for a long time.... The system as it was almost guaranteed, from a design standpoint, a low common denominator vehicle. There were just too many voices involved in what the vehicle was finally going to look like.... In some cases ... process is not the right answer...creativity cannot be reduced to a process.... I'm going to be seriously questioning a lot of the sequential steps that we have in the product creation process ... sometimes you do some great design and don't worry about by what process you got there.'

We began this chapter with a quote (1985) from Peters and Austin:

there are only two ways to create and sustain superior performance over the long haul. First, take exceptional care of your customers ... via superior service and superior quality. Secondly, constantly innovate. That's it. There are no alternatives in achieving ... or sustaining strategic competitive advantage.

As we saw with McDonald's in Chapter 1, General Motors is another great marketing corporation that may have lost sight of that perspective, and whose 'business model' may have passed its use-by date. But not necessarily. Slowly, there are signs that it is changing. It has to, for the 'economics of corporate life and death' mean growth remains a priority. General Motors is attempting various domains of growth, all of which require the building – or rebuilding – of relationships. For example, it is pursuing a strategy of growth from within, and in particular changing the process by which models are designed, developed and brought to market. It is attempting to work more closely with the increasingly important supplier groupings that are now taking shape. It is also actively pursuing growth by external acquisitions and alliances, such as its recent Saab-Impreza collaboration. Will it succeed? As we shall examine in the next chapter, growth by mergers and acquisitions in particular is often seen as an appealing, quick-fix alternative to the slower growth gains possible from within. It is also fraught with difficulties however, and may do little to address the fundamental need to grow and thereby actually create more value.

## CHAPTER 4

# Growth and Value

## CHAPTER OBJECTIVES

This chapter discusses growth and the paradox that growth does not necessarily generate value or profit. For example, external growth by a policy of mergers and acquisitions (M&A) may be attractive in the short term in terms of boosting top line revenue. However, the reality is that managing the complexities and uncertainties of M&As when under the unremitting scrutiny of the stock market may detract from, rather than enhance, corporate performance.

We continue our Chapter 3 discussion of the automobile industry by examining the issues that companies such as General Motors face when pursuing external growth opportunities through mergers and acquisitions. We do this by looking at the celebrated example of DaimlerChrysler. Both the academic and the business media discourses generally agree that M&As are fraught with difficulties: they simply do not work out in most cases. Is DaimlerChrysler any different, or is this new entity now better positioned to deliver greater value, for example, to its customers and its owners?

We then turn our attention to the issues of strategy and the creation and delivery of value. We do this by using the framework of Bear, Benson-Armer and Hall (2000), three examples culled from the business media discourse, and look at three critical factors: the pressure to deliver more shareholder value; establishment of the corporate 'context' that ensures increased value creation and strategic direction; and the dramas associated with organizations attempting to ensure performance accountabilities and implementation.

Finally, we consider what these three issues might mean for how organizations are rethinking their organization 'model' – are they shifting from value 'chains' to value 'nets', perhaps? This rethinking of the organizational model is occurring as they simultaneously rethink what value 'discipline' (Treacy and Wiersema, 1993) may now be most appropriate to deliver the new forms of value that customers are demanding.

Managing for value thus suggests an even greater need to generate internal growth and constantly reinvent the business. Concurrently, such activities need to be managed against the diverse needs of customers, employees, shareholders and other stakeholders as value extends beyond the addition of value to raw materials through the production process, and the creation and delivery of value is managed within a series or network of both transactions and embedded relationships.

It is perhaps no wonder then that marketing and marketing practices appear to have got more difficult in terms of what is involved, more urgent in terms of execution, and even more demanding in terms of what is expected! It may also be no wonder that the growth option of mergers and acquisitions has been so attractive.

## THE ATTRACTION OF EXTERNAL GROWTH STRATEGIES

Mergers and acquisitions within the automobile industry have been prevalent since it began to develop beyond small-scale manufacturing over a hundred years ago. In fact, General Motors was turned into a corporate colossus on the basis of a series of acquisitions in the first quarter of the last century. As noted in Chapter 2, during the 1970s and 1980s GM entered into a number of strategic alliances with Japanese competitors, in particular, to gain access to their small car models and their technologies, including manufacturing. Another incidence was the acquisition of premium players such as Saab of Sweden, and of equity stakes in major players such as Fiat, the perennially troubled Italian car company. Despite their many attractions, however, external growth strategies through acquisitions are no guarantee of success. For example, under cost pressure in Europe GM in 2003 merged Saab's engineering, sales and marketing operations with Opel in Europe, thereby potentially compromising what GM had purchased in the first place: the Swedish maker's 50-year effort to carve out its own special brand identity in respect of engineering excellence and individuality of design. Today, are these likely to be attributes that readily spring to mind when the name General Motors is mentioned? And since Fiat has been in dire straits for so long will it just be a continuous drain on GM's resources? Why then, have M&As been so attractive to companies like GM?

Mergers and acquisitions make for big businesses, and a number of strategic and financial pressures have driven many organizations into the cycle of growth through this means (Wolfe, 2002). These pressures include increasing international competition, rising customer expectations, rapidly changing technologies and, above all, shareholder demands. Increased sales, revenues and market share, along with lower costs through scale and greater operational efficiencies through synergies, are some of the expected outcomes of mergers and acquisitions. They also offer the acquiring company speed and time benefits, such as quicker entry to markets, faster access to R&D, and other operational competencies and marketing advantages such as broader product lines and service offerings. Most importantly, M&A's are seen as a quick way to increase corporate value for shareholders (Millman, 2000).

Mergers and acquisitions are also very risky. Recent evidence suggests the claim that M&As drive revenue growth is a myth (Bekier, Bogardus and Oldham, 2001). Frick and Torres (2002) report that M&A deals in the high-tech industries are more likely to destroy corporate value than to create it. Using data from Standard and Poor's (part of the McGraw-Hill Group) and deal tracker Mergerstat, Henry (2002) analyzed 302 major mergers over six years between 1995 and 2001. His conclusion? 'If CEOs had kept their checkbooks under lock and key and simply matched the stock market performance of their industry peers, shareholders would have been far better off.'

Why were mergers and acquisitions so prevalent in the 1990s (Tetenbaum, 1999)? Why was there a slow-down (Frick and Torres, 2002)? Why did so many M&As go wrong? And why do so many companies appear not to have learnt from the well-publicized mistakes of the likes of BMW and AOL Time Warner? These are all questions now receiving increased attention. Unfortunately, according to Bower (2001), 'we know surprisingly little about mergers and acquisitions, despite the buckets of ink spilled on the topic'. The topic is conspicuously absent from mainstream academic marketing journals, and in the textbooks it is often relegated to a cursory mention at the bottom right-hand corner of the traditional 2x2 product-market matrix in the box labelled 'Diversification', as shown in Figure 4.1.

If the recent M&A record of many firms – as so avidly portrayed in the business media discourse – is so suspect, why are M&As also so common? To answer that question it is useful to consider the behaviour of companies trying to maintain 'the 15 per cent delusion'.

## THE HARD LESSONS OF M&AS

Many companies have found out the hard way that successful growth is hard to come by from the external route. For example, early in 2000 BMW was extricating itself from what the *Economist* (2003a) termed the 'botched

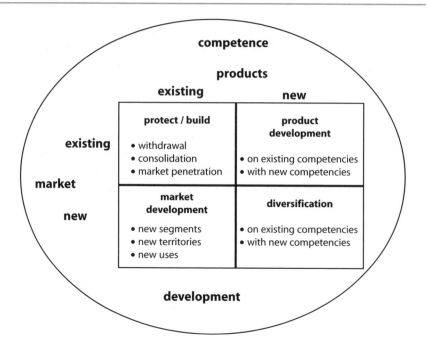

**Figure 4.1** Directions for strategic development

*Source:* Johnson and Scholes, 2002

purchase' of Britain's Rover Group, with billions lost trying to revive its 'English patient'. As one senior BMW executive commented (Ball and Miller, 2001): 'You have to decide whether you are in the premium market or the volume market.... You cannot build enough bridges to combine those.' He believed the acquisition of Rover involved 'a deflection of management attention that is something that I think is underestimated. You can't put a dollar stamp on it, but this is something which is a reality. We learned the lesson.'

BMW is a quick learner. By 2003 the company's strategy was once again focused on internally designing and building vehicles to support its long-standing promise of making 'ultimate driving machines'. A consolation prize from Rover was the super-mini Mini Cooper which, as a result of a better than expected American reception, helped push BMW's sales volume to a million units for the first time. Recent new models included the X-5 SUV, the Z8 roadster, and what some critics considered an overly technical new top-of-the-line 7-series luxury sedan. Into this vehicle BMW packed extremely sophisticated – and expensive – electronic systems. Most controversial was the new command centre technology called iDrive, consisting of a silver knob on the centre console connected to a menu of options presented on a computer screen in the centre of the dash. The knob is similar to a PC's mouse in that it allows the driver to select and navigate through any of eight activities: communications (phone), navigation, in-car entertainment, interior climate, roadside assistance, vehicle maintenance, help (with iDrive) and configuration (all the programmable systems on the car). It allows the driver to pre-set and fine-tune everything that is electronic – air conditioning, the sound system, traction control, and so on – to suit the individual.

According to BMW, iDrive 'opens up a new perspective on driving, with more technology for greater comfort and safety, more driving pleasure and performance in a new context that is less complicated, more comfortable, more individual'. Others suggest it redefines what is a car. As Sloane (2002) noted: 'The car is as much a mobile communications centre as it is transport'. Many drivers and motoring journalists have found the system less intuitive than the company expected. BMW appears to have learned quickly from these criticisms, as it looked for cost-effective ways to move the technologies down to the next tier models. Thus, its revamped 5-series saloon, launched in early 2003, had a reworked and simpler iDrive-type system.

## THE LESSON OF DAIMLERCHRYSLER

BMW's acquisition lesson is one that DaimlerChrysler is also learning. In May 1998 the US$36 billion merger between Daimler Benz and Chrysler was announced. Said the *Economist* (1998): 'the deal between Chrysler and Daimler is the largest merger in industrial history and will create the world's fifth largest car maker. Daimler's strengths in Europe and in the market for luxury cars complement Chrysler's American base and its reputation for family-carrying minivans and sport-utility vehicles.' The *Economist* (1998) also pointed out an apparent contradiction in the industry that manufacturers had to reconcile: 'The immense fixed costs of developing and manufacturing vehicles mean that making profits from cars goes with making lots of them ... the most profitable manufacturers will be those that satisfy the urge for individualism, but from one basic design.'

As it turned out, the merger was the beginning of an eventual takeover of Chrysler by Mercedes-Benz. That did not occur by chance, and was always on the German company's agenda, given its need to grow. In 1985 Daimler-Benz's revenue was DM52 billion, double what it was ten years earlier. By 1995 it was double again, at DM125 billion. It had achieved this growth largely by embarking on a diversification strategy that turned it into an integrated technology conglomerate (Waller, 2001).

By mid-1997, however, with a new CEO in charge, this strategy was acknowledged as failing. It had cost the company and its shareholders some DM100 billion over the past decade and it realized it had to offload some of its acquisitions, including AEG, the massive electrical engineering group which made everything from computer chips to fridges to trams, and Fokker, the venerable Dutch manufacturer of commuter aircraft.

Daimler-Benz also concluded that the corporate growth target of DM250 billion for 2005 could not be met by a reversion to the Mercedes brand alone. To achieve it would require a significant expansion into the mass market for automobiles and a more global outlook (*Economist*, 2003a). The issue was, with whom should the company partner? According to Jurgen Schrempp, the new CEO, the criteria for joint arrangements were: any potential partner had to provide profitable growth; their products and geographic markets should not overlap; and Daimler-Benz must be the leading partner (Waller, 2001; Vlasic and Stertz, 2001).

An internal study team was set up to consider five merger possibilities: Toyota, Honda, General Motors, Ford and Chrysler. The team was given three months to complete their assessments. They had full access to the new Mercedes-Benz state-of-the-art corporate information and communications centre, which had electronic links to two thousand databases, all internal reports and tens of thousands of employees worldwide. A second team was set up to assess where the automobile industry was heading in the next ten years. By mid-November their tasks were completed. They concluded Mercedes-Benz had to find a mass-market partner, and Chrysler was their preferred choice.

On 12 January 1998, just prior to the Detroit Motor Show, Schrempp visited Robert Eaton, CEO of Chrysler, and in a one-to-one meeting outlined the proposal that their companies should merge. Even though Chrysler had not been considering the possibility of a merger with Mercedes-Benz, Eaton's reply was: 'It makes some sense. Just give me a week, or two. I'll call you.' The entire encounter took 17 minutes. Marvelled Schrempp: 'He didn't even have the chance to offer me coffee' (Vlasic and Stertz, 2002). Ten days later, Eaton called Schrempp to say the two companies should commence formal discussions. Four months later, what the two partners pointedly termed a 'merger-of-equals' was officially announced.

Two years later the deal was in tatters. DaimlerChrysler's market capitalization was about half what it was when the corporation began trading as a single stock in November 1998; two major credit-ratings agencies had downgraded its debt rating; the cyclical US auto industry was signalling a downturn; the Chrysler group was losing money by the truckload and discounting virtually every model in its line; and the top executives of both companies realized they had underestimated the difficulties of merging two distinct corporate- and country-based cultures. As the *Economist* (2000a) asked: 'Could a bunch of process-led German engineers work effectively with Chrysler's hunch-inspired, risk-taking bosses?' At the time, they could not, and by the end of 2000 Eaton and most of the US management board that had been responsible for Chrysler's stunning transformation during the 1990s had either resigned, retired or been made redundant; Chrysler was being run by an astute German CEO from Daimler, officially ending the merger-of-equals 'spin'; and some very angry US shareholders were threatening to sue the company for fraud.

## HONDA: A BETTER BET, AND SLOAN'S FOURTH WAVE?

If Daimler-Benz were looking for a low-cost global auto partner that operated on the value creation side of the diagonal line in Figure 2.1 in Chapter 2; that earned most of its revenues in the American market; and that possibly represented the next – or fourth – wave of the automotive industry, it is perhaps unfortunate that it did not purchase Honda. The Japanese company was on its original list and, as the *Economist* (2003a) reported:

> One of its competences was a network of factories around the world, all hooked into the same supply chain. Each operates in the same way, so each is able to make any vehicle in the product range according to demand. That gives the company tremendous flexibility, thanks as much to slick logistics as to excellence in manufacturing.... Honda pays meticulous attention to detail to help ensure that its products are made on time. It has special data systems installed in each of its factories to monitor weather forecasts. These allow factory managers to talk in advance to parts suppliers about bad weather and how it might affect deliveries. They can decide what and when to stock up.

If 'mass-class' represents Sloan's third period of the automobile industry (Sloan, 1963), then Honda may represent what might be termed the 'flexible-customizable' fourth phase. It is the cumulation of nearly two decades of development in global manufacturing, logistics and supplier relationships. It is also what Bylinsky (1983) had identified as 'a logical extension of a manufacturing philosophy that views the production of goods as a seamless activity that starts with product design and ends with support in the field – a philosophy, as the Japanese put it, of making the goods flow like water'.

The system requires Tier 1 suppliers to become an extension of the design–development–engineering processes of an OEM. Firms such as Honda thus become assemblers of pre-tested, pre-assembled modules. They also tap into a greater talent pool, even if they are not under the direct line control of the OEM's vehicle development group. Nor are they part of the OEM's fixed cost structure. What is emerging is the virtual automobile organization, as the worldwide resources of multiple companies (OEM, Tier 1, Tier 2, and so on) begin by focusing the sum of their collective capabilities on a new vehicle being developed, and finish by delivering, just-in-time, all the necessary 'plug-in' modules to the OEM's assembly lines, wherever they are located. Benefits include fewer labour costs at final assembly and the flexibility continuously to upgrade the components that go into the module, such as dashboards with the latest in electronics.

In terms of the marketing implications, McKenna (1991) predicted more than a decade ago – and well before the Internet appeared – that:

> In a world of mass manufacturing, the counterpart was mass marketing. In a world of flexible manufacturing, the counterpart is flexible marketing. The technology comes first, the ability to market follows. The technology embodies adaptability, programmability, and customisability; now comes marketing that delivers on those qualities.

Unfortunately for General Motors and its continued reliance on 'move-the-metal' special deals, this flexible-customisable approach may be some time away. However, under the prodding of believers such as Lutz, it is moving in that direction. Moving too slowly could potentially be catastrophic, for if the believers are correct, 'mass customisation' presents all kinds of possibilities for the creation, development and delivery of new forms of value. Is marketing, and are marketers, ready and able?

## THE PRESSURE TO DELIVER VALUE

A possible lesson from the M&A 'bubble' is that internal growth strategies make marketing more important than ever, especially in today's information age (Doyle, 2000). Despite the criticisms of marketing's shortcomings, such as we saw with GM, the core purpose of marketing remains unchanged. In her well-reviewed book *What Management Is*, Magretta (2002) said: 'Value creation is the animating principle of modern management and its chief responsibility.... Management's mission, first and fore-most, is value creation.... Value is defined not by what an organization does but by the customer who buys its goods and services.'

As markets become more open and competitive, customers more knowl-edgeable and expecting, and shareholders and regulators' demands more exacting, there is greater pressure on the marketing function to be more disciplined and accountable in the pursuit of value-based marketing strate-gies – especially in the academic discourse (for example, Treacy and Wiersema, 1993; Parasuraman, 1997; Anderson and Narus, 1998; Hamel, 1998; Kim and Mauborgne, 1999; Bear, Benson-Armer and Hall, 2000; and Doyle, 2000).

These pressures require that marketers' tasks become more difficult and complex, as they juggle the goals of:

- generating more profitable growth and shareholder value
- maintaining superior buyer value in existing markets and engineering quantum leaps in buyer value for new markets, and
- building greater customer intimacy, loyalty and returns from their most valued customers.

Given such demands on marketing, Whitwell, Lukas and Doyle (2003) argued that there were several reasons why 'marketing professionals should now have become more important in the top councils of business'. For example:

- Crucial issues for companies are the ways in which they understand and adapt to rapidly changing markets, customer expectations, direct and indirect competition, the information technology revolution, and so on. Said Whitwell, Lukas and Doyle (2003): 'If senior management are not focusing on customers and markets, it will mean other issues fill the agenda.'
- Marketing – rather than production – skills have become critical to creat-ing a competitive advantage, such as, for example, the importance of understanding the power of branding and brand equity, and of going beyond product and service augmentation, by offering tailored solutions for individual customers, and so on.
- Marketing performance is at the heart of creating shareholder value. However, as Whitwell, Lukas and Doyle (2003) argued, paradoxically, marketing's influence in the boardroom is less than it should be: 'Several factors account for this paradox of the growing importance of marketing with the lack of influence of marketing professionals in top

management. Of fundamental importance has been the failure of the marketing discipline to incorporate the concept of shareholder value.' As a result, said the authors, top managers have tended to be preoccupied with two strategic approaches: cost-cutting 'sometimes disguised by more appealing names such as reengineering, downsizing or right sizing' and acquisitions, despite the evidence 'that three out of four acquisitions fail to add value for the acquiring company'.

Why should the lack of marketing influence at the boardroom level matter? Because, as Whitwell, Lukas and Doyle (2003) also argued:

> If senior management are not focusing on customers and markets, it will mean that other issues fill the agenda. Evidence suggests that managers become preoccupied with short-term budgets, [with] operating rather than strategic issues and, when difficulties arise, retrenchment rather than renewal. Such myopia is, in the long run, antithetical to genuine value-creating strategies.

Echoing Iaccoca's (1984) earlier negative comments about financial managers in control at General Motors, Gummesson (2003) has warned, somewhat trenchantly: 'Obsession with measurement means handing over the future of a company to the accounting tribe, abolishing vision and leadership.'

## STRATEGY AND THE ART OF CREATING VALUE

At the risk of stating the obvious, in order to create and deliver value, and to manage fast growth, organizations need a strategy (von Krogh and Cusumano, 2001). According to Norman and Ramirez (1993): 'Strategy is the art of creating value. It provides the intellectual frameworks, conceptual models, and governing ideas that allow a company's managers to identify opportunities for bringing value to customers and for delivering that value at a profit.'

In a review of value delivery, Piercy (1998a) identified three organizational processes to do with 'going to market' – first, value defining; second, value developing; and third, value delivering – in order to illustrate the different dimensions to the creation and delivery of value. Whitwell, Lukas and Doyle (2003) also suggested that there are three drivers of value in a business that will deliver greater shareholder value: first, financial value drivers; second, marketing value drivers; and, third, organizational value drivers. These are shown in Figure 4.2. They argued that 'the most fundamental determinant of shareholder value is the anticipated level of free cash flow', something which helps us to understand General Motor's recent emphasis on incentives to 'move the metal'.

While acknowledging the importance of metrics that show marketing's contribution to the firm's success, the academic discourse has tended to emphasize the various dimensions of the value construct and the organizational delivery of value, as will be discussed in more detail below, when we

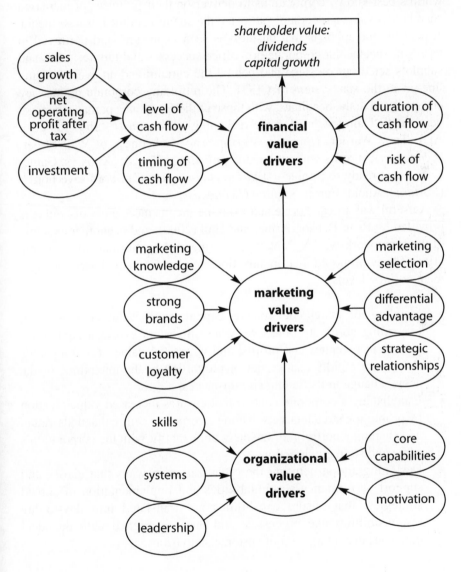

**Figure 4.2** The drivers of value in a business

*Source:* Whitwell, Lukas and Doyle, 2003

also draw on the business media discourse. This exercise is timely and useful in terms of providing a framework within which to examine the changing nature of marketing practice.

While Payne and Holt (1999) have cautioned that the nature of the inter-relationship between, for example, customer value and shareholder value is still not clear, and therefore requires further study, the failure of many of the world's best-known corporations to deliver on their promises of increased shareholder value has certainly attracted the attention of the business media. A possible metaphor is that business is seen as theatre, and portrayed in terms of: spectacular corporate box-office successes and failures; plots and subplots acted out on-stage and behind the curtain; and an ever-changing line-up in the star system of CEOs. The unfolding corporate dramas are encapsulated in the headlines, with those of the *Economist* perhaps the most percipient: 'DaimlerChrysler: the reckoning' (*Economist*); 'Show time for AOL Time Warner' (*Business Week*); 'The wickedness of Wall Street' (*Economist*); 'Profits without honour' (*Financial Times*); 'Xbox vs. Game-Cube – get ready to rumble' (*Wall Street Journal*); 'Can Ford save Ford?' (*Fortune*); Ahold: Europe's Enron (*Economist*).

A useful way to categorize and examine the business press discourse is provided by Bear, Benson-Armer and Hall (2000), and is another example of the framework-type of thinking recommended by Norman and Ramirez (1993). They proposed that organizations implement value-based manage-ment at three levels:

- Standing for shareholder (market capitalization) value creation as an overriding corporate objective, where investors expect a continuous growth in revenues and profits, and where the value of a company's shares can rapidly change out of proportion to the magnitude of the actual change in its trading circumstances.
- Establishing a corporate context that ensures increased value creation by promoting stretch targets; having a corporate centre that adds value; and shaping a portfolio of business units that fit with the corporation's goals and strategic direction.
- Designing and structuring the organization in ways that clarify and support performance accountabilities and implementation of agreed strategies; that ensure capabilities are translated into day-to-day responsibilities and processes; and that are aligned with the ideal outcomes that a target set of customers envisions.

Examples from the business press discourse allow us to consider each level in the context of a particular issue facing organizations.

## The dramas associated with standing for shareholder value creation as an overriding corporate objective

The 1990s can be characterized by the elevation of shareholder value as the key driver of business activities, the ubiquitous spread of short-term business thinking, and the consequent focus on the next half-year – or quarterly in the USA – financial results. A contributing factor was the combination of CEO and top management incentive schemes, such as stock options, that discouraged growth and development based on long-term investment. Instead these encouraged short-term behaviour, such as growth by acquisition in order to maximize shareholder returns and increase the firm's share price, and an executive predilection for making brash predictions about future earnings. Loomis (2001) termed this 'the 15 per cent delusion' and said if the forecast panned out the result was the firm starred in the stock market and its CEO was 'given, so to speak, ticker-tape parades'. 'And, hey', she added, 'why settle for a measly 15 per cent?'.

By 2000 the signs that the economic growth bubble was about to burst began to appear. As noted by Colvin (2000):

> As significant as the number of companies warning of bad news was Wall Street's merciless response. Here were firms admitting profits wouldn't meet expectations for a single quarter, and their stocks were getting taken down 10 per cent to 15 per cent.'

For example, in late July 2000, when Nokia announced that its sales revenue for the quarter to the end of June had increased by more than 50 per cent over the same period in the previous year, its shares fell by 26 per cent, the largest single-day drop in value ever experienced by a European company. Apparently what most concerned Nokia's predominantly American investors was the concern that the company's annual sales growth of some 50 per cent per year since 1997 was finally slowing down (*Economist*, 2000b).

Three years later, the bad news continued. For example, early in 2003 Intel warned that its first-quarter results would fall short of its earlier forecast, as demand for its flash-memory chips used in cellphones and digital cameras continued to decline. The *New York Times* (2003) reported that Intel was losing sales to rivals after it had raised its prices by as much as 40 per cent, whereas 'Customers want lower-priced chips as faltering economic growth, made worse by the prospect of war with Iraq, hurts their profits.' After the announcement, Intel's share prices fell 28c to US$16.70, and the *New York Times* (2003) reported that Intel's share price had dropped some 49 per cent in the past year.

Early in 2003 Volkswagen, Europe's biggest car maker, announced that first-quarter earnings would fall 'significantly', as buyers started to cut back on discretionary spending, and as the euro strengthened against the US dollar. Further, even though it would be introducing the Touran mini-van, a revamped Audi 3, and a revised version of its top-selling Golf in 2003, Volkswagen disclosed it would be cutting investment in new plant and equipment by some 10 per cent. As a result, reported the *Herald* (2003), 'Volkswagen's shares fell to the lowest in more than six years on the news.'

When IBM announced early in 2003 that its sales and earnings for the first three months of the year would fall below Wall Street expectations, the announcement knocked some 10 per cent off its share price. Some analysts suggested that, under its new leadership, IBM might be 'managing earnings downwards ... so that later comparisons will look more impressive'. Another said: 'This brings to the surface the old question about IBM – for all that Gerstner (its previous CEO) did, it is not a growth company' (Lohr, 2003a). Shortly afterwards, when IBM announced that its first quarter revenue for 2003 had risen by some 11 per cent from the quarter a year earlier, Lohr (2003b) reported IBM executives as saying that the company was 'on track to meet Wall Street's consensus estimates for profit of about US$4.30 a share for the full year'. However, Lohr also noted that some analysts were pointing out that, after excluding the benefits of an additional US$1 billion in revenue brought in from its acquisition of PricewaterhouseCoopers Consulting in 2002, plus a fall in the exchange value of the dollar in the year, 'IBM may well have experienced a decline in revenue instead of an 11 per cent increase.'

These are extreme examples, but such falls and such criticisms may reflect the anomaly that the market capitalization value of many publicly traded companies may have exceeded both their book value and their ability to deliver expected returns on equity (Bary, 2000; *Economist*, 2001a). They may also help to explain recent concerns such as:

- the role of financial analysts in hyping the prices of technology stocks (Elkind, 2001)
- the investment community's call for common financial and business measures in order to eliminate what have been termed 'opaque, questionable accounting reports in the wake of the Enron debacle' (Farrell, 2002) and, more recently, the overstating of the earnings of Royal Ahold, leading the *Economist* (2003b) to warn: 'The Ahold scandal shows that Europe is not immune from America's corporate ills'

- and possibly even the need for a new financial theory of the firm (Zingales, 2000).

## The dramas associated with establishing a corporate context that ensures increased value creation and strategic direction

As an example, Unilever, the Anglo-Dutch company, was formed in 1929 through the merger of Lever Brothers and Margarine Unie. It was a massive global company at the time, with operations in some 40 countries. However, according to Beck (2000):

> Over the decades, Unilever continued acquiring companies, moving into chemicals, packaging, market research and advertising. The result: a hodgepodge of businesses and a complex management matrix (including two chairmen), which, until recently, gave enormous power to country managers to set their own priorities and tailor products to local tastes.

Said one former consultant to the company: 'Unilever's brand structure is confusing. It doesn't bring clarity in the consumer's mind' (Beck 2000).

During the 1990s Unilever's annual sales growth rate was only 2 per cent, and in the last half of 1999 its market capitalization value fell from US$85 billion to some US$55 billion, as investors shifted out of low-growth traditional manufacturing to higher-growth technology shares. In an effort to stem the decline, early in 2000 Unilever officially announced a massive restructuring that would cut some 10 per cent from its 250,000 workforce worldwide, close some 100 of its 380 factories, and reduce its 1600 brands to 400 global 'power' brands, such as Persil, Dove, Lipton, Magnum, and Calvin Klein (Beck, 2000; Bidlake, 2000).

Unilever's co-chair, Niall FitzGerald, explained their future strategy (FitzGerald, 1999):

> Our businesses will mass their marketing muscle and advertising support behind these power brands. They will be run by our best people, and will drive our R&D programs. We will leverage them across geographies, categories and channels, building strength on strength.... Our aim is to build a core portfolio of no more than 400 leading brands, each one No. 1 or 2 in its market or segment.

The company would be organized into 'innovation centres', to 'concentrate on a small number of big hit innovations. At their core will be a deep understanding of where consumers are going, so that we can be there when they arrive' (FitzGerald, 1999).

Brands selected for the top 400 had to display 'brand appeal' (strong current performance and the ability to sustain growth) and 'brand scale' (the critical mass to justify further R&D and marketing support). They would be classified into three groups: 'international brands' that would have a common international brand positioning strategy (for example, Lipton Tea); 'international brand positioning', whereby different brands could have the same international positioning (for example, Flora low-fat spread in the UK is called Becel in Germany); and 'local jewels', whereby brands with strong local positions would still be supported (for example, Marmite and Oxo cubes in the UK). Unilever was also reported as predicting the recent annual growth rates of under 5 per cent for the power brands would increase to more than 6 per cent by 2004 (Bartram, 2000).

FitzGerald believed that the power brands would only succeed if the company worked in partnership with retail groups: 'This is a fast-moving consumer goods business focused on a relatively small number of big brands. You get synergies with the retail trade by bringing to them the big brand leaders which draw traffic through their store' (Voyle, 2000).

In 2000 Unilever announced it had earmarked some €200 million to expand electronic commerce and other Internet services, including an on-line purchasing system that was expected to 'transform the way in which the firm obtains its products and materials. Within two years (predicted FitzGerald) half of all purchasing will be done on the Internet' (*Economist*, 2000a).

In 2000 Unilever also announced a series of web alliances, such as a US$200 million joint venture with iVillage, 'an American portal aimed at women aged between 25 and 54, who are prime consumers of lucrative personal-care products. Another alliance will test how European teenagers interact with brands on the Web.' While Unilever was unsure whether the Internet would ever become a major channel for direct selling to consumers, 'until the answer is clearer, Unilever will experiment', said the *Economist* (2000a).

More recently (Dignam, 2002), FitzGerald was reported as having introduced changes in the way Unilever reports information on individual brand performance worldwide, to include data on growth, sales and, sometimes, market shares. This information was seen as crucial for analysts, investors and the public to assess how well Unilever's 400 core brands were performing in terms of their target of accounting for 95 per cent of company revenues by 2004. As Unilever's financial director said: 'Unilever was one of the forefathers of branded goods. That is our heritage and we must focus the business on our core brands' (Hayward, 2002). To this end Unilever in 2000 alone sold some 27 businesses worth close to US$1.3 billion, even though in the same year it paid more than US$20 billion for Bestfoods, the US maker of leading brands such as Knorr (soups), Hellmann's (mayonnaise) and Skippy (peanut butter). Argued FitzGerald: 'The deal is transforming the industry because it literally combines the best player in the US with our business. Since the industry was going to consolidate anyway, it's much better to lead that consolidation and choose the best partner with which to do it' (Voyle, 2000).

Has Unilever's emphasis on power brands paid off? In 2001 the company's overall revenue increased 8.6 per cent, to €52.2 billion. Its operating margin (before exceptional items and goodwill amortization: BEIA) for 2001 rose to 13.9 per cent, up from 11.2 per cent at the beginning of 2000. The company also reported €7.5 billion in cash flow from operations, up 11 per cent from €6.7 billion in 2000. In the same year, what the company now termed its 'core' brands achieved a sales revenue growth of 5.3 per cent, compared with a 3.8 per cent growth in 2000. It also announced that its 'core' brands made up 84 per cent of group sales in 2001, up from 75 per cent of sales at the beginning of 2000, and were on track to achieve its target of 95 per cent for the year 2004 (Ellison, 2002).

Early in 2003 Unilever announced it would beat its own targets for 2002 sales and profits. Despite 'difficult market conditions', its sales revenue grew by 4 per cent; operating margin was 14.9 per cent; cash flow was €7.9 billion; and sales growth of its core brands was 5.4 per cent, representing 89 per cent of group sales. The company also announced that in 2002 its restructuring programme had delivered procurement savings of €1.6 billion, 'ahead of schedule', and it had reached its full Bestfoods integration savings target of €0.8 billion, 'again ahead of plan'. Predicted the company: 'The momentum in our all-round performance in 2002, underpinned by strong innovation and further cost savings, gives us the confidence that our 2004 Path to Growth targets will be achieved in full' (Unilever, 2003).

Is the strategy working? In mid-2002 the chair of Unilever UK, speaking at the Institute of Directors' annual convention, said of the company's Path to Growth strategy: 'This is good business. We have the economies of scale in terms of manufacturing, marketing and advertising that come from a concentration on a group of leading brands' (Kinsella, 2002).

Later in 2002 FitzGerald added: 'The focus on our leading brands with sustained rates of innovation will drive accelerating top-line growth' (Ball,

2002a). To support this kind of leverage, Unilever also reported that it had invested €7.3 billion in worldwide advertising and promotion in 2002, up 8.5 per cent from 2001 (Hayes and Ball, 2003).

As an example, part of the revenue and top line growth of Unilever's power brands came from the success of Dove which, over the past three years, had expanded into a US$2 billion business by moving from its original bar soap and into deodorant, body wash, facial cleaner and, in early 2003, shampoo and conditioner. The head of Unilever's hair-care business in North America said that the advertising for the new Dove shampoo and conditioner would also feature the personal testimonials approach of the other Dove brands, adding: 'We will get a very, very fast awareness build because we have so many consumers who already know the brand' (*Wall Street Journal*, 2003).

Despite the continued growth, some analysts were more sanguine since part of the growth in revenues was from price rises as opposed to volume growth and brand extension initiatives. As one analyst said: 'Innovation is good to keep a good category bubbling, but it's never a cure for a fundamentally low-growth category' (Ball, 2002b).

## The dramas associated with (re)designing and (re)structuring the organization in ways that clarify and support performance accountabilities and implementation, and which are aligned with meeting market requirements

For many companies it is critical that news of their performance receives favourable reportage. An interesting sideline to the 1998 Daimler-Chrysler merger is the extent the new company went to in order to build relationships with the various stakeholders affected by the merger, and to control the resulting business discourse. Waller (2001) reported that the two companies made the story as succinct as possible, and provided a complete 'package' of information, based on a series of bullet points, for key influencers, including politicians, journalists, academics, consultants, financial analysts and employees. Above all, 'the deal had to be wrapped in a cloak of consensus'. One theme stressed was 'the creation of a leading global automobile company' serving:

- shareholders – it enhances corporate value
- customers – premium brands with excellent potential
- employees – new growth opportunities through sales in global markets.

Even the timing of the announcement was deliberate, according to Waller:

The deal was announced on a Thursday with the aim of making the communications process easier. It would give reporters relatively little time to contact potential sceptical third parties such as financial analysts and academics. On Thursday, they would be too busy reporting the facts, leaving Friday as the only full working day of the week in which to put together a balanced assessment of the deal. In the meantime, DaimlerChrysler would itself be contacting opinion-formers. The hope was that they would be singing from the official hymn-sheet by the time reporters caught up with them over the weekend or on Monday of the following week.

The initial business media discourse was mostly positive. However, stung by the slowness of the integration process (Muller, 1999), and in an effort to rebuild share market confidence in the merger, late in 1999 Daimler-Chrysler announced new performance measures which it claimed would set new standards for the industry (Burt, 1999). One initiative was a US$48 billion R&D investment package to cover several broad areas that the company believed it needed to invest in so as to stay competitive: new propulsion technologies; new design concepts; new materials; new manufacturing technologies; new traffic management systems; in-car internet access; and what it termed 'mechatronic control systems'. Burt (1999) also reported that, despite the high market and technological uncertainties surrounding these investments, they would still be subject to the company's overriding 12–15 per cent return requirements.

However, a year later, and beset by falling demand, a market capitalization value some 20 per cent less than at the time of the merger, and a domination of Chrysler's senior echelons by German turn-around specialists, DaimlerChrysler announced a US$500 million third-quarter loss, with a similar amount projected for the following quarter. In one initiative to stem these losses, the company that had once been lauded for building close relationships with its suppliers (Vlasic, 1996; Kisiel, 1997) said that it would now require suppliers to reduce their prices by 5 per cent from 1 January 2001, with a further 10 per cent cut required over the next two years (Burt and Tait, 2000). Another announcement was that it would pare its product development funds from US$48 billion to US$36 billion (Tierney, Karnitschnig and Muller, 2000).

Industry financial analysts were not convinced of the company's priorities. Said one: 'Not only do there appear to be no shareholder initiatives in the pipeline, but DaimlerChrysler appears intent on making investments that are likely to generate little or no return' (Burt and Tait, 2000). A former Chrysler chief who helped build the company's well-known close relationships with its suppliers added: 'I worry what the long-term damage will be from a short-term dictatorial approach' (*Herald*, 2001).

Two years on, it appeared that some substantive results were beginning to emerge. While it lost US$1.9 billion in 2001, the company reported an operating profit (excluding charges) of US$1.3 billion in 2002. The financial news was positive for Chrysler, and reflected its abilities in the 1980s and 1990s to think creatively about ways to design and build new vehicles on limited budgets. Said Taylor (2003):

> In a world awash in manufacturing capacity, global carmakers keep building assembly lines and launching new models in the hope that their own cars will steal market share from rivals doing exactly the same thing. Instead, the automakers end up slashing prices to move surplus merchandise at sharply reduced margins...Chrysler is attacking this problem from an angle: Instead of reducing the supply of cars, it is reducing the cost of making them.

Two initiatives illustrated this. One was the launch of its new US$35,000 Crossfire sports car, which was the first jointly-developed car and could be a harbinger of the future. Said Taylor (2003):

> The Crossfire is a Mercedes in a Chrysler body – 39 per cent of its parts, including the engine, transmission, suspension, and electrical components, are made by Chrysler's corporate stable mate Mercedes-Benz. Crossfire comes to market after just 24 months of work, for the budget price of US$280 million (vs. the US$1 billion Chrysler would normally expect to spend). Better still, Crossfire is assembled not at an expensive plant (in the US) staffed by union autoworkers but by an outside supplier using its own employees at its own factory (in Germany).... If Chrysler can make the new formula work, it will spend less money, employ fewer workers, and reduce the amount of assets devoted to engineering and building cars.

The other initiative was illustrated by an announcement early in 2003 that Chrysler's next generation of small (Chrysler PT Cruiser/Dodge Neon) and mid-sized (Chrysler Sebring/Dodge Stratus) models would be developed from a single platform, rather than two, and that the platform would be the one that its Japanese partner, Mitsubishi, was using for its redesigned Lancer model. Kranz and Connelly (2003) said the decision would reduce both automakers' costs of vehicle development and assembly. For example, each new platform, including its related engineering, tools and other costs, normally costs about US$1 billion. Another benefit was that the decision to use one platform for both small and mid-sized vehicles would allow the company to share a new four-cylinder engine that would be built not just for the new Chrysler and Mitsubishi models, but also for another partner, Hyundai Motor Company. Finally, the move 'would allow the automaker to produce a wide range of models on the same assembly line, matching production of each model with consumer demand'. If successfully executed, however, such a situation would turn the 'logic' of a hundred years of automobile manufacturing on its head, namely, the notion of the special-purpose factory turning out hundreds of thousands of near-identical vehicles to the same standard year after year.

While the financial results for Chrysler may have turned positive, it saw its market share slip from 16 per cent in 1998 to 13 per cent in 2002. In other words, it might have taken costs out of its development and manufacturing processes, but it still needed to design and make vehicles the market would accept without demanding a discount. Otherwise, it faced more cycles of rebates that would continue to erode its bottom line, and thus require further cost cutting. The Crossfire represents a major shift in strategy for Chrysler, and an attempt to redefine its value proposition to the market, by calling on the expertise and resources of its German parent company.

Tierney (2003) called it an 'audacious plan' and said:

> The logic is simple: Stylish, well-built, reliable cars retain their value longer, command higher prices, and are more profitable.... Moving into the ranks of premium carmakers would allow Chrysler to leave those promotions behind, or at least offer fewer of them.

Logical, yes. Difficult, definitely. After a decade Ford has still to obtain the market and financial returns it expected when it purchased ailing Jaguar. It took Audi more than a decade to be accepted as a premium-priced brand and to compete with the likes of BMW and Volvo. Lexus has become a premium brand because Toyota was prepared to change its name, and invest in a decade of continuous evolution without ever compromising on quality standards.

To make its strategy and its initiatives work, Chrysler has to reconcile increasingly complex and potentially conflicting imperatives. For example:

- It has to ensure its platform teams coordinate the development, engineering and manufacturing done by insiders and outsiders, and share their learning experiences.

- It has to manage communications and data networks with its partners worldwide.
- It has to rebuild damaged relationships with both its global suppliers, who will still be expected to reduce costs continuously, and its employees, who are likely to fear that more outsourcing will mean more job losses;
- It has to ensure that, even as it moves away from the vertically integrated structural 'model' that characterized the automobile industry for a century, it still retains ownership, direction and control over its core competencies and assets, including icon brands such as Jeep.
- It has to ensure that, by focusing on cost reductions through the sharing of key components and by building a range of models on common platforms, it does not alienate its customers by eroding the characteristics of its individual brands, or compromising their respective quality standards, as General Motors did in the 1980s.
- It has to balance the need to deliver increased returns to impatient stakeholders against the imperatives – and costs – of being competitive on a day-to-day basis in its home market, where its main competitor is spending vast sums on rebates 'to grow. We don't care who we take it from' (Welch, 2003).
- It has to maintain relationships with its existing customers, by continuing to offer them updated and improved – and possibly discounted – brands of models they know and understand, and yet also come up with innovative brands of models that will attract premium prices and expand their customer base.

No wonder that companies like Chrysler are now finding their marketing practices more complex in terms of what is involved, more difficult in terms of execution, and even more demanding in terms of the results that are expected. Is this the new marketing reality?

## THE NEW MARKETING REALITY

As illustrated by the above examples, and as discussed throughout this book, with a greater managerial emphasis on value creation, development and delivery there is a growing realization that marketing has less to do with the traditional 4Ps and economic transactions, and more to do with building and maintaining relationships, networks and continuous interactions between players throughout an entire business value system.

This wider approach has been termed 'relationship marketing' and it is integral to a firm creating, developing and delivering greater product and service value, and in turn gaining and keeping its most valued customers, at a sufficient return to all parties, including the firm's owners. In other words, value can be present and accounted for in a firm's net worth, in its tangible and intangible assets, including its brands, and in its relationships with current and future partners, including employees, suppliers, intermediaries, competitors and customers.

Whatever it is labelled, this approach to marketing also reflects the shift from a focus on the traditional metrics such as sales and market share growth, profit margins and return on investment, to issues more concerned with: increasing the firm's market value; realigning the information 'intensification' of products, services and processes; managing the outcomes of customer expectations, experiences, satisfactions and dissatisfactions; building long-term relationships and loyalty; and capturing a greater proportion of the lifetime value of a firm's most-valued customers. In effect, it may be about the use of power, as discussed in Chapter 5.

Caulkin (2002) argues that companies that focus solely on driving up shareholder value are more likely to destroy value instead, particularly when executives' remuneration is tied to share price performance:

> To meet their numbers, marketing people will raise prices or lower value for money, salespeople will push short-term promotions at the expense of long-term customer value, and production people will squeeze suppliers and cut corners on materials. In finance, they will outsource, shift assets, buy earnings and fiddle with the balance sheet. Note that none of this is illegal, ill-meaning or even dramatic – in the short term.... You do not need scandal-plagued Enron and WorldCom to prove the point. They are just more extreme versions of the fundamentalist thinking that has driven the auto-destruction of many companies such as Hanson and Westinghouse, liquidated by their directors to the greater glory of shareholder value.

Based on Caulkin's (2002) comments, companies post-Enron in the USA and post-Ahold in Europe may start to take on the following characteristics:

- *Purpose:* they will have a purpose beyond the share price. For some companies the purpose used to be termed the 'vision'. Companies are starting to realize that vision is too insubstantial. Likewise they will have goals beyond the 15 per cent delusion, and built instead around the balanced scorecard concept.
- *Strategy:* they will have a clearly delineated strategy designed to create and deliver superior customer value, however that is defined, which is

predicated on the best utilization of the resources of the firm, and which requires the wise use of the power they possess.

- *Innovation:* they will constantly innovate, in order to create new value as opposed to stealing share of existing value from others. This process of innovation may require companies actively to seek discontinuities to their existing technologies and traditional ways of doing business.
- *Change:* innovation will be fuelled by a commitment to change and continuous improvements in products, services, processes and strategies in order to maintain the apparently contradictory twin goals of continuously reducing costs and improving quality.
- *Learning:* the company will value the need for continuous learning. For example, said Caulkin: 'Workable innovations, whether to products, processes or strategy, can only emerge from the interactions of people who are busy learning from their contacts with customers and suppliers, including internal ones.'
- *People:* the company will be people-centred, and this is central to companies adopting a more relational approach to their marketing. For example, creating and maintaining internal and external relationships based on understanding, trust and commitment will be the prime requirements for long-term success of the organization. Caulkin suggests people-centred organizations may require a different type of leadership as a result: 'Leadership is still important, of course, but it is quiet leadership that asserts purpose and enables improvement, not the heroic stuff that often ends in disaster.' Or in the headlines of the business media discourse.
- *IT:* information technologies will play an integral part in the continuous learning process, where 'IT facilitates the acquisition, processing, storing, delivery and sharing of information and other digital content' (Ward and Peppard, 2002).

## CREATING VALUE IN THE KNOWLEDGE ECONOMY

As companies attempt to create value in the new information-rich 'knowledge economy' and achieve profitable growth many are realizing they need to break out of 'the competitive and imitative trap', as we saw with Chrysler (Kim and Mauborgne, 1999). An extreme view is a reinvention of the entire industry model (Hamel, 1998), in order for enterprises to leverage numerous sources of value, including intangible assets based on customers, suppliers, employees, patents and ideas (Boulton, Libert and Samek, 2000) and in order to balance the needs of industry, society and the environment (Senge and

Carstedt, 2001). According to Gulati, Nohria and Zaheer (2000): 'The image of atomistic actors competing for profits against each other in an impersonal marketplace is increasingly inadequate in a world in which firms are embedded in networks of social, professional, and exchange relationships with other organizational actors.' Nevertheless, as Senge and Carstedt (2001) cautioned: 'Innovative business models and products must work financially, or it won't matter how good they are ecologically and socially.'

Porter's 'value chain' framework (Porter, 1985) has been a commonly accepted means of representing the logic of value creation at the individual firm level, and is still used as a convenient framework (see, for example, Ghosh and John, 1999). However, as firms move from the material–industrial age and into the information age, alternative approaches to value creation other than that which is associated with the value chain and its emphasis on industrial production are being mooted (Rayport and Sviokla, 1995; Ramirez, 1999; Allee, 2000; Berthon, Holbrook and Hulbert, 2000).

In the industrial age companies created value by transforming tangible assets, such as raw materials, into finished products. In the information age firms are creating value by transforming intangible assets, such as customer relationships and employee know-how (Srivastava, Shervani and Fahey, 1998; Allee, 2000; Kaplan and Norton, 2000). Critical to their success is continuous access to information (Goodstein and Butz, 1998). This issue will be examined in more detail in Chapter 7, when we consider what managers in our study perceive as some of the main changes driving how they now practice marketing.

One argument is that, as strategy increasingly focuses on the service aspects of relationship building (Gummesson, 2003), the logic of how organizations manage relationships and configure value can now perhaps be better understood in terms of industry frameworks, such as value networks (Achrol, 1997; Holm, Eriksson and Johanson, 1999; Allee, 2000). For example, Brandenburger and Nalebuff (1996) build on Porter's work on value chains (1985, 1996, 2001), by arguing that the process of creating value in the marketplace involved four types of players interacting in what they termed a value net: customers, suppliers, competitors and complementors, where complementors are seen as other firms from which customers might buy complementary products or services, or to which suppliers might sell complementary products or services. The addition of complementors helps explain why many firms are joining into strategic alliances, in order to gain access to other firms' competences.

We can extend the framework of Brandenburger and Nalebuff (1996), by adding M&A partners. As suggested in Figure 4.3, M&A partners can be embedded (that is to say, they are still visible) or completely subsumed (they

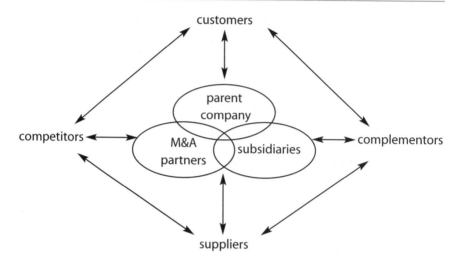

**Figure 4.3** The value net

*Source:* based on Brandenburger and Nalebuff, 1996

disappear altogether) into the parent company, or may sit adjacent to it, depending on the amount of independence and separate identity that has been granted. To some extent, this may depend on what customers now want in terms of value delivery. Does a new car buyer in Europe want a Saab from General Motors, a Saab from Opel, or a Saab from Sweden? Or does it matter anymore, so long as the brand honours its promise? For example, General Motors is using its international web of connections to install a 3.2-litre V6 from its Australian subsidiary, Holden, in Alfa Romeo's new Kamal, a four-wheel-drive BMW X3 competitor. Given its 20 per cent financial stake in Fiat, GM is also likely to put the Holden engine in other large Alfa and Fiat sedans, and possibly those from Opel and Saab as well.

## WHAT DO CUSTOMERS NOW WANT?

We finish this chapter by asking a basic marketing question: what do customers now want?

Nowadays they appear to want everything! According to Treacy and Wiersema (1995b):

> Customers today want more of those things they value. If they value low cost, they want it lower. If they value convenience or speed when they buy, they want it easier and faster. If they look for state-of-the-art design,

they want to see the art pushed forward. If they need expert advice, they want companies to give them more depth, more time, and more of a feeling that they're the only customer.

Moreover, they want everything right now! As the Head of Interactive Marketing and Electronic Commerce at Unilever plc (Darling, 1998) predicted:

> The future of marketing in 2020 is instantaneous, two-way, personal, integrated and seen everywhere.... People increasingly want things instantaneously – 24-hour news, 24-hour shopping.... They also want things personal. There's no longer a tolerance for things that aren't for me...or for 'I can't get things where I want it.' If I want it on my mobile phone, I'll have it there. On my TV? I'll have it there. The technology can enable these things.... The fundamentals of marketing remain unchanged – consumer understanding, brand innovation, brand communication, media. They all stand. The challenge is, how we do all these things is changing.

Treacy and Wiersema (1993) believed that firms deliver this by crafting generic strategies based on what they term 'value disciplines', and as described in more detail in Table 4.1:

- *Operational excellence:* delivering relatively high quality and achieving the best cost structure, a position sought with relentless efficiency by the likes of Wal-Mart and Virgin Blue.
- *Product leadership:* offering the best product or service through technical leadership and continuous innovation, a position sought by the likes of market builders such as Nokia and Sony, and niche players such as Apple.
- *Customer intimacy:* building reciprocal relationships with customers by being the most dependable and responsive to their individual needs, a position sought by the likes of IBM as it attempts to transform itself from a computer manufacturer to a technology conglomerate driven to provide 'solutions'.

They also believed that:

> Companies that have taken leadership positions in their industries in the last decade typically have done so by narrowing their business focus, not broadening it. They have focused on delivering superior customer value in line with one of three value disciplines – operational excellence, customer

**Table 4.1** Value

|  | Operational excellence | Product leadership | Customer intimacy |
|---|---|---|---|
| Core business processes that … | Sharpen distribution systems and provide no-hassle service | Nurture innovation, translate ideas into products and market them skilfully | Provide solutions and help customers run their businesses |
| Structure … | Centralized authority and a finite level of empowerment | Decentralized, pushes empowerment close to frontline customer contact | Ad hoc, organic, loosely knit and ever-changing way |
| Management systems that … | Emphasize standardization of operations | Reward individual innovation and success | Measure cost of providing service and maintaining customer loyalty |
| Culture that … | Values conformance: 'One size fits all' | Encourages experiments and outside-in thinking | Fosters flexibility: 'Have your way' |

*Source:* Treacy and Wiersema, 1993.

intimacy, or product leadership. They have become champions in one of these three disciplines while meeting industry standards in the other two.

Later (Treacy and Wiersema 1995b), they added:

We have identified three distinct value disciplines, so called because each discipline produces a different kind of customer value. Choosing one discipline to master does not mean that a company abandons the other two, only that it picks a dimension of value on which to stake its market reputation over the long term.... Then it can identify core competencies and reengineer the processes that make up the operating model required to get the job done.

To get that job done, as we have seen, many are having to redefine their traditional business 'models' in order to concile the various pressures to do with growth and shareholder value. They are simultaneously cutting costs, improving efficiencies, pushing up quality and enhancing their technical advantages, in order to build 'power' brands and deliver a higher level of composite value. They are identifying their most important customers and building closer relationships with them. And they are also doing it by establishing a stronger purpose and relevancy within a network of other players and partners, including those by mergers and acquisitions.

As we have seen in this chapter, the pursuit of excellence and competitive advantage has gone up a notch. Today, when it comes to considering a generic value discipline, such as advocated by the likes of Treacy and Wiersema, it may no longer be an issue of preference, choice, or even emphasis. Rather, in the context of their own industry and its dynamics, the pressure is now on companies to achieve, and then continuously improve on, a balanced standard of excellence and competitive advantage in all three disciplines – operational excellence, product and service leadership, and customer intimacy – and to achieve this by leveraging advantage. This will be the subject of the next chapter.

## CHAPTER 5

# Finding and Creating Advantage

## CHAPTER INTRODUCTION

Customer attitudes and expectations have changed. At the same time competition has increased as the marketplace has switched from one of demand pull to supply push. There are more subtle changes as well, with the attitudes and expectations of customers becoming ever more stringent.

This chapter considers how companies can develop a basis for competition and address the stark contrast between customers' requirements for better service, lower prices and short-term benefit against the response by suppliers to improve relationships and offer higher levels of involvement. This may be the end point and outcome of a supplier's response, but a clearer understanding of the sources of advantage required to achieve this is needed.

## THE STRATEGY DEBATE

Of course, what we all seek for ourselves and our business is advantage. Writers from the field of strategy talk about competitive advantage and even sustainable competitive advantage, watchwords that are increasingly used in the context of marketing. While the marketers may complain that others have stolen their intellectual assets (Whittington and Whipp, 1992), this is perhaps just another example of how marketing has failed to take the initiative and lead the debate in developing new and insightful ways of understanding businesses, customers, competitors and the changing business environment. So let us start this discussion of advantage by borrowing some ideas from the field of strategy, and seeing how the strategy gurus can help our understanding before moving further into more clearly defined marketing territory.

A debate that has continued for many years in the field of strategy concerns the question of what it is that causes profit. If we know the answer to that, then development of the business could be significantly advanced. The question is a good one, but one that does not necessarily resolve itself into a simple and straightforward answer; business of course is never that simple, although there are many purveyors of management recipes to trap the guileless. The strategists offer three fundamental answers to this intriguing question. First, that it is concerned with the structure of the industry and the influence this has on strategy; second, that each firm has resources it can use to generate advantage; or, third, that business is so complex that somehow strategy happens as part of the way we compete.

While these explanations overlap and intertwine it can be seen that as the pressures on business referred to in Chapter 4 continue to increase, so the responses required become more demanding. The previous chapter also asked what customers now want and drew on the work of Treacy and Wiersema (1995a), who identified three value disciplines. In their work they also emphasize the need to strike a suitable balance between them. From a marketing rather than a strategy perspective we consider how to develop advantage, create and manage value, and what this might mean in the way we think about relationships between network members. We also refer back to these themes in future chapters and consider issues such as the drivers of change, the influence of power in relationships, and the organizational responses to these dominant forces.

## STRUCTURE, CONDUCT, PERFORMANCE

The first explanation is one which is summarized by Michael Porter (1980). His original book – *Competitive Strategy* – discusses a large field of work in the area known as the 'structure–conduct–performance paradigm'. This analysis is conducted at the level of the industry and encompasses familiar tools such as those for analyzing the external business environment, including PESTLE (political, economic, social, technological, legal, environmental), and the competitive environment, including Porter's Five Forces Model and Generic Strategies.

The composition of the industry, the balance between large and small players, their relative power and the ease with which companies can enter and exit the industry will determine their conduct, or strategy, and hence their performance. Good performance then feeds back into the structure of the industry as the poorer performers either exit or are acquired by the better and increasingly larger performers. Hence, the structure of the industry changes as the balance of competitive forces shifts. This therefore argues that advantage is gained by differentiation, adopting a niche and specializing within it, or perhaps becoming a large player in the industry and being comparatively more efficient. This would apply in areas such as cost utilization and other efficiency factors (Bain, 1951), but also it would entail being more effective in accessing routes to market and maintaining presence with customers. According to this argument, industries can be dominated by a few large companies, with the possibility that they act in concert or even collusively in order to maintain prices, keep competitors out and enhance profits still further (Demsetz, 1973).

All of this makes reasonable sense, since we can see examples of this happening all around us. Industry giants seem only to get bigger as industries relentlessly rationalize in order to reduce fixed costs and lever efficiencies. A good example might be the pharmaceutical industry, where we have seen ongoing acquisitions, mergers and rationalizations as companies struggle to compete. The driver in this particular case is the quest for new pharmaceutical products. Every pharmaceutical company wants the next big burner product. Previous big burners include Zantac, Prozac and the 'Pfizer riser' – Viagra. However the cost of developing a new pharmaceutical product is dauntingly high, and the timescale is a long one that can easily take half the patent life of the active chemical ingredient. Recovering the development cost, which could be as high as US$750 million, paying for the products that fall by the wayside, and providing funds for the next development can be an increasingly steep and slippery slope to climb. In these circumstances one company may acquire another in order to obtain its stream of new products, or voluntarily merge with another to maintain and increase firepower.

It is easy to be cynical about this process since the discovery of new drug products can only be targeted at diseases of the rich. Such is the sophistication of the marketing process nowadays that when a therapeutic benefit is discovered in respect of a particular disorder, pharmaceutical companies may be accused of 'inventing' new disorders so that a market can be developed for a new product. This is a one-sided view, however, since development costs are driven by the regulatory requirements that call for the demonstration of quality, safety and efficacy, something that requires long-term studies. Consequently the structure of the industry, and the nature of the products produced as a result of the strategy adopted, are both heavily influenced by the external environmental factors.

## RESOURCES

Another explanation for why a business is profitable is that each one is unique and individual, and possesses different resources and capabilities. The argument for this approach is that an industry is simply an arbitrary collection of firms, and that there is greater variation in profitability between firms than there is between industries. As a consequence there is more to learn by conducting the analysis at the level of the firm, rather than at the level of the industry.

The resource-based argument introduces the concept of the firm as a bundle of resources, competences and capabilities, however appealing and yet confusing these jargon terms may be. To add yet more to the confusion, it is unclear how particular types of resources can be used in different ways to produce benefits. The process by which the resources are engaged is somewhat vague, and masked by the blanket terms: resources, strategic assets, competences, capabilities, and so on. To take this further we first need to understand these terms, despite the fact they are used interchangeably within the strategic management literature.

A resource might be regarded as an organizational asset, the kind of thing that might be written in the 'strengths' box of a SWOT analysis. It may be tangible, such as a state-of-the-art manufacturing plant, but also – and perhaps even more importantly – intangible, such as a brand or unique intellectual property. Not only can resources be intangible, they can even stretch outside the firm to include special relationships and personal contacts. Resources have a number of distinctive features. They are valuable to the firm in its environment, but they are also rare since otherwise they are generic and offer no differential advantage. For the same reasons they are imperfectly mobile and imperfectly imitable (Ambrosini, 2002). Resources must, of course, be used in order to deliver competitive advantage, and hence this ability to utilize resources may be termed a 'capability'. The resource-based concept was popularized by Hamel and Prahalad with their 1994 book *Competing for the Future* (Prahalad and Hamel, 1990; Hamel and Prahalad, 1994a), and they introduced the term 'core competences' which they saw as a bundle of skills and abilities, a hybrid between a resource and a capability.

While resource-based theory is an appealing and engaging view, it has at least one thing in common with relationship marketing – there is a significant lack of empirical evidence to demonstrate and explain it in practice. This is needed to develop and test the theory and to help in the development of resource-based tools and techniques of use to managers. As Ambrosini (2002) says, 'there is little doubt that ... theoretical work is still needed, the future of the resource based view lies very much in the search for empirical evidence'. This takes us back to the lack of clarity discussed earlier.

The ability to turn resources into competitive advantage is intuitively understood. How else can a firm compete other than by having better resources and/or using them more effectively? This is a question that is still to be answered, but is finessed with the concept of 'causal ambiguity' (Lippman and Rumelt, 1982). This acknowledges the inability to connect resources to their application and results. In fact, it is argued that it is this causal ambiguity which is actually the source of competitive advantage: if the process could be understood then it would be transparent to competitors and easily copied. Our ability to use our resources may be due to our tacit knowledge (Polanyi, 1966). Tacit knowledge does not mean that we know more, but is more a matter of know-how. By its very nature it is knowledge gained by experience and is inherent within each of us. Members of a firm have knowledge about their business and industry, and perhaps one of the main reasons why competitors find it difficult to imitate our strategy is that they may well see what we do, but they do not know how we do it.

---

### Eli Lilly – Turning Resources into Advantage

In the second half of the 1990s it was increasingly apparent to Sidney Taurel, Eli Lilly's new CEO, that the pipeline of new products would be insufficient to sustain the company when its blockbuster product Prozac came off patent in 2001. The loss of revenue could be up to some $2.5 billion. The pharmaceutical industry is characterized by successive takeovers and mergers as companies fight to maintain their position in the industry and their investment in new product development. If the innovation process is not delivering, then companies are inclined to acquire competitors whose development pipeline could fill their revenue gap.

Eli Lilly conducted a rigorous analysis of this pattern of takeovers and mergers, and concluded that it was more profitable to grow organically by discovering and developing new products, than to invest in acquiring competitors. Eli Lilly invested heavily in development resources and staff to kick-start its pipeline of new products. The company has been extremely successful in this strategy, with eight new products coming to the market from 2003 onwards. Some of these have particular value in the marketplace: for example, a product for attention deficient/hyperactivity disorder (ADHD) is not classed as a stimulant under the (American) Controlled Substances Act and therefore can be much more widely marketed and promoted. Another is a competitor for Viagra, which also offers benefits over this so far unique product. Other new products will also be available for the treatment of depression and osteoporosis. This complements current products in the areas of sepsis and diabetes, for example, that also have significant growth potential. As a consequence Eli Lilly stock is trading at a substantial premium to other members of the 'Big Pharma' group.

(Arndt, 2001)

While resource-based theory has yet to contribute practical management tools as such, it does give great insight into why firms are able to compete, and helps in understanding that some, or perhaps most, of our resources may be intangible. Our most precious resources may lie in that complexity of intuitive knowledge, the unconscious but inherent approaches to doing things, and the network of relationships that is built over time and managed by experience. Paradoxically, those resources that we do not understand or know that we possess may be our most important ones. Our conscious lack of intangible resources may also help to explain why the apparently simple things that competitors do are so difficult for us to imitate, and explain why change can be so difficult to achieve, since the unconscious foundation of tacit knowledge has yet to be built to sustain the new processes and techniques introduced.

## EMERGENT STRATEGY AND GAME THEORY

In the course of our work we find that managers are more comfortable working in a rational and logical manner. If a framework, model or process is discussed then this can be applied, perhaps in a case study, or by means of a project as a way of learning how to apply the technique. What this suggests is that analysis, planning and making rational decisions between alternatives lead to strategic choice and, hopefully, desired outcomes.

This is just one way in which strategy may be regarded. Mintzberg (1998) introduces us to the idea that strategy is not necessarily developed from analysis. That is to say, it does not come about through the application of a logical, detached and objective process, but it simply happens or emerges in response to the complexity of events as they unfold. Business is simply too complicated and fast moving for us to make logical, detached decisions. In any case, there are many more things liable to change than we can possibly take into account, and how many such rational plans are actually put into place anyway?

After all, surely many plans simply represent a variation of that bizarre ritual 'the budgeting process'? In that process we minimize our commitments upwards while maintaining as much freedom and flexibility as possible downwards, knowing that in any event profit and cost targets are likely to be imposed by 'them' anyway. This results in a set of numbers, divorced from the reality of the marketplace, accompanied by gung-ho statements about what we are going to do and how we are going to do it, knowing that we have 12 months either to negotiate away our target and/or seek opportunistic ways of fulfilling it. If we reach the target then the plan has worked; if we do not then we have a logical post-rationalization that explains the variance from the plan. Hence the process is seen to have worked and rolls forward to the next planning period.

It could be argued that on some occasions managers make decisions which suit their own best interests, but which can later be post-rationalized against the facts as they saw them at the time. This is the concept of bounded rationality (Simon, 1957).

---

### Self-serving bounded rationality or an economically rational decision?

I have carefully explained to my boss that the purchase of a new Mercedes as my next company car is an economically rational decision. Over the lifetime of the vehicle and when all costs are taken into account, despite the high initial purchase price and service costs, the car shows the lowest cost per mile due to its high reliability, low depreciation and long life. As a bonus there is the safety, security, comfort and reliability afforded by such a high quality vehicle. Could anybody reasonably accuse me of wanting to buy a luxurious car, one bearing the all-important three-pointed star on the bonnet, in order to boost my sagging ego and impress our friends and neighbours?

Consider the cases of WorldCom loaning its CEO, Bernie Ebbers, $400m, or city analysts making positive buy recommendations whilst privately disparaging the performance of the same stock in intra-office emails.

Are these examples of self-serving bounded rationality or rational business decision taken in the interests of shareholders and clients?

---

While game theory is derived from economics and is applied in many fields other than strategy, it does have in common the notions that strategy is a process of interaction and that the choices made by managers are not necessarily rational and logical. In thinking of business as a game we then see our own firm arrayed against a competitor. Game theory helps us to understand that our choices as to future direction also depend on how we see our competitor reacting to our decision. In fact, there are occasions when we compete but also cooperate. Brandenburger and Nalebuff (1996) wrote a commendably short but readable book on the application of game theory to business under the title of *Co-opetition*. Within an industry competition can be anticipated between firms, but there are also issues on which firms will cooperate. For example, they may work together through a trade association to make the case against legislation that may increase operating costs for all players in an industry. Competition and cooperation lie at the heart of networks as companies seek to survive and prosper in the new business environment.

These perspectives help us to understand that strategy is not necessarily a stepwise process. It can be incremental and involve trade-offs between different points of view that involve compromise, politics and negotiation (see Figure 5.1). Implementation as an outcome of the strategy process is fundamental, and marketing activities occur as part of our wider organizational strategy and direction. Elegant discussions of marketing intent without a wider understanding of these issues will almost certainly lead to disappointment, and the isolation of the marketing function. Marketers must form views about the trade-off between the desirable, the achievable and the possible.

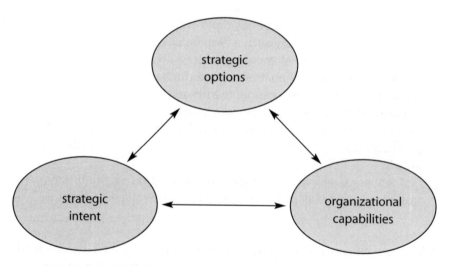

**Figure 5.1** From strategy to implementation

## MARKETING ADVANTAGE

There is an interesting framework that helps us to identify various sources of marketing advantage (Christopher, 1996); these are illustrated in Figure 5.2. Of course, these are not necessarily distinct but overlap one with another, and the context in which the firm operates may vary the value of each approach.

## THE CONSUMER FRANCHISE

Classically, transactional marketing was led by the development of branded fastmoving consumer goods. In the business-to-business sector we can think of reputation as being analogous to a brand, although many business-to-business organizations recognize the value of brands and actively develop and promote them (for example, Intel). In a business-to-business organization the company name often represents the reputation and sometimes the brand for a company. The distinction between reputation and brand is that a brand has personal involvement, and creates emotions that characterize an individual understanding – what thoughts come into your mind when you think of McDonald's or BMW, for example?

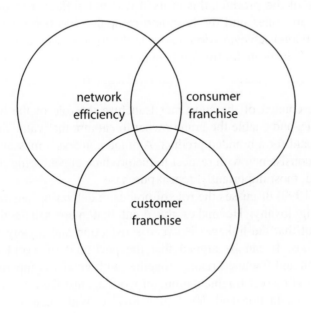

**Figure 5.2** Marketing advantage

*Source:* Christopher, 1996

> ### Ingredient branding
>
> The DuPont Corporation are largely credited with initiating the concept of 'ingredient branding', whereby awareness and understanding of a business-to-business product is generated at the consumer level. They have successfully established brands for products incorporated into further manufactured items. DuPont own brands such as Teflon and Lycra, well known to consumers and incorporated into a wide range of products.
>
> Dennis Carter of Intel initiated the branding programme for otherwise anonymous computer components known as microprocessors. These gloried in such names as the 386SX. These simple descriptive terms were not judged to constitute intellectual property, and could be used by any manufacturer. Intel initiated their programme in 1991 through television advertising and the co-sponsorship of their customers' advertisements, which included the now well-known logo; several hundred manufacturers are now licensed to use the symbol on their products. The brand stands for technological leadership, quality and reliability, and in four years recognition of the brand by computer purchasers reached 80 per cent. While technological innovation is at the core of the product, this in itself was not sufficient to generate interest and sales, and the branding campaign has been one of the factors in Intel achieving dominance in the microprocessor market.
>
> (Institute for the Study of Business Markets, www.intel.com)

Within the context of the consumer franchise the role of the brand is to create value, and enable the brand owner to capture that value through the premium paid for a branded product. A brand conveys a message of reliability and consistency with respect to the product, encouraging preference, loyalty and, most importantly, repeat purchase.

Oliver (1999) discusses the role of brands in delivering satisfaction and encouraging loyalty. He makes the point that mere satisfaction is not enough, but that the linkages between satisfaction and loyalty are somewhat tenuous. It can be argued that the post-modern world of instant gratification and fractured reality, together with greater competition, price pressures and market fragmentation, all work against the role of brands in delivering satisfaction and developing loyalty. With such a wide choice available to consumers, of such high quality and low price, why should they buy just one brand – and take the time and trouble to visit the outlet where that particular brand is sold – rather than simply buy another that is conveniently available?

However, Oliver argues that loyalty is also a natural human state: people like to belong. Encouraging loyalty to a brand in the future may involve incorporating the brand into a more social context, so that the brand is part of the experience and taps into the social network that has formed. In 2003 many Harley-Davidson motorcyclists participated in HOG (Harley Owners Group) events to celebrate the hundredth anniversary of the brand. Manchester United Football Club is a global phenomenon, with supporters around the world who watch the match, wear the shirt and share the experience. Thus, brands have a future, but for more mundane domestic and household products loyalty cannot often be said to be their characteristic feature (Oliver, 1999).

So the rules of the game have changed, and brands no longer have the pulling power that they once had. Philip Morris owns Marlboro, one of the most famous brands in the world. Cigarette sales were suffering due to the competition of generic no-name products and, over ten years ago now, Philip Morris decided to reduce the price of Marlboro cigarettes by around 20 per cent – a tacit recognition that the brand was no longer achieving the premium in the marketplace of which it had been capable. Consumers no longer attached such a high value to the brand. The significance of this was not lost on the stock market, where companies relying on brands suffered a reduction in stock price. If one of the most famous brands in the world was not capable of sustaining its premium, then this had implications for other, lesser brands.

Brand-led companies have continued to rationalize their product portfolios. Unilever has a strategy of reducing the number of brands that it will support from 1600 to 400. This is a reflection of the cost of maintaining a brand in the marketplace against the multitude of competing promotional messages, the generic competition and the greater choice that is now available.

As retailers have increased their dominance as a distribution channel to consumers their one-time, generic own-brand products have evolved to become brands in their own right. These sit on the supermarket shelf alongside more expensive manufacturers' brands. In the 1990s there were several well-publicized battles in the UK between manufacturers and retailers with the manufacturers making accusations of 'passing off'. Retailers were producing products with similar packaging and names to manufacturers' brands. For example, Asda (now owned by Wal-Mart) produced a chocolate covered biscuit under the name of 'Puffin' that competed with the 'Penguin' biscuit brand produced by McVitie's. Sainsbury's locked horns with Coca-Cola shortly after the introduction of their own-brand cola in bright red cans with swirl-style logos. However, in the USA it is quite common to see retailer own-label products with remarkably similar packaging to manufacturers' own brands. This may be an undesirable situation for manufacturers, but is at least preferable to the thriving market in fake and counterfeit goods found in Far Eastern street markets. Perfectly workable copies of Microsoft Office or Adobe Photoshop, ignoring the odd virus complication or two, can be obtained for just a few dollars alongside designer clothes, trainers, watches and so on. This even extends into the business-to-business sector with, for example, fake products such as medicines or braking system components being sold as manufacturers' original products.

## THE CUSTOMER FRANCHISE

We live in a world where many products are notable for their similarities in terms of appearance, features and benefits – as a visit to any department store or car showroom will demonstrate – rather than their differences. Those that can gain a design edge, such as Apple Computers or Dyson vacuum cleaners, set a high standard for others to achieve as the bar inexorably rises. As the value of brands becomes eroded by attack from retail or own-label products, and competitor products offer similar features and benefits, then other sources of advantage must be found.

The fundamentals behind Unilever's decision to reduce their number of brands have been explained by the company. They have progressively disposed of non-strategic businesses in order to improve margins and focus to their core capabilities. Rationalization of the portfolio will lead to simplification of the business, and a reduction in manufacturing complexity; this in turn will reduce costs. At the same time, with fewer brands to support, Unilever can aggressively promote those that remain, and eventually develop a smaller number of global 'powerbrands'.

Implicit in this is the understanding of where new sources of value can be found: not solely in investment within, in products and brands, but looking even beyond customers and upstream into manufacturing, and downstream into distribution. In order to achieve this a much greater understanding of the supply and value chain is required, along with a more comprehensive insight into the needs of, and activities performed by, each member of those chains.

This implies a very different way of working. Developing a consumer franchise requires significant investment in brands. Unilever, for example, invest well over 10 per cent of their turnover – not profits – in advertising and promotion. To gain greater insight into value and supply chains requires a mindshift of management thinking and reallocation of resource. Gaining the necessary insight and understanding also means that different and more insightful market research techniques are needed. In fact, this goes beyond research and into market understanding.

---

**Monsanto and value capture**

Monsanto have an outstanding track record over many decades for the development and successful commercialization of agricultural chemicals for weed, pest and disease control. Their brand leading product, 'Round-up', is successfully marketed around the world and has revolutionized agricultural practice and productivity.

A more recent discovery is a product for controlling an otherwise uncontrollable fungal disease of cereals commonly known as 'take-all' – even its name indicates the severity of the disease. It causes withering of the roots of wheat plants, in particular, and severely reduces output. The intensity of the attack depends on the soil type and weather conditions, so a farmer never really knows how reliable his yields will be. The product is highly effective but must be applied to the outside of the seed before planting, and this inevitably means a further processing step in the route to the farmer. Sophisticated fungicides are normally available from specialist advisers, while seed treatments have long been regarded as near-commodities.

The market is mature and indeed declining, and there is not sufficient business to sustain all the intermediaries who process, wholesale and retail agricultural seeds as volumes and margins continue to decline. This posed a dilemma for Monsanto and Jeff Cox, Manager for Northern Europe responsible for the product. How could Monsanto introduce the product to a commodity-driven market with little understanding of the product technicalities, the disease or with the capability to assist end-users – farmers – in using the product to best effect? An additional concern was the need to pay back the costly development and registration costs involved, as well as to provide the revenues to sustain further investment.

The supply chain suffers the near universal problem of maturity: demand has declined but supply chain members overhang their excess capacity and competition is reduced to a bitter price war. Even innovative new products are quickly discounted and profitability is reduced as it is negotiated away by price-orientated end-users, and value is destroyed as the technical service package that supports optimum product usage is discounted away. Monsanto's insight told them that processors within the chain were frustrated by their inability to achieve even minimal levels of profitability, yet end-users needed their expensive technical advice, provided by field staff employed by processors and retailers. This posed a conundrum as to how to achieve these contradictory objectives. Low prices, minimal margins and poor results in use meant that every participant in the supply chain was dissatisfied to a greater or lesser extent.

Monsanto's response was to fully investigate and understand every element of the supply and value chain, what was valued and where value was created and destroyed, and the route by which products reached the farmer as the final end-user. They used a range of sophisticated qualitative and quantitative research techniques, and continually reviewed and revisited the data to ensure that their understanding was correct. In addition, detailed studies were undertaken to understand the economics of wheat production and take-all infection at the farm level, while building up a valuable technical information resource in the process

Building on this understanding Monsanto then took responsibility not just for the next step in the supply chain, the conventional supplier/buyer relationship, but for incentivizing the whole network to help end-users obtain the best performance from the product. Specialist sales agents used sophisticated computer models to diagnose the optimum treatment, taking account of soil, weather and farm conditions; processors were audited to ensure that the product was appropriately applied to the seed; and financial incentives were offered to motivate members of the network to ensure best results. To achieve this, the product was sold directly to farmers, complete with the technical advice package, and network members received fees in return for their achievement of objectives. The overall focus on value generation at the end-user level meant that farmer satisfaction with the product was high as excellent results were achieved, and the extra value generated could be divided as incentives between all the network participants.

The product was initially launched in Ireland, then in Poland, and is now being successfully used in a number of countries. Initially sceptical of the changed terms of business, but seeing the opportunity provided by a genuinely innovative product, the traditionally conservative supply trade has been remodelled as a result of this customer- and value-led initiative.

One of the techniques for developing this helicopter overview of the value and supply chain is to prepare a market map. Mapping as a management technique has a number of applications, for example in segmentation (McDonald and Dunbar, 1998) or strategy development (Kaplan and Norton, 2000). This particular application is an applied version of the value chain proposed by Porter (1980).

The map is developed based on the way that the product flows through to the end-user. Various judgments have to be made when developing such maps: for example, should the role of influencers and authorizers be included? If considering prescription drugs, then clearly the role of the medical practitioner is pivotal as an authorizer, although the physical product flow may be somewhat different. Similarly, in considering the opportunities for architectural fittings such as door handles and power sockets, then the view of the architect or designer would be very important. In such cases judgement has to be applied. The market map gives a helicopter overview and helps in the identification of intermediaries and routes to market that may or may not be used with respect to the product in question.

Value mapping can then be undertaken by the following steps:

- Input cost – at the beginning of the chain identify raw material and other costs entering the chain.
- Process steps – identify the process(es) that the product or service undergoes at that point in the supply chain.
- Process costs – estimate the costs associated with each process step.
- Output cost – ascertain the cost or price at which the product or service is transferred from or leaves that part of the supply chain.
- Value creation/destruction – add all the costs incurred and subtract from the output cost/price to ascertain value created or destroyed.
- Frictional costs – as products and services are transferred between supply chain members this may involve transport/storage/processing/administration costs. Identify these frictional costs associated with moving products or services through the supply chain, and cross-check against input cost to the next supply chain member.
- Continue until each element of the chain has been analyzed.
- Identify product volumes associated with each step of the chain to give an understanding of value build by unit and in total.
- Review findings to identify:
  - alternative, cheaper methods of processing
  - supply chain members adding more cost than value
  - alternative or cheaper routes to market.

- Estimate value capture compared to net value created.
  - Consider reconfiguration to improve value capture.

All this would appear reasonably straightforward when written down in a simple checklist such as this. In practice, it is reasonably easy to estimate the market overview quickly, but it becomes increasingly more difficult to identify the costs and processes associated with each step. It can be a good process to undertake as a management team, with the sharing and pooling of ideas triggering new insights. Another useful practical technique is to start with the end-user and work up the chain; this can be helpful in identifying all routes to market.

Identifying processes and other costs is a matter of insight, experience and estimation. It may be difficult to identify costs specifically; supply chain members may be reluctant to disclose such information, and accessing this may involve shrewd questioning and comparing and contrasting various views in order to arrive at a best guess. It is particularly important to understand how costs are viewed and managed by the various supply chain participants.

One particular exercise clearly demonstrated that a wholesaler and processor was destroying value. The input cost plus all processing costs was greater than the price at which the product was sold. This was a source of great concern and confusion to the researchers, but checking and rechecking the rather disparate data that we had clearly demonstrated that this was the case. After further discussions it became clear that the basis on which we were determining costs was different from that used by the wholesaler/processor. In this marginally profitable business the calculations had been made by allowing for machine utilization with respect to the processing equipment. It became apparent that the processor made no such allowance. In this particular business success was meeting the wages bill at the end of the month. Subtleties concerning the fully allocated costs of operating processing machinery were ignored. When this large and expensive piece of equipment eventually expires the funds will not be available to replace it and this particular player will exit the industry, as others have done previously.

This technique can be widely used, and only requires a little imagination to adapt it to the context in which it is being used. Here are a few examples:

- A manufacturer of bathroom suites was experiencing unsatisfactory performance. An analysis showed that this company was more effective at selling its products to builders of new houses because of its presence in the large builders' merchants route to market, as compared with its competitors, who were better positioned to access the do-it-yourself bathroom replacement market because of their strong relationship with the retail 'sheds' (retailers such as B&Q in the UK and Home Depot in the USA). The analysis also highlighted a new, emerging channel: the complete installer. These companies had some high street presence and also advertised in magazines and so on, offering a complete bathroom replacement service including plumbing, redecoration and, of course, the bathroom suite itself.

- A credit card and retail sales processing company was experiencing high volumes but low margins. The analysis showed that processing costs for debit/credit/store card sales are individually extremely low – an electronic pulse over a telephone line. However the fixed costs of systems and staff are high. Very large retailers were disinclined to pay for the service on a transaction basis, preferring instead to negotiate a fixed price for a period irrespective of the number of transactions. The tendency to accept such terms meant that large contracts such as these were being marginally priced, and the company had a high share of this particular market sector. The type of customers they targeted, and their contract terms, were reviewed.

- A plastics packaging company reviewed the supply chain and researched consumer opinions as to their attitudes to packaging. As a result of their findings they prepared new designs for packaging, using their products, with product details printed where consumers had indicated they wanted to see them – on the side of the pack, where they were visible when stacked on a supermarket shelf. As a result of their value analysis, they were able to offer savings of over 3 cents per pack to the retailer by omitting the use of a cardboard outer pack. The retailer then specified the use of its product to the manufacturer of its own-label products.

## NETWORK EFFICIENCY

The understanding of networks where marketing is concerned has been considerably enhanced by the work of the IMP (Industrial Marketing and Purchasing) Group (Ford, 1998). Their work has been conducted within the context of business-to-business markets, which of course constitute the majority of relationships. We should first differentiate the understanding of a network from that of a supply chain. Typically a supply chain is seen as a linear series of relationships with raw-material suppliers at the top of the chain, intermediaries such as processors and wholesalers within the chain, and finally retailers selling to end-users. Networks do not conform to this linear view, but rather represent a constellation of relationships that constitute a series of interdependencies among those involved in the network.

As industries diffuse and become less distinct, the role of networks becomes more important. A few years ago it was clear that telecommunications, computing and video games, for example, were distinct and discrete technologies. Now we have PDAs (personal digital assistants) and even mobile phones that can perform all these functions and more besides. This demonstrates how technologies and industries have merged and overlapped in order to provide new products, thus adding complexity to relationships as networks change and adapt in response to this technology push.

Another factor driving the development of networks is the need to seek new sources of value. If we regard companies as bundles of resources, then this provides the incentive to seek new opportunities to apply those resources. In the UK supermarkets have chosen to enter the personal banking sector, offering cheque accounts, personal loans, credit cards, insurance, and so on. Their growth has been dramatic as they capitalize on their resources, namely, strong brands trusted by consumers, easily accessed premises, good retail locations, ready availability of cash, frequent customer visits – 17 million visits per week – and long opening hours. Even more potential can be realized if companies choose to pool their resources in order to do together what they cannot do separately.

The almost breathless pace of technological change, and the relentless drive for value, emphasize the importance of understanding networks. It is said that in the future it is not companies that will compete, but companies and their constellation of relationships, that is to say networks. The clear implication here is that if we do not understand the rules of the network game, and manage ourselves within a constellation of relationships, then we will either be managed by those more adept than us, or we will simply fade away. If we return to the example of the airline alliances discussed in Chapter 2, we see that there are two major alliances competing against each other – Star Alliance and One World. Swissair was not a member of an alliance network.The management team at Swissair made a number of poor management decisions, include buying-in to SABENA, the national airline of Belgium, in an attempt to build links with other airlines. Swissair failed to establish itself in an effective alliance, and the consequences of 11 September and the dramatic downturn in airline travel were sufficient to take the company into bankruptcy.

work of the IMP group characterizes relationships in three ways:

1.  Activity links: it can be understood that a transaction involves the sale
    of a product or service, with no connections extending beyond that. For
    activity links to emerge this involves the development of more inte-
    gration between buyer and seller. Generally speaking, security services
    at factories and offices are contracted out to specialist companies.
    However, the staff involved may act as part of the customer team and
    wear the appropriate corporate uniform.
2.  Resource ties: a company may be competent at a particular task, but
    not particularly capable with respect to others. Order capture and
    processing was a typical capability of many dot.com retailers but fulfil-
    ment – delivery of the order to the customer – was a clear problem. To
    be truly effective other members of the network, or potential members,
    may have better resources and capabilities that can be utilized. Manag-
    ing the position of a company within the network may be regarded as
    a capability in itself.
3.  Actor bonds: of course it is not one company that buys from another,
    but people. People form personal bonds and relationships, and are the
    personification of the culture, attitudes and values of the company they
    represent. Hence the personal relationships that develop over time are
    an intangible but important part of what characterizes a network.

As personal relationships develop, the resources and capabilities of the
various partners in the network become better understood and activity links
develop. Networks become complex and interwoven, and as shared meaning and understanding develops the network becomes an increasingly
effective unit of competition.

Two main types of network can be identified, depending on the location
of the prime mover around whom the network is built. A supplier network
would typically be driven by a large retailer such as Wal-Mart, or a
manufacturing organization, of which Toyota or Honda would be a good
example. Distribution networks operate from the perspective of a seller
rather than a buyer, and are largely constituted by the various supply chain
intermediaries and routes to market that the members of the network represent. A financial services company typically has many different routes to
market in order to optimize the opportunities for its products and services.

A significant benefit of a network is the opportunity to lever in the
capabilities of its component members. However, such are the forces of
competition that even this may not give sufficient differentiation to the product in the market. One of the most important intangible benefits of a network

is the opportunity to reduce the time it takes to get the product/service to market. Product parity is a feature of many markets, and perhaps the only way to retain a customer is to improve the speed with which the product or service reaches the customer. It is now possible for an individual to obtain a mortgage – in order to undertake the largest personal transaction of their life – in an hour. Japanese manufacturers such as Toyota and Honda have the capability to drive product innovation using the power of the network of relationships they have built. It may be that the relationship that you have with the customer is the only difference between you and the competitor, and your ability to serve the customer more quickly may be the only way in the future that you will keep them. In concluding this discussion on sources of advantage, Table 5.1 summarizes some of the distinctive features of each element.

## THE INTERACTION OF POWER AND ADVANTAGE

We have discussed how we may generate advantage, but this is often within the context of strategy. In other words, it is a longer term perspective that requires a clear vision of what is to be achieved, and the change and reallocation of resources as a consequence. In the short term many managers are faced with the stark day-to-day reality of the application of power, either exercising it or responding to it. The relationship 'triangle' diagram (Figure 1.4) demonstrates how in some types of relationships power can be aggressively and ruthlessly applied. Figure 5.3 suggests the sources of that power within the supply chain.

Here is a quotation from the chief executive of a large American business-to-business organization supplying ingredients to a multinational corporation:

> The X company were most needy people, so demanding, and the thing that killed me, when she was talking about it, was how aware and conscious they are of what they're doing to their suppliers. Taking, take, take, take, take, they know it. It's a plan, they train their people to do it and we allow it. You know we bend over – how far? Okay, a little further, no problem.

There are members of networks and supply chains who will feel a degree of empathy with the situation this chief executive finds himself in. As the triangular diagram of relationships also demonstrates, power may be present in a relationship but not used in such an aggressively naked way. This is a comment made by a manager from a different part of the same organization concerning his relationship with one of his customers:

**Table 5.1** Sources of marketing advantage

|  | Consumer franchise | Customer franchise | Network efficiency |
|---|---|---|---|
| Basis of competition | Develop loyalty and repeat purchase | Improve value offering | Improve channel coverage Product velocity |
| Focus | Brand development | Service and quality | Responsiveness Low cost to serve |
| Product differentiation | Features and benefits | Value-in-use | Service enhancement |
| Route to profit | Brand premium | Increase and retain value | Reduce costs below umbrella of price |
| Promotion | Awareness, involvement with brand Broadcast | Communicate value proposition Narrowcast | Presence/ dominance to purchaser via channels |
| Service | Routinised | Customised | Class leading |
| Route to market | Differentiate by channel | Channel neutral | Ubiquitous |
| Processes | Supporting | Enhancing | Transforming |

I can think that actually, in my limited experience with x, that if you're adding value to their business they will reward you.

As this quotation suggests, this very large customer has ample power to lever short-term advantage from this particular supplier but they may refrain from exercising that power in response to the possibility that the supplier may be able to add value. This illustrates that if marketing advantage can be generated in the longer term, then that can be used to counteract the short-term pressures produced by the overt application of power. This is summarized in Figure 5.4.

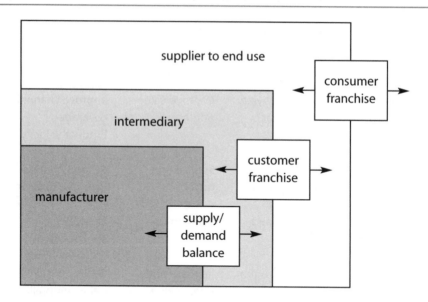

**Figure 5.3**  Power within the supply chain

We are familiar with the idea of competition and cooperation when thinking about relationships, the interaction between a buyer and seller. This discussion concerning marketing advantage introduces us to the expansion of the idea from individual relationships into supply chains and networks. Dempsey (2000) talks about the 'collaboration chain', suggesting that this is a way in which the requirements to reduce costs and time to market can be balanced against the increasing complexity found in the supply chain. As manufacturers have rationalized and continued to reduce their number of suppliers, this is counter-balanced by the pressures of increased component complexity, in the electronics industry, for example, and the move to global sourcing. This means that despite moves to reduce the supplier base and outsource activities, life does not seem to get any easier, and relationships have to be considered in a different way.

In order to encompass this idea that supply chains and networks, rather than individual relationships, operate differently in order to improve effectiveness, we shall introduce the concept of the 'decision involvement unit' (DIU). The DIU is a term which encompasses both conventional, linear supply chains and the more complex networks, but at a generic level. It refers not just to the buyer and seller involved in an individual relationship, but to the parties or firms involved in the relationship between, and also beyond, the supplier and the buyer. Having understood what constitutes marketing advantage, the concept of the DIU helps us to understand how it may be obtained.

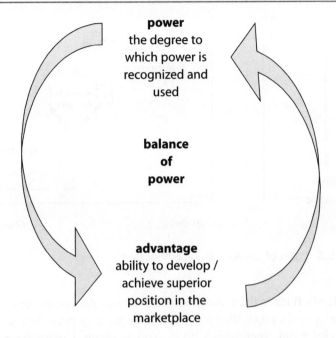

**power**
the degree to
which power is
recognized and
used

**balance
of
power**

**advantage**
ability to develop /
achieve superior
position in the
marketplace

**Figure 5.4** Power and advantage

Figure 5.5 shows three stylized representations of different types of DIUs
that span both supply chains and networks.

These can be classified into three types: reinforcing, enhancing and
transforming. These demonstrate the degree to which those involved in the
buyer and supplier relationship and beyond – in other words the DIU –
compete/cooperate in order to generate marketing advantage:

- *Reinforce:* this is represented as a typical, linear supply chain. The interaction between the various players in the chain is largely competitive; in
  order for one to win another has to lose. In this circumstance we can see
  an overt, aggressive use of power with a considerable emphasis on price.
  A characteristic of this type of DIU is that advantage is gained through
  the consumer franchise at the retail level; consider for example the 'category killer' retailers such as Toys 'R Us or Wal-Mart, and their ability to
  dominate an area of the market. Alternatively, or possibly additionally,
  power is held via a customer franchise, typically by a large brand owner,
  able to counterbalance the power of the retailer. A value chain analysis
  will show that value largely accumulates with either or both of these
  supply chain members. Upstream suppliers are increasingly at risk. They
  experience considerable price pressure, and integration within the chain

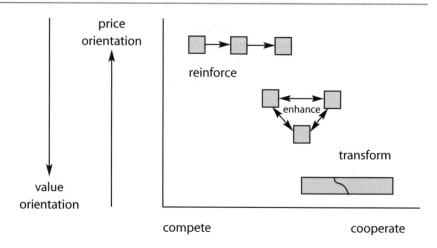

**Figure 5.5** Types of decision involvement units

reduces further their competitive position. As companies within the supply chain rationalize and become larger they push their product and service requirements back up the supply chain. Unless these upstream suppliers have sufficient critical mass to meet the changing needs of these larger and more demanding companies, then merger or alliance with a competitor may be the optimal solution.

- *Enhance:* this type of DIU suggests that relationships are more open, with multiple levels of discussion and not simply a focus on price. Here companies work more cooperatively to share information, and generate a more comprehensive understanding of the relative needs of players within the network. With a more comprehensive, agreed understanding of end-user and intermediary requirements it is possible to develop solutions that add value by generating new forms of value, rather than by simply transferring value between buyer and supplier by reducing price. Market research and other forms of customer insight are ways in which the discussion can be positive and progressive. By actively recognizing the resources and capabilities of each player in the network, these can be creatively brought together to provide new solutions for the end-user.

- *Transform:* in this particular form of the DIU the understanding goes beyond customer needs, and to the shared realization that mutual objectives can be achieved by adjusting the boundaries of the businesses that the various players represent. This allows otherwise inaccessible value to be created, although this may reduce flexibility by increasing the degree of integration and mutual dependence, the benefits may be judged to outweigh the disadvantages. This type of DIU could take the form of new, joint venture businesses drawing on the resources of both partners, or other forms of asset rearrangement (Table 5.2).

**Table 5.2** Characteristics and examples of DIU types

| | | |
|---|---|---|
| *Reinforce* | Characteristics | Competitive |
| | | Gain power and advantage |
| | | Capture value |
| | | Market significance/size important |
| | Example | *Unilever* |
| | | Stated policy is to rationalize and focus on major brands, increase spend behind each brand, reinforce position in the market. |
| *Enhance* | Characteristics | Cooperative |
| | | Create advantage |
| | | Increase value |
| | | Role of resources |
| | Example | *Monsanto* |
| | | Create value in the market, actively seek to change and adapt relationships in order to create value. |
| *Transform* | Characteristics | Cooperative |
| | | Gain advantage, counteract power |
| | | Create mutual value, prevent value destruction |
| | | Synergistic resource combination |
| | Example | Merger of *Carrefour & Promodes* (see Hendrickson et al., 2001) These two French companies, both retailers, chose to merge in order to combat the perceived threat of WalMart's continued expansion. The merged businesses have market leadership in a number of South American, European and Far Eastern countries. The merger created the second largest retailer in the world. |

## CHAPTER 6

# Organizational Transformation

## OBJECTIVES

In this chapter we examine recent developments in information technologies (IT) and how these are affecting organizations. In particular, we are interested in understanding whether there is likely to be a widespread 'organizational transformation' as companies adapt to what are known as 'inflection points'. The Internet is an inflection point. As we will show, companies as powerful as IBM and Intel, and even Microsoft, are neither immune nor immutable when confronted by an IT-induced inflection point.

We will attempt to answer questions such as: what are inflection points, and how might they impact on industry leaders, as they try continually to create and shape the future to their advantage? What are information technologies, and the nature of their increasing 'pervasiveness' into every aspect of running a business? What is digital convergence and its significance in terms of the question: What business are we in? What are the impacts of IT, not just on adding value to existing forms of products or services, but on creating new forms of value through IT-enabled interactivity brought on by the Internet? In fact, are we in agreement as to the impacts of the Internet? For example, is it really no more than a 'tool' or is it 'changing everything'? In other words, are IT transforming the nature of products, services and marketing, in particular; or are they merely reinforcing or possibly enhancing the organizational status quo? Answers to the last question will come in a later chapter.

## CREATING THE FUTURE

According to Hamel and Prahalad, writing a decade ago (1994b):

> Organizational transformation must be driven by a point of view about the
> future of the industry: How do we want this industry to be shaped in five

or ten years? What must we do to ensure that the industry evolves in a way that is maximally advantageous for us? What skills and capabilities must we begin building now if we are to occupy the industry high ground in the future? How should we organize for opportunities that may not fit neatly within the boundaries of current business units or divisions?

Microsoft is one company that appears to understand the imperative of shaping one's future.

Early in 2003 Microsoft announced that it would offer a complete suite of software to automate practically every aspect of business for small and mid-size companies. It believed the market to be about 45 million businesses worldwide, and saw it as the biggest untapped software market left (Greene, 2003). It also said that it expected its revenue from this business in 2010 to be in the order of US$10 billion, or about the size of its desktop Windows business in 2002. Claimed a top Microsoft executive to *Business Week*: 'If we do a good job, we'll build the next big growth business at Microsoft.' Replied a top industry analyst: 'It would seem optimistic to me to think (that division) is going to be bigger than SAP in seven years. That's an awfully ambitious goal.'

According to Greene (2003), Microsoft faces a number of challenges with this new initiative:

- *Integrating recent acquisitions:* over the past two years Microsoft made its largest acquisitions ever when it acquired two companies that make software for small and mid-size companies. It will need to leverage both their technical and their market expertise.
- *Persuading customers to buy:* many businesses in this sector already use basic packages for purposes such as tax, payroll and accounting, plus Microsoft's own products, including Windows and Office. Persuading them to upgrade to a more sophisticated and complete suite of packages via a multitude of resellers may prove difficult, particularly in tight economic conditions.
- *Keeping resellers happy:* to reach this market Microsoft said it would train the 24,000 resellers who already sell its other software. The challenge was to come up with products for them to sell that are both powerful and easy to use and administer, since the resellers will not be able to afford large numbers of technical and service specialists. The risk was that the thousands of resellers currently selling other small-business software would favour products from Microsoft's rivals, such as the German giant SAP or Intuit, the maker of the popular Quick-Books accounting software for small business.

- *Handling software partners:* the acknowledged key to its success would be in creating a base layer of small-business technology, called the Microsoft Business Framework, for, say, order processing and inventory management. Its challenge would be in persuading other software makers to shift their strategies to focus on applications that cater to specific customer segments. To this end, Microsoft announced that some 160 software makers had already signed up to develop specialized applications for Microsoft's customer relationship management software. Its risk was that its biggest rivals such as SAP and Intuit would not use the base software, thereby relegating them to niche markets.

- *Dislodging entrenched competitors:* Microsoft would be competing against other industry giants such as Oracle and SAP, specialists such as Intuit, and a host of local players in every geographic market it enters. Its risk is that, when it goes head to head with tough industry leaders, as it has done recently, for example, with Sony, with its Xbox versus Sony's PlayStation2, all of its great resources and size may still not be sufficient. What matters is whether it can offer something that is of sufficiently compelling value to convince millions of small businesses to buy it.

- *Continuing to invest:* Microsoft has committed some US$2 billion in 2002/3 to build this market through the resellers. This is similar to the approach it used successfully in marketing server software to small and mid-size businesses a decade ago. Whether this investment is enough is not known. One thing, however, is known: Microsoft is persistent, has deep reserves and uses its weight.

Given these issues, why would Microsoft set an 'awfully ambitious' goal like this for itself? Isn't it secure enough in its current dominant position and, at 12 per cent in 2002, still growing sufficiently to satisfy investors? Some might argue it has no choice, if history is any indicator. A decade ago, Loomis (1993) referred to a troika of leaders (General Motors, IBM and Sears) as industry 'dinosaurs':

> What swept over these companies was profound change in their markets, to which they were required to adapt. None did, neither fast enough nor fully enough, in part because the erosion of their positions was so gradual as to leave them unaware that they were descending into a state of crisis.

As a top computer industry executive told Loomis: 'There is at least one point in the history of any company when you have to change dramatically to rise to the next performance level. Miss the moment and you start to decline.' For Microsoft that moment might be something with the innocuous name of Linux. Does Microsoft know this?

## THE VIEW FROM THE TOP

A problem is that many companies do not recognize the potential significance of what might turn out to be profound changes, when at first they appear merely as innocuous, irrelevant or inferior. As Rothstein (2001), writing for the *New York Times*, commented:

> It's lonely at the top, but it also seems secure. The view is intoxicating. Every potential challenge is visible. The perch seems to guarantee invulnerability.... But then, from an unexpected direction, comes an almost insignificant challenge, one that at first can seem a minor annoyance, hardly worth concentrated attention. And then unexpectedly the leader is toppled.

Bill Gates does not intend Microsoft to be toppled, and the decision to enter the market of small and mid-size companies reflects that. And that is only one of several recent moves by the company. Why is that? In 1999 Gates stepped away from his job as CEO and became what he termed the company's 'chief software architect'. Writing in *Fortune* Schlender (2002), said that not being CEO freed up Gates to:

> focus on the big things.... His new role plays to perhaps his greatest skill – that uncanny ability to foresee how emerging software technologies can be woven together and parlayed into must-have 'industry standard' products, which, in turn, reinforce demand for other software from Microsoft and its allies.

In other words, Gates's job is to protect his company from challenges from unexpected directions. In a 2001 interview (Gengler, 2001) he explained the need to constantly reshape the industry for Microsoft:

> Part of what I did was a way of looking at things that the existing companies didn't have.... And of course, through things like Microsoft Research and working with universities all over the world, we try to make sure that we don't miss anything and that we're there getting involved – whether it's interactive TV stuff we got into super-early, or video games that we're now getting into, or small devices that we're in.... We try to make sure we're

not missing anything.... But certainly my impact was that I found something that all the existing companies didn't see ... and they didn't see that computers would be compatible across all platform manufacturers, they didn't see that the microprocessor guys would be driving the hardware, that somebody could create a platform that was a high-volume, low-priced platform, and literally get the software on the street and be one hundred times bigger.... Maybe there's something like that out there that I'm missing today but I don't think so.... I say that there are more solutions that will come out of the PC industry this decade than have come out in the entire past. This is the decade you'll look back on and say: 'Of course you don't get bills on paper, and you don't buy music on CDs and you don't do photos with a chemical developer.'

Whether Gates is correct only time and circumstances will tell. Our examination of General Motors in Chapter 3 showed that it was not suddenly and unceremoniously toppled from its lofty position, like some Saddam Hussein statue in a central square. Rather, its decline has been inexorable, as its market shares, profits, and even its capacity to use its weight slowly diminish. Nevertheless, it remains the biggest automaker. Not all companies are so fortunate. For some, if a potential threat suddenly appears, how they react may eventually stigmatize them as yet another declining empire, where arrogance vies with intransigence.

In 1981 Sony introduced the Mavika, which looked like a conventional 35 mm camera, but stored pictures on a miniaturized computer floppy disk. While the resolution was poor, Sony and other Japanese electronics firms continued with their development. In 1984 one firm, Hitachi, offered the marketing rights to Polaroid Corp. The offer was rejected, and one of Polaroid's top scientists told *Business Week* (Beam and Port, 1985): 'The prints aren't very good. A true photographic company can't come out with a product that's mediocre.'

How do companies organize for opportunities or threats that don't fit neatly within the boundaries of their current business models, as Gates is trying to do for Microsoft? All companies face change or the threat of change: consumers' needs, values and behaviours may quickly shift as a result of some exogenous factor; new competitors challenge existing markets with better products or services, or new insights and capabilities; new technologies redefine existing products or services, or create the possibility of new markets if the needs can be identified; new regulations – or deregulations – force shifts in successful practices, or create opportunities for others; mergers or acquisitions may lead to cooperation, trust and new relationships, thus creating avenues for growth, and so on.

These changes are interrelated, with information technologies (IT) constituting an underlying factor. Information technologies are not new. What is new is their growing pervasiveness in virtually every aspect of running an organization, and their potential to create an 'IT-enabled business transformation' (Venkatraman, 1994), to be a 'disruptive force' (Downes and Mui, 1998), or to have a 'disruptive impact' (Ward and Peppard, 2002). Another way to label them is as 'inflection points'.

## INFLECTION POINTS

What happens when the organization is faced with an event that has the potential to topple even the entrenched leader? Andrew Groves, co-founder of Intel Corporation, coined the term 'strategic inflection point' to 'represent what happens to a business when a major change takes place in its competitive environment.... A strategic inflection point causes you to make a fundamental change in business strategy' (Puffer, 1999). The *Economist* (2000c) labelled the merger between AOL (market capitalization US$163 billion) and Time Warner (market capitalization $US83 billion) an inflection point: 'one of those events that have the potential to change the competitive landscape so fundamentally that nothing can be the same again.'

Groves said that the challenge is to identify what is a strategic inflection point from all the other changes and pressures that impact on a business. While obvious in hindsight, otherwise blind alleys serve only to divert resources, time and managerial attention as such opportunities become deflection rather than inflection points. The French utilities group Suez had undertaken a vigorous growth campaign by an aggressive series of takeovers, only to find that economic circumstances changed. Profits and the share price plunged, and the group and the highly respected CEO Gerard Mestrallet once again had to prove himself by turning the business round (Rossant, 2003). This is a story that could be repeated many times over with respect to such companies as the UK-based Marconi group, destroyed by its unwise exposure to the telecoms sector, or Australia's insurance giant AMP, crippled by acquisitions that turned unexpectedly sour.

The Internet has been identified by Groves as an inflection point impacting on Intel. He also warned that a strategic inflection point almost always 'hits the organization in such a way that those of us in senior management are among the last to notice' (Puffer, 1999). It may be no coincidence that he was once quoted as saying that in business only the paranoid survive.

## DID COMPAQ MISS AN INFLECTION POINT?

Compaq Computers provides a useful case study of this warning. In 1993 Eckhard Pfeiffer became its chief executive after the previous CEO had been ousted for not responding to a major inflection point of the time – the onslaught of assemblers of cheaper PC clones. Between 1993 and 1999 Pfeiffer is credited with transforming the company from a struggling maker of over-priced desktop PCs, with an annual turnover of US$3.3 billion, into the world's biggest PC maker – which was also in the process of remaking itself into a full-service company – with annual revenues over ten times the total for 1933.

Early in 1999, however, the *Economist* (1999a) reported: 'Mr Pfeiffer's standing as a titan of high-tech proved no protection once Mr Rosen (chairman of Compaq since its inception in 1983) began to suspect he was losing the plot.' A few weeks earlier, on 9 April, Pfeiffer had warned industry analysts that, as a result of greater price competition and slowing computer sales, first-quarter earnings were likely to be half what they had expected. Shortly afterwards Pfeiffer was gone, the result of a boardroom coup highly reminiscent of the one that led to the ousting of the previous CEO.

Some industry observers felt that Compaq had been losing two plots. As identified by the *Economist* (1999a), the first was that it had not been successful in transforming itself 'from a hardware company into an integrated firm like IBM' and, secondly, it had failed in its attempts 'to match the built-to-order efficiency of Dell in the mid-market for PCs'. These issues did not suddenly emerge in 1999 to strike at Compaq. Nearly two years before, writing in *Fortune*, Kirkpatrick (1997) argued that while Compaq had two advantages – its well-engineered machines and its strong brand name – at the time it was being hamstrung by two failings: its inability to provide the necessary support for the increasingly complex networks of machines being installed in organizations, and its inability to compete on price. As the CEO of a Compaq reseller told Kirkpatrick, 'Every time Eckhard loses a sale, it's because of either Dell's price advantage or HP's and IBM's service and support.' At the time a top Compaq official admitted that, 'We don't have a linkage with our customer.'

To create that linkage Compaq embarked on a two-pronged change in strategy. First, it announced it was going to appoint 2000 new sales and service employees. Then, in January 1998, Compaq announced it would purchase Digital Equipment Corp. in a US$8.7 billion deal, the largest ever in the computer industry, thus taking it into higher-margin markets and turning it into a full-service supplier of complex corporate information systems, making it second only to IBM in computer sales. In a *Business*

*Week* article headed 'How the Compaq-Digital deal will reshape the entire world of computers', McWilliams (1998) said:

> Compaq's timing couldn't be better. The merger comes just as corporations are grappling with wrenching change in their computing options and the way they do business. The move away from mainframe-style computing to cheaper, powerful servers tied to banks of PCs is accelerating as companies buy new equipment to ward off potential software problems posed by the year 2000. At the same time, the race is on to figure out how to link a mish-mash of corporate networks to the Internet for speedy access to customers and suppliers. Compaq will now be able to offer solutions on all fronts – low cost, powerful computing systems, along with a cadre of consultants to install and maintain the high tech gear.

The second prong of the strategy was revealed when Compaq announced it would shortly be building and shipping some customized PCs once a reseller had confirmed a sale. This was a move designed both to reduce costly and increasingly obsolete inventories, and to reassure the company's resellers (whether consumer-oriented outlets or business-oriented value-added-resellers, or 'VARS') that it was not about to commence ousting them by dealing direct with customers in the same way that had made Dell Computers such a potent force. While Kirkpatrick (1997) suggested that 'it's just a short step from there to cutting out the reseller altogether', the CEO of one major reseller told *Fortune*, 'I don't think Compaq is 100% clear on what it wants to do right now.'

Then, late in 1998, Compaq announced a third prong to its strategy, in that one of its product lines aimed at small businesses would be available only on its website.

## COMPAQ'S STRATEGY COMES UNSTUCK

By early 1999 all three prongs of the strategy had come unstuck. First, as Burrows (1999) concluded, Pfeiffer's 'plan to use Digital to put Compaq on an equal footing with IBM and Hewlett-Packard has been bogged down by troubles melding the two organizations, product delays, and an incoherent strategy.' Second, Compaq had been unable to come near Dell in its order–produce–deliver cycle (12 days versus Dell's 3.1 days), and many of the resellers who had invested heavily so as to do final assembly operations in response to their customers' orders found that Compaq was not fully supporting them. Third, Compaq changed its mind about selling via the

Web when sales did not materialise as fast as expected, and when many resellers began to complain about the double standards of Compaq saying, on the one hand, it was dependent on them, while on the other actually competing against them (Kirkpatrick, 1999).

What may also have helped Compaq to come unstuck was the mistaken belief that sales growth would come mainly from finding more new PC customers, when the two most successful direct-sellers of PCs at the time, Dell and Gateway, were trying to find ways to take advantage of their close connections with their existing customers. As the CEO of Gateway told *Fortune* (Kirkpatrick, 1999), 'Everybody's looking for some form of ongoing revenue stream from their installed base. As prices come down the box itself is a smaller percentage of the overall solution you offer customers.'

Kirkpatrick (1999) explained:

Gateway doesn't just sell PCs. It sells a broad range of software, such as packages for doctors, lawyers, and other small-business people. It sells Internet access; it gets additional revenues from customers who pay in instalments; it gets ad revenue from its Website.

At the same time, value-added solutions providers such as IBM were also heavily discounting their PCs in order to sell extra services, and thereby lock in profits for years to come. Kirkpatrick concluded: 'The basic facts of Pfeiffer's firing are well known. The PC industry has been getting more challenging, and Compaq has been handling the challenges poorly.'

The ousting of Pfeiffer was a clear signal that the Internet was transforming the business landscape, and that Compaq had not understood that organizations who had built up their sales forces to serve intermediaries had also had to reconcile the potential opportunities of the Internet. Compaq's attempts to integrate the Internet into its overall strategy without alienating its resellers was seen as half-hearted when compared with the likes of Dell. Reuters (1999) reported that 'even before there was a Worldwide Web, Dell was growing quickly as a 'made-to-order' company.... Giving Dell the Internet just put their strategy on steroids. It built a $US3 billion a year Internet ordering business before competitors like Compaq even responded.'

Reuters (1999) summed up Compaq's situation as follows:

- The ousting of Pfeiffer 'gives one of the clearest signs yet that the Internet has transformed the business landscape and the corporate boardroom'.
- Compaq 'has seen its profits squeezed in recent years as upstart

competitor Dell Computer dramatically outperformed its bigger competitor by adopting more quickly to e-commerce'.

- Compaq's business model was different from Dell, in already 'having a big, active network of distributors who made them the world's largest personal computer seller'.
- Even before the Web, Dell's more focused strategy was as a made-to-order company, building PCs only when it had orders for them. And as noted before, the Internet put its strategy 'on steroids'.

This example is not meant as a criticism of Compaq. The history of information technology developments these past few decades is the story of a series of strategic inflexion points, and how companies have responded – or not, as Groves observed.

## NOW, IT'S HEWLETT-PACKARD'S TIME

An illustrative example is the business media reportage of the recent acquisition of Compaq Computers by Hewlett-Packard, the largest merging of two computer companies up to that date. On 4 September 2001, HP announced a deal to create a company with a combined revenue of US$90 billion, second only to IBM, and which henceforth would become a much stronger competitor for Sun Microsystems and IBM in the server computer market, and for IBM, Dell and Gateway in the personal computer business. Hewlett-Packard claimed that it would not only now be a global leader in digital imaging and printing, but, most importantly, by building on their joint capabilities, the new enterprise would also become a major player in the rapidly growing services and 'solutions' category. This involves working closely with clients to set up, organize and maintain their computer and data networks, in order to make their investment in IT more productive. The new enterprise was also expected to trim some US$2.5 billion annually in costs, through 15,000 redundancies, merging various operations, shutting surplus plants, eliminating overlapping products, and by realizing the benefits of greater economies of scale (Sorkin and Norris, 2001).

The *Economist* (2001b) said that even though the earlier merger of DEC and Compaq 'proved to be a total disaster, distracting management at a time when the merged firms' core businesses badly needed more attention', there were solid reasons for the merger. In effect, they had no alternative since both were being 'buffeted by three powerful forces':

- *The slump in IT expenditure*, as the world economy was slowing down, and as companies looked for ways to squeeze efficiencies out of existing investments.

- *Cut-throat competition:* for example, the *Economist* predicted that Dell, with its greater strength in the PC business, would possibly drive Compaq out of business anyway.
- *Technological shifts* that were turning hardware, the main strength of both companies, into a commodity. IBM was seen as the new business model and, claimed HP's chair and president, Carleton Fiorina: 'For the first time in a very long time, IBM will have a competitor that is strong enough to take it head-on.'

Fiorina also said: 'Clearly the potential of this combination is compelling, but we understand the magnitude of the challenge and the need for discipline and speed' (Sorkin and Norris, 2001). It took seven months for Fiorina finally to declare the narrowest of victories in March 2002. Over that time she was unable to convince many in the investment community, and most of the founding Hewlett and Packard families of her first claim (a compelling deal) as to the justification for the merger. She greatly underestimated the magnitude of the second (challenges); she was sorely tested on the third (need for discipline); and she didn't really achieve the last (speed).

The saga kept the business media enthralled, as illustrated by a sample of headlines from the *New York Times*: 'Wall St. finds fault with computer merger' (5 September 2001); 'Hewlett chief battles for her deal and her career' (10 December 2001); 'Hewlett heir issues letter denouncing planned deal' (14 December 2001); 'He said. She said. It just gets uglier.' (17 March 2002); Hewlett-Packard is accused of misleading holders' (24 April 2002). The *Financial Times* even ran an online discussion, www.ft.com/hp.

In the rapidly changing IT industry, was the Hewlett-Packard takeover of Compaq good strategy, and will it succeed? For many industry observers, the odds are against it. The day after the announcement of the acquisition the price of HP and Compaq shares fell 18 per cent and 11 per cent respectively, while those of Dell and IBM rose.

Shortly after the deal was finalized two industry observers (Waters and Kehoe, 2002) said:

Ms Fiorina's success now hinges on her abilities to pull off a management feat that has never before been achieved in the computer industry: the efficient and rapid integration of two large companies with multiple product lines and global operations – without letting competitors take advantage of the inevitable internal focus and disruption that accompany such a combination.

Earlier, a financial analyst commented to the *New York Times* (Norris and Sorkin, 2001), 'Two losers don't make a winner.'

Is the new Hewlett-Packard a winner? A year after the deal was sealed HP announced that it had cut its workforce by some 17,000 and its costs by some US$3 billion. More importantly, it had just signed a US$600 million services contract with the Bank of Ireland, another of about US$1 billion with Ericsson, and had beaten IBM to a US$3 billion services contract with Procter & Gamble. While the company was thus commended for exceeding its original promise, and for taking on IBM in the IT solutions business, one senior analyst from Merrill Lynch cautioned that, when compared with IBM, HP was relatively inexperienced at negotiating and managing such large service contracts. Thus, he saw HP as running the risk that at some point it would be caught out by unanticipated costs. As a result, Merrill Lynch downgraded HP's shares shortly after the P&G deal was announced (*Economist*, 2003c).

What is it that makes the impact of inflection points so difficult for companies? Is there an organizational transformation occurring that is forcing companies such as HP to reconsider: what business are we now in? And, if HP cannot please the analysts with its answer, what company can?


## INFORMATION TECHNOLOGIES

Nearly two decades ago Porter and Millar (1985) defined information technology in terms that formed the basis for what we now understand, saying that IT is:

> more than just computers. Today, information technology must be conceived of broadly to encompass the information that businesses create and use as well as a wide spectrum of increasingly convergent and linked technologies that process the information. In addition to computers, then, data recognition equipment, communications technologies, factory automation, and other hardware and services are involved.

A more comprehensive view of information technologies was provided by Morton (1991) in the seminal study of information technology and organizational transformation by MIT:

> The Management of the 1990s Research Program used a very broad definition of IT, including computers of all types, both hardware and

software; communications networks, from those connecting two personal computers to the largest private and public networks; and the increasingly important integrations of computing and communications technologies, from a system that allows a personal computer to be connected to a mainframe in the office to globe-spanning networks of powerful mainframe computers.

Ward and Peppard (2002) offer an updated version of the Porter and Millar (1985) and Morton (1991) definitions:

IT refers specifically to technology, essentially hardware, software and telecommunications networks. It is thus both tangible (e.g. with servers, PC, routers and network cables) and intangible (e.g. with software of all types). IT facilitates the acquisition, processing, storing, delivery and sharing of information and other digital content. In the European Union, the term Information and Communication technologies or ICT is generally used instead of IT to recognize the convergence of traditional information technology and telecommunications, which were once seen as distinct areas.

Orlikowski (2000) makes a useful distinction between technologies as artefacts (that is, tangible) and technologies in use (that is, intangible). Brady, Saren and Tzokas (1997) add that: 'The focus is on IT as the answer to business problems, on how it supports and changes business operations, rather than on a focus on the technological aspects of IT.'

## IT AND EARLY PREDICTIONS OF AN ORGANIZATIONAL TRANSFORMATION

Rockart (1988) and Cecil and Hall (1988) warned that IT would become inextricably intertwined with business, moving from the back end of the business system to the front end (that is, from accounting to production to selling and marketing to servicing). They foresaw that IT would help link companies and their suppliers, distributors, resellers and customers into what might be termed 'seamless' networks of relationships and interactions throughout an industry's entire value system.

It was predicted that the transformation taking place in the late 1980s and early 1990s would not only add value to existing forms of products or services, but would also create new forms of value (Normann and Ramirez, 1993). For example, IT might be used to instil intelligence and capabilities into products in order to enhance their functionality and purpose. IT might even become an important facilitating factor in building relationships, if not the aspect of a relationship most valued by customers (Cecil and Hall, 1988). As a result, instilled IT would create competencies critical in enhancing the competitiveness of the organization (Morton, 1991). What they did not foresee a decade ago was the impact of the Internet on the process of organizational transformation.

## NOW, THE DIGITAL REVOLUTION AND THE INTERNET AS AN INFLECTION POINT

As argued by Groves earlier, the Internet represents a strategic inflection point. Hall (1998) saw the Internet as part of something even more telling, something that 'represents the basis of ... a fundamental evolution of capitalism itself from an industrial to an informational era'. According to Hall, there are four main elements to this:

1. *The digital revolution*, or what Hall termed the 'most fundamental' shift, which is that 'almost all information is becoming digital'.
2. *The Internet*, or what Hall termed 'a new infrastructure of communication'.
3. *Increasing interconnectivity*, or what is generally known as the digital revolution and the convergence of four IT streams via the Internet: computers, consumer electronics, telecommunications and software. In this 'always-on' world computers link with televisions, VCRs, scanners, MP3 players, mobiles, printers, cameras and any number of other hand-held or fixed forms of communications devices.
4. *Killer applications*, that is, on the basis of this convergence and interconnectivity, the development of 'the so-called killer applications that will constitute the new basic industries of the information age'.

As shown in Table 6.1, three 'drivers' of the relentless march of an IT-led transformation are:

1. *Moore's Law* (after Gordon Moore, a founder of Intel), which states that computing power and capacity double every 18 months
2. *Metcalfe's Law* (after Bob Metcalfe, inventor of the Ethernet), which states that the value of a network is roughly proportional to the number of users squared

**Table 6.1** Drivers of IT change

| *Moore's law:* Computing power and capacity double every 18 months | *Metcalfe's law:* The value of a network is roughly proportional to the number of users squared | *Increasing bandwidth:* The cost of data transmission halves every 12 months, i.e. faster than Moore's law |
|---|---|---|
| *Implications*<br>• Ubiquitous diffusion, from fridges to phones<br>• Increasing application sophistication; everything is getting 'smarter'<br>• The technology leads; the market follows, perhaps | *Implications*<br>• Each new node adds more value to the total<br>• The network is worth more to groups<br>• The more people become involved, the more involved they become | *Implications*<br>• Local response times now possible globally<br>• Global operations can be run from anywhere<br>• More and more of anything digital can be transmitted faster and faster |

3. *Increasing bandwidth*, which states that the cost of data transmission halves every 12 months.

What is special about the Internet and digital convergence is not that the dotcom 'bubble' went through a period of hype and growth, starting in the mid-1990s, before its collapse and uncertainty by the end of the decade. Rather, what is special is that the most challenging question for organizations is still: what business are we in? And in answering that question, is there a need for organizational transformation?

Greenwald (2000) said:

It is as if God placed upon the earth these tools – movie studios, television networks, telephone companies, record labels, cable companies, Internet providers – and then stood back and waited for silly mortals to figure out how they all fit together.... The idea here is similar to what compelled Viacom to buy CBS and AOL to merge with Time Warner: joining content with distribution. In some sense, it is technology – or fear of technological change – that is driving these partnerships. Who knows in the high-speed, always-on, wireless world what is more valuable: content or distribution, programming or cable, music or the means to get the tunes to the listener?

Some might argue – or fear – that Bill Gates and Microsoft are best positioned to figure it all out.

In this new digital world information has morphed into both products and services, whether it is an automobile, banking facility, computer, elevator, pizza home-delivery, refrigerator, telephone or vending machine. A problem is that throughout the history of information technologies a common theme is that the innovators did not have a clear idea of what it was they were unleashing, nor what the potential market reaction was. They may not even have had the full support of their organization. The development of the Internet is no exception.

For example, for its 80th anniversary edition in 2003, *Time* selected 80 days in the years since its launch for events that it called 'turning points ... that changed the world'. One of those days was 6 August 1991, according to Grossman (2003):

> Nobody was paying attention to Tim Berners-Lee and his pet idea. He was a young British scientist at CERN, a high-energy physics lab in Geneva, and he had a radical new way for scientists to share data by linking documents to one another over the Internet.... But he wasn't getting interest from his bosses. His proposal came back with the words 'vague but exciting' written across the cover ... so Berners-Lee took his invention to the people. He posted a message to a newsgroup – a kind of electronic public-access bulletin board – announcing the existence of the 'WorldWideWeb(WWW) project'. The message included instructions on how to download the very first Web browser from the very first website, http://info.cern.ch.... He posted it and we came. From that day forward traffic to info.cern.ch rose exponentially, from 10 hits a day to 100 to 1000 and beyond. Berners-Lee had no idea that he had fired the first shot in a revolution that would bring us home pages, search engines, Beanie Baby auctions and the dotcom bust, but he knew that something special had happened. 'Of all the browsers people wrote', Berners-Lee remembers, 'and all the servers they put up, very few of them were done because a manager asked for them. They were done because somebody read one of these newsgroup messages and got that twinkle in their eye.'

If Berners-Lee's creation in 1991 was one strategic inflection point on the way to the Internet as we now know it, another was some special graphical interface software created by Marc Andreessen and his co-workers at the National Centre for Supercomputing Applications (NCSA) at the University of Illinois. In 1993 they posted on the Internet the first major web browser, 'Mosaic'. Levy (2003) termed it 'the most important computer application ever'. The problem with previous web browsers was that they were text-based only and relatively cumbersome, and therefore up that point the Web was used mainly by the research community as a way of digitally distributing papers. Mosaic handled graphics and sound, and was relatively easy to use. It was also free. Within six months more than a million people had downloaded it. Said Levy: 'Before Mosaic, there were only a few hundred websites. But when huge numbers of people were able to access colorful pages, there was incentive to create innovative sites. That provided web surfers with more reason to stay online.'

Andreessen, who was a programmer at NCSA at the time Mosaic was posted, admitted to Levy (2003): 'The most satisfying thing was just seeing how we assembled a couple of building blocks that people could then pick up and do things we never anticipated. The process by which the whole thing completely spun out of control was very satisfying.'

What Andreessen certainly did not anticipate was that within a year he would team up with Jim Clark, an entrepreneur in Silicon Valley, and together they would build a faster, more stable browser that bore the company name, Netscape. On 9 August 1995, they made a public offering of their shares and thereby became another of *Time*'s 'turning points'. Their share price was expected to open at US$12. Instead, it came in at US$71 and, according to *Time*, this event marked the beginning of the dotcom boom: 'this deal changed everything. We began to classify every company as new economy vs. old economy' (Cramer, 2003).

And what became of Netscape? Its share price peaked at just under US$98 in 1999. Unfortunately for Netscape, by the time it had its historic share offer, Microsoft also had a browser ready for its new operating system, Windows 95. As Bill Gates commented earlier in this chapter: 'We try to make sure we're not missing anything.' Added Levy (2003):

> That was the first shot in the so-called browser wars, a conflict that saw a remarkable explosion of innovation compressed into a brief period.... Microsoft, aided by its Windows monopoly, prevailed, and a struggling Netscape was bought by AOL. The loser was the user, as innovation slowed.

Given that Microsoft emerged from its recent antitrust case in the USA relatively unscathed, and that Gates is committed to ensuring he misses nothing, is it inevitable that it will always prevail?

Microsoft faces an inflection point that possibly does have the potential to topple it, especially from its operating system perch. The interloper is Linux, an operating system that was developed by a young Finnish programmer, Linus Torvalds. It was written by him as a stripped-down version of Unix for the PC in 1991, and was offered free to computer hobbyists as an alternative to systems from the likes – or dislikes, if you're a computer geek – of Microsoft and IBM (Kerstetter, 2003). As Torvalds said (Kerstetter, 2003): 'If someone had told me 12 years ago what would happen, I'd have been flabbergasted.'

What has happened is that Torvalds' little programme was very quickly adopted as a cause 'by a ragtag band of open-source programming volunteers scattered around the globe – and hooked up via the Internet'. It has been developed and refined to the point where it now is an operating system that is big and flexible enough 'to run everything from an IBM supercomputer to a Motorola cell phone'. While it can still be downloaded and updated from the Internet for free, its second-stage inflection point impact is that, increasingly, it is being bought by corporations as part of a services package from the likes of Dell, Hewlett-Packard and IBM who, in effect, are legitimizing it as an alternative to Windows. Kerstetter (2003) said there were three main reasons for this: the downturn in technology spending by clients was forcing IT companies to provide lower-cost solutions; Intel, the key maker of processors for PCs, decided it would optimize for both Linux and Windows; and, in simple terms, 'widespread resentment of Microsoft and fear that the company was on the verge of gaining a stranglehold on corporate customers'.

Whether Microsoft can coexist with Linux, and vice versa, is an issue that has yet to be played out. Regardless of the outcome, though, the threat of more inflection points from the likes of Andreessen and Torvalds shows that an increasing challenge for companies – whether new or old economy, and whether an industry minor or a Microsoft – is how to organize for an Internet-determined world of commerce. Are organizational transformations inevitable?

## ORGANIZING FOR THE INTERNET

Despite the dotcom bubble bursting, the Internet remains a potent force for organizational transformation. The issue for many companies is still how they should organize for it. For example, Hagel and Singer (1999) predicted that: 'As more business interactions move onto electronic networks like the Internet, basic assumptions about corporate organization will be overturned.' However, as Child and McGrath (2001) admitted:

> We have posited that the underlying transformation creating the necessity
> for new ways of organizing is the shift from a physical economy, which

was served well by the principles of bureaucracy, to an information-intensive economy, whose structural implications are not yet clear.

In describing the new digital landscape as the 'e-lance economy', Malone and Laubacher (1998) claimed that:

> Nowhere would the changes be as great as in the function of management itself.... As more large companies establish decentralized structures, the boundaries between companies will become much less important. Transactions within organizations will become indistinguishable from transactions between organizations.... An e-lance economy, though a radical concept, is by no means an impossible or even implausible concept.... What is lagging behind technology is our imagination.

Possibly one reason for this, suggest Evans and Wurster (1997), is that over the past decade managers may have focused on adapting their operating processes to new information technologies when in fact they should have been rethinking the 'strategic fundamentals of their businesses', that is to say, 'what business are we now in?' In his early work on IT transformation Morton (1991) concluded that 'none of the potentially beneficial enabling aspects of IT can take place without clarity of business purpose and a vision of what the organization should become'.

## WHAT BECAME OF IBM?

History shows that information technology breakthroughs, when thought of as strategic inflection points, have a way of forcing the question: what business are we now in? This is one of the issues that drove Hewlett-Packard to merge with Compaq. It was also an issue that changed IBM some four decades ago, and as we will see in the next chapter, forced it to change again over the past decade.

Louis Gerstner, who is credited with turning around IBM in the 1990s, told how IBM introduced its mainframe System/360 in the 1960s. This new family of fully compatible computers brought the world 'into the digital computer age' according to Gerstner, for IBM was the first to incorporate the high-density integrated circuit – what we now know as the semiconductor chip – into computing. IBM did not invent this chip; what its executives did however was 'bet the company' on its possibilities. The marketing breakthrough was that, previously, a company's computers were based on the supplier's proprietary technology. Even computers from the same supplying company were unable to work with each other. Thus, if a client wanted to upgrade it literally had to start over.

Said Gerstner (2002): 'System/360 represented an entirely new approach.' Because it was built with high-performance integrated circuits the machines were more powerful, more reliable and less costly than anything else currently available, thereby changing the prevailing price/value 'model'. System/360 represented a family of computers, from very small to very large, and software developed for one processor could run on any other. All peripheral devices, such as printers and punch-card readers, could also work with any processor in the family. A key benefit to customers was that they could easily make upgrades as their needs changed, or grew. A key benefit to IBM was that once a relationship with a company was established, it was unlikely to be terminated quickly. The Big Blue line 'No one ever got fired for buying IBM' thus held for decades.

What changed it all in the 1990s, and nearly brought IBM down, was a combination of a number of external inflection points and IBM's internal shortcomings: the critic's argument of arrogance vying with obduracy again? The first inflection point, and according to Gerstner (2002), the one that posed the greatest threat to IBM, was not the emergence of the PC, but the rise of UNIX:

> an 'open' operating environment championed by companies like Sun and HP. UNIX offered customers the first viable, economically attractive alternative to IBM's mainframe products and pricing.... In the open, plug-and-play world of UNIX, many, many companies could make parts of an overall solution – shattering IBM's hold on architectural control.

Added Gerstner, 'After UNIX cracked the foundation, the PC makers came along swinging wrecking balls.'

What this meant for IBM was that the vertically integrated mainframe computer industry it had dominated was about to end. Gates (1999) explained the changed nature of the industry, as shown in Figure 6.1:

> A major shift in the computer industry has made end-to-end business solutions much more feasible. The realignment of the computer industry from vertically integrated vendors to horizontally integrated, customer-driven solutions has brought prices down dramatically and offered more choice.

Gerstner (2002) believed IBM's own failings meant it did not fully grasp the possibilities of the PC as a strategic inflection point. He explained these failings as:

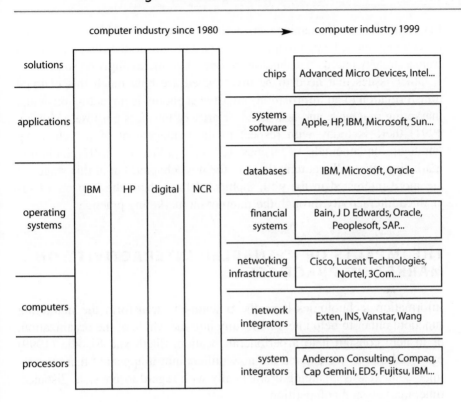

computer industry since 1980 ⟶ computer industry 1999

| | | | | | | |
|---|---|---|---|---|---|---|
| solutions | | | | | chips | Advanced Micro Devices, Intel... |
| applications | IBM | HP | digital | NCR | systems software | Apple, HP, IBM, Microsoft, Sun... |
| | | | | | databases | IBM, Microsoft, Oracle |
| operating systems | | | | | financial systems | Bain, J D Edwards, Oracle, Peoplesoft, SAP... |
| | | | | | networking infrastructure | Cisco, Lucent Technologies, Nortel, 3Com... |
| computers | | | | | network integrators | Exten, INS, Vanstar, Wang |
| processors | | | | | system integrators | Anderson Consulting, Compaq, Cap Gemini, EDS, Fujitsu, IBM... |

**Figure 6.1** The new computer industry

*Source:* Gates, 1999

- *Market and marketing myopia:* eventually PCs would shift from the hobbyists, home-use market to the business-use market: 'We failed to size up the market properly and did not make it a high corporate priority.'
- *Product and organizational myopia:* said Gerstner: 'IBM was consistently reluctant to take new discoveries and new technologies and commercialize them. Why? Because during the 1970s and 1980s that meant cannibalizing existing IBM products, especially the mainframe, or working with other industry suppliers to commercialize new technology.... Because we did not think PCs would ever challenge IBM's core enterprise computing franchise, we surrendered control of the PC's highest value components: the operating system to Microsoft, and the microprocessor to Intel.' Gerstner added that, despite neither of these two companies inventing their respective technologies, by the time he arrived at IBM as CEO (1993), they 'had ridden this gift from IBM right to the top of the industry'.

In Chapter 9 we will examine Gerstner's contribution to IBM in terms of the inflection point he helped shape over the past decade, as the company shifted from a strategy based on technology to one based increasingly on solutions.

Other issues that need to be investigated are how much this claimed transformation to an information-intensive economy is impacting on actual marketing practices, and how much 'clarity of business purpose' (Morton, 1991) there is today with respect to the management of the changing 'strategic fundamentals' of business (Evans and Wurster, 1997), including marketing. We will examine these in the next chapter, but at this stage we are more interested in the philosophical debate about the impacts of IT-enabled interactivity through the Internet on marketing practices.

## THE IMPACTS OF IT-ENABLED INTERACTIVITY ON MARKETING PRACTICES

Information technologies have the potential to transform the marketing function: either to help integrate it fully into the whole of the organization, or to help consign it to a peripheral location. Sheth and Sisodia (1999) proposed that as we entered the new millennium it appeared that marketing's context was changing dramatically with regard to physical distance, time, markets and competition.

Ward and Peppard (2002) say three aspects make the Internet distinct from other technologies:

1. *It is pervasive.* The Internet directly reaches consumers in any number of locations and potentially at any time – at home, at work, at leisure, and so on. It therefore facilitates the conduct of business in ways never before possible.
2. *It is interactive.* This is important, said Ward and Peppard, for 'much business activity consists of interactivity'. IT-enabled interactivity occurs in a variety of formats, including human and technical communication, data gathering and sharing, collaborative problem solving, negotiating, and so on.
3. *It is a new medium.* The Internet has characteristics different from the physical world – what Ward and Peppard term the 'marketspace': 'The marketspace denotes the transformation in business activity as moving from the physical marketplace with fixed locations, inventories and products to an information-defined transaction space. This shift ranges from basic business transactions such as ordering and invoicing to utilizing sophisticated business-to-business (B2B) exchanges and electronic

marketplaces.... This has implications for organizations' brands, for understanding trust, for product and service pricing, for issues of location, for collaborative ventures, for collecting duties and taxes, etc.'

Ranchhod, Gurau and Hackney (2000) say the Internet bypasses the limitations of physical space and time, and this makes it different from traditional media. As Roth (1998) notes:

> While in traditional media content is king, in new media it's turned out to be a pawn. At first the Internet was seen as an offshoot of 'real' media, an alternative distribution vehicle, another way to get your content into the hands of customers. But in the past 12 months or so, it's become clear that the Internet has little to do with traditional media. Online, what counts is not text but tools and transactions. People go to the Web for services: they want to buy a used car; search movie listings; track their stock portfolio; learn how to clean their dog's teeth; buy plane tickets.

Another feature of IT-enabled interactivity, as the *Economist* (2000c) explains, is that 'everything can be recorded: not just every transaction, but which web pages a customer visits, how long he spends there and what banner ad he clicks on'. What is termed 'tacit' knowledge (Wind and Mahajan, 2000) about customers is thus more accessible. For example, specific customers' shopping and information search patterns, interests and activities, payment transactions and chatroom discussion comments are all available from on-line-based research and data-mining techniques. This can produce a formidable array of data that makes possible one-to-one marketing, directing sales pitches at particular individuals, and mass customisation – changing product or service specifications for anything from autos to computers to jeans to travel destinations, in order to match supply to the individual customer's preferences. Under such circumstances, the added value to customers of shopping electronically is bound into the combination of products and services that are being offered simultaneously (Deighton, 1996a; Taher, Leigh and French, 1996). Quinn (2001) sums up this situation by arguing that fundamentally the Internet has 'changed the experience of the customer'.

The Internet may also change 'the experience' of those who supply the goods and services. By using technologies such as interactive communications, electronic networks and sophisticated software programmes, organizations are finding new ways to build closer relationships not only with their customers, but also with their employees, suppliers and other players in their 'marketspace'.

## DOES THE INTERNET REALLY CHANGE EVERYTHING?

A McKinsey international study of the machine tool industry (Gutermann, et al., 2000) concluded that the traditional options for growth, as outlined in Figure 4.1 in Chapter 4, were no longer feasible. One reason was that market saturation was being reached for many companies; another was that existing segments were under attack from competing technologies. A third, perhaps more significant, threat was the Internet as a strategic inflection point for, as Gutermann et al. (2000) pointed out:

> The threat to traditional machinery companies from this source is that the Internet inflates every competitor's market territory from a regional niche to the whole world overnight, as customers can much more easily shop for products and research company qualifications. Firms with cozy local relationships may find themselves suddenly competing with every corner of the globe.

In other words a new way of marketing was about to be undertaken, based on a different perception of space and time.

The interactivity potential of the Internet is seen as particularly well-suited for building business-to-business (B2B) relationships, such as B2B service industries (Bauer, Grether and Leach, 2002), where person-to-person interactions are likely to be critical. For example, Jap and Mohr (2002) say that emerging IT-enabled technologies such as the Internet can be combined to improve relationships through the technologies' capabilities for improving processes such as reaching customers, providing customer service and information sharing.

Furthermore, say Jap and Mohr (2002), by properly matching the B2B context with Internet technologies, organizations can free up scarce human resources to provide extra 'value-added' services. This value-adding potential of IT-based interactivity is supported by Marcolin and Gaulin (2001) who add that:

> Typically the staff responsible for buying and selling functions in organizations spend 25–40 per cent of their time on traditional transactional activities. Automation releases a significant proportion of man-hours which can then be invested in negotiating better contracts, improving customer relations/service and R&D.

However, it is not only the possibilities of value-added services and improved relationships that characterize the Internet. Kaplan and Sawhney

(2000) argued that the Internet had the potential to improve both the efficiencies and the effectiveness of business-to-business operations: 'The appeal of doing business on the Web is clear. By bringing together huge numbers of buyers and sellers and by automating transactions, Web markets expand the choices available to buyers, give sellers access to new customers, and reduce transaction costs for all the players.'

The above discussion might suggest there is likely to be a common view of the potential of IT-enabled interactivity. However, not everyone appears to agree on the extent of the impact of the Internet, even before the bursting of the dotcom bubble. For example, Coviello, Milley and Marcolin (2001) examined four different schools of thought:

1. *It changes everything.* One school of thought is captured by the likes of Venkatraman (2000) in that 'the Internet changes everything'. Gates (1999) agrees: 'The successful companies of the next decade will be the ones that use digital tools to reinvent the way they work. Those companies will make decisions quickly, act efficiently, and directly touch their customers in positive ways.'
2. *It's a tool.* A second school of thought suggests that new IT offer tools to support or augment traditional approaches to the market. As cautioned by Porter (2001), firms need to move 'away from the rhetoric about "Internet industries", "e-business strategies", and a "new economy" and see the Internet for what it is: an enabling technology – a powerful set of tools that can be used, wisely or unwisely, in almost any industry and as part of almost any strategy'. Early proponents such as Rust and Varki (1996), Schultz (1996), and Peterson, Balasubramanian and Bronnenberg (1997) also predicted that tools such as the Internet would be likely to have a major impact on marketing communications.
3. *It's a new channel.* A third school of thought is that interactive technologies basically offer a new channel to the market (Elofson and Robinson, 1998; Ghosh, 1998), and one with the ability to bypass or complement existing channel members and allow direct access to customers. In his review of the practices of Federal Express, Quinn (1999) thus notes that the Internet is 'nothing more than a fourth sales channel ... integrated into other channel strategies'.
4. *It offers a balance of opportunities.* A fourth school of thought is more holistic, in that the notion of a balance means IT-enabled interactivity offers organizations opportunities according to their contexts (Haeckel, 1998; Nilsson, 1999). Gulati and Garino (2000) say that when firms are faced with the decision to integrate or separate their 'bricks and clicks' activities, they need to tailor marketing approaches to the needs of their

particular customers and to their own market and competitive situation. Mandel and Hof (2001) add that they need to do this in a 'balanced' manner.

According to Cairncross (2000), the broader view of the Internet suggests that the Internet:

> is not simply a new distribution channel, or a new way to communicate. It is many other things: a marketplace, an information system, a tool for manufacturing goods and services. It makes a difference to a whole range of things that managers do every day, from locating a new supplier to coordinating a project to collecting and managing customer data. Each of these, in turn, affects corporate life in many different ways. The changes that the Internet brings are simply more pervasive and varied than anything that has gone before.... At the root of the change is a dramatic fall in the cost of handling and transmitting information.

Such a transformation requires not only active acceptance by customers and possible shifts in regulatory authorities' attitudes toward the collection and use of confidential information; it may also require a major shift in how organizations manage their internal priorities, processes and relationships to build and maintain external relationships with customers. However, as Jap and Mohr note (2002), referring to a specific business-to-business environment, 'establishing successful B2B on-line strategies can be tough and complicated'. As we will examine in Chapter 8, this statement may represent a range of industries and situations. In effect, it depends on the situation or context.

How should we think of the Internet then? Peter Hall, who is a Professor of Planning at the Bartlett School of Architecture and Planning, University College London, has a slightly different perspective on the impact of the Internet when compared with the four views considered by Coviello, Milley and Marcolin (2001). Hall (1998) predicted:

> The creation of this system will be one of the great pieces of infrastructural construction in history, paralleling the railways of the 1830s and 1840s, the metros and subways of the 1890s, and the motorways and freeways of the 1950s and 1960s; and its effects will be equally momentous.

He argued that the technology is important

because without it, there would be nothing.... Yet what is really crucial, as before in history, is not the basic infrastructure, but what that infrastructure enables.... We are mistaken when we focus merely on the production of technology.... It was not the internal combustion engine that was finally important, but the entire chain of impacts that it wrought on living and working. It is the applications that will again prove crucial.

If Hall is correct, the Internet *is* changing everything, and so there will be more inflection points not only for the Hewlett-Packards, Intels and Microsofts directly involved in information technologies, but also for the General Motors, McDonald's and all the rest. As a result, they will be forced continually to ask the question: What business are we in? Equally important, if structure follows strategy, in their quest for improved value creation marketers will also continually be asking the question: What amount of organizational transformation is needed?

The above discussions suggest it could be worthwhile to consider not just the extent that firms are incorporating IT-enabled interactivity, based on the Internet, into their marketing operations, but also what managers think about the role of IT in their organization as a whole. In particular, the extent to which IT is used to reinforce, enhance or transform the status quo (Orlikowski, 2000) must be considered. According to Orlikowski, each role reflects a different level of IT integration in the organization. For example, when IT is used to support/preserve current marketing efforts it *reinforces* the status quo; when IT is used to extend/improve existing marketing efforts it *enhances* the status quo; and when IT is used to redefine/drive the marketing efforts it *transforms* the status quo. What IT role is required for most effective marketing practices today?

In the next chapter we consider what managers tell us are the critical changes they see as forcing them to rethink their marketing practices. There are five changes in total, and in examining them we are also considering the academic and business media discourses on the topic. There appears to be general agreement on these. In Chapter 9 we then consider the extent to which IT is used to reinforce, enhance or transform their organizational status quo. From that analysis we will then discuss the issues to do with management of change. If Hall and others are correct, and the Internet is changing everything, then marketers may need to be comfortable with leading change in their organizations if marketing is to be everything, as McKenna (1991) once claimed.

## CHAPTER 7

# Contemporary Marketing Practice and the Five Changes Challenge

## OBJECTIVES

In the last chapter we examined 'inflection points' and their implications. When considering the impacts of the Internet and IT-enabled interactivity as an inflection point, we ended up asking whether this was leading to an organizational transformation, and concluded there were a number of differing views on this. For example, the Internet is seen as: changing everything; as a tool; or as a channel. For others, its impact is seen in a more balanced fashion, in that companies need to integrate both their 'bricks' and their 'clicks' according to their situation. From that we asked the question, do organizations see an organizational transformation as necessary in order to incorporate IT-enabled interactivity, or is it merely a case of using IT-enabled interactivity either to reinforce or to enhance the status quo?

In this chapter we consider this last question by revisiting the contemporary marketing practices (CMP) study. We wanted to understand from our companies under consideration what was the extent of their possible organizational transformation as a result of their commitment to IT-enabled interactivity. In particular, were there any factors that were driving these changes in their marketing practices? The results of our studies show that, on the basis of what executives have told us, there appear to be up to five major changes affecting marketing practice today. In presenting these findings we also delve into our other two discourses, in the academic and the business media. What is most apparent is the high degree of agreement between all three discourses. Finally, we consider how these changes might be interrelated, and how they might impact on organizations overall. In particular, we consider whether their collective impact is likely to reinforce, enhance or transform the organizational status quo.

## ALL COMPANIES FACE CHANGE

As we have stressed in several chapters, all companies face change: consumers' living and buying patterns change; new competitors challenge existing markets; new information technologies create inflection points, and force companies to rethink what business they are in; new regulations force shifts in successful business practices; and so on.

The CMP research into contemporary marketing practices shows that the dominant trend in the organizations being studied is that towards developing relationships. We have determined there are at least six inter-related aspects of marketing practices today, and one of them is a variation of the traditional transactional marketing practice. As we have seen, there can be considerable variation in the way relationship marketing is practised within firms, and both relational and transactional approaches can coexist. What binds them together is the need by companies to get closer to – and better understand – their customers. And while some firms appear to be less relational than other firms, relationship marketing in some form is both relevant to – and practised by – all the firms we studied.

What they also have in common is that a number of changes, or drivers, are affecting how they do their marketing practice – in fact, how they 'do' business. A close examination of our research results shows that, for many companies, up to five major changes are occurring simultaneously, and therefore their response to these changes in terms of marketing practices needs to take all five into account.

These changes are:

1.  Financial accountability, loyalty and customer value management.
2.  Increasing emphasis on service aspects of all products.
3.  Organizational transformation.
4.  Retail power and systemic relationships.
5.  Interactive media and mass customization.

When we asked our executives to assess these impacts, the general view was that the increased emphasis on greater financial accountability was probably the most pressing. This is consistent with the arguments about growth and value that were examined in Chapter 4. We also asked how these changes might interact with each other, and one such model or frame-work that was presented to us is shown in Figure 7.1. Information tech-nologies were also seen as an underlying force behind these changes, as, for example, in terms of facilitating relationships.

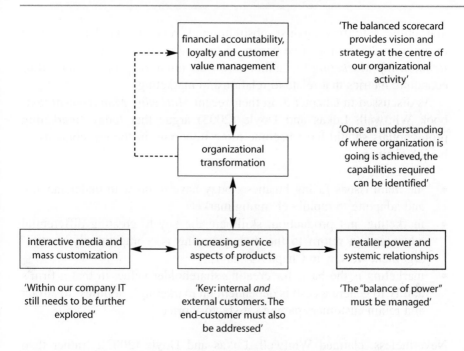

**Figure 7.1** Integrating the five changes (telecommunications company)

## CHANGE 1: FINANCIAL ACCOUNTABILITY, LOYALTY AND CUSTOMER VALUE MANAGEMENT

While marketing's expected contribution to an organization's overall financial performance is an issue that receives sporadic attention in the academic discourse, it is of great importance to executives. In a study of top managers' views of the major issues facing marketing management, Webster (1981) found that the second- and third-ranked issues respectively were the decreasing productivity of marketing expenditures, and that 'marketing managers are generally unsophisticated in their understanding of the financial dimensions of marketing decisions and lack a bottom-line orientation'. Has anything changed?

Twenty years on, similar concerns are still being raised. In a special edition of the *Journal of Marketing*, Moorman and Rust (1999) argue that the marketing function could improve its contribution to the firm by, amongst other things, placing more emphasis on issues of financial accountability. In the same edition, and citing the Marketing Science Institute's (MSI) 1998–2000 research priorities, Day and Montgomery (1999) said that 'the most important was developing metrics that might be used to help academics, managers, and governments judge the performance of marketing activities against absolute and relative standards'. More recently, in 2002, in all five papers in the charter issue of the *Journal of Relationship Marketing* the authors drew attention to specific financial or economic metrics that relate to relationship marketing.

As discussed in Chapter 3, in their recent *Marketing Management* textbook Whitwell, Lukas and Doyle (2003) argue that today 'marketing professionals should have become more important in the top councils of business' since:

- the main issues facing business today have to do with understanding and adapting to rapidly changing markets
- marketing, not production, skills are the key to creating differential advantage (a return to the manufacturing is 'competitively neutral' argument we saw in Chapter 4), and
- marketing is the basis for creating shareholder value, in that a firm's ability to generate cash is dependent on marketing's abilities 'to attract and retain customers paying satisfactory prices'.

Nevertheless, claimed Whitwell, Lukas and Doyle (2003): 'rather than gaining in influence, marketing professionals, whose expertise is in identifying these market opportunities and building customer relationships, appear to have lost influence in the boardrooms of industry.' As we also saw in Chapter 4, a criticism of industry today is its preoccupation with short-term revenue growth and financial returns at the expense of long-term position and health.

Not everyone agrees that this should be so. As markets become more open and competitive, consumers more demanding, capabilities and operations more compelling, and the concepts of value and loyalty more elusive, managers have been challenged to accept that an emphasis on a limited range of mainly financial measures is inadequate as a means of determining the overall performance, and well-being, of a company and its brands. And, re-quoting Gummesson (2003): 'Obsession with measurement means handing over the future of a company to the accounting tribe, abolishing vision and leadership.' Ghosh and John (1999) argue for a move away from the traditional 'transaction cost analysis' approach to 'governance value analysis' as a way 'to address marketing strategy decisions, especially with respect to strategies grounded in cooperative relationships'. Kaplan and Norton (1992) argued, 'what is required is a balanced presentation of both financial and operational measures'.

In nearly a decade of writing, Kaplan and Norton (1992, 1993, 1996a, 1996b, 2000) have advocated a management reporting system called the 'balanced scorecard' that brings together the disparate elements of a company's competitive and performance measures. These include measures of four broad perspectives of the business:

- *Customer:* measures that show how customers view and relate to the organization and its offerings.
- *Internal business:* measures of what technologies, competencies and processes a company must excel at to meet the expectations of its customers, and to beat its competitors.
- *Innovation, learning and growth:* measures that tell a company that its ability to develop employee satisfaction and motivation for innovation, learning and growth will ensure long term competitiveness and success.
- *Financial performance:* measures that track whether a firm's strategy, tactics and processes are contributing to bottom-line improvement, along with other indicators of success required by shareholders, in particular.

As explained by the executive from a telecommunications firm, and as shown in Figure 7.1, their balanced scorecard reflects an attempt to put vision and strategy, not control, at the centre of their organization's activities. As a result, the measures are intended to act as collective goals so executives will take appropriate actions to realize them. A factor seen as critical to this implementation is the issue of managing the organization's *internal* and *external relationships*, such as the building of commitment and loyalty (Hart et al., 1999).

Another important issue is how to put 'hard' measures, such as accounting rates of return on capital, on what may be considered 'soft' measures of the intangible (market-based) assets of an organization (Srivastava, Shervani and Fahey, 1998), for example: an organization's ability continuously to generate intelligence and to consider learning as an investment (Slater and Narver, 2000); the added value of supplementary services (Anderson and Narus, 1995); the value of brand equity (Aaker, 1996; Berry, 2000) and customer equity (Rust, Ziethaml and Lemon, 2000). According to Mendonca and McCallum (1995), companies recognize that the heavy initial expense of acquiring a new customer makes it vital to maintain customer relationships as long as possible, hence the increased interest in metrics to do with 'customer relationship economics' (Storbacka, Strandvik and Gronroos, 1994) and 'life-time value' (Heskett et al., 1994), including the 'return on relationships' (Gummesson, 2003).

While the balanced scorecard has received widespread coverage and support in both the business press and academic studies, according to

Goulian and Mersereau (2000), 'the literature to date has tended to be mainly normative, focusing more on the advantages of the approach than on the details relating to actual implementation'. Further, in their controlled study Lipe and Salterio (2000) found that where a corporation's balanced scorecard contains some measures that are common to multiple units, and some that are unique to individual units, only the common measures are likely to affect superiors' evaluations of each unit, and these are the more traditional financial measures. In other words, when it is a choice between marketing pull and financial push, push normally wins.

## What the Managers Told Us

In our research, this issue was one that struck an immediate chord with executives. As a result we though it appropriate to include their voice in this section. Examples include the following:

- The need to move from a focus on financial measures of success when the main drivers of strategic success have increasingly to do with innovation and growth:

    As a future-oriented company, we may be hampered by measuring our company success on a purely historical financial basis, which ignores the real company assets of innovation and new product and service development.

    (Telecommunications equipment company)

- The need to have a more integrated set of measures in order to ensure that the relationships between strategy success (effect) and the drivers (causes) of success are more clearly articulated:

    The key performance indicator is achieving sales targets for the year, followed by reaching the specific targets of each unit within the section.... There is, however, no link between the performance level in achieving our strategy targets (effect) and the drivers (causes). As a result, the effort and priority that the drivers get is not in proportion, nor is it a given fact that limited resources are targeted to gain maximum impact. This filters down to the staff as often they do not have a sense of direction – they are unsure as to what they should be setting out to achieve.... For example, there is a link between sales and integrators/consultants specifying our work. End users are largely influenced by what these people recommend. The cause and effect of this is that if we train the integrators and consultants about our products they will become more knowledgeable about the benefits our technology can deliver. If they recommend our systems then our sales will increase.... Thus the allocation of resources to educate integrators is important.... The performance of the section given the responsibility to train integrators should be part of the overall performance measure.

(Medical equipment manufacturer)

- The need to move away from an emphasis on centralization and cost cutting, which has reduced the business unit's ability to offer 'value' and retain customers when what is required is the development of new offerings and the building of brand equity:

Due to the current price competitive environment in which we compete, senior management have been focused on the reduction of internal costs.... Unfortunately, this has been to the detriment of sustaining customer satisfaction, as the cost cutting initiatives are now affecting the service and 'value' we are providing.... To achieve an advantage, we must look to measuring our current merchants to understand their motivation for staying, and their future requirements, to ensure we continue to redevelop our services for the different markets which are now emerging. The retention of our current merchants is vital as we are aware of the additional costs we incur from acquiring a new merchant.

(Trading bank)

- The need to redress the negative impacts that recent emphasis on financial performance has had on staff morale and satisfaction, in order to move toward a customer value management system that, if successful, will still deliver the financial requirements:

Staff satisfaction and commitment are elements that have been let down during the past few years.... While our financial success has been reasonable, the impact on staff and the decline in staff relations is now impacting on our ability to deliver real value to our trading partners and, in some areas, their customers.... One area of comfort is that, given the financial pressures on a lot of carriers operating this theatre, they are also apparently lacking the ability to move in this direction quickly, the exception being the American carriers who have well-developed internal structures to measure staff and customer satisfaction against

financial measures.... Post-modern thinking by senior management is
now even more vital to ensure the negative effect of this decline in dedication to staff is turned around quickly.... Customer Value Management
through effective use of IT solutions associated with loyalty
programmes will be able to directly link customer needs with our ability to deliver satisfaction to them. The lifetime value of the customer
will be more easily established once customer travel trends are
analyzed. However, the ability to use this information to our advantage
will still be the telling factor. Information is meaningless unless it can
be translated into strategic thinking and action.

(Airline company)

- The need to categorize customers into value groupings, and to have a
more integrated set of measures in order to ensure that the relationships
between satisfaction and loyalty are linked to employees' positive
attitudes and efforts:

We are still a very financially driven organization with traditional
measures of success, that is, revenue, market share, connections,
winbacks, and return on investment.... While we measure customer
satisfaction, and participation by customers in loyalty programmes, we
do not correlate the data between these two measures, satisfaction and
loyalty. Consequently, we spend significant marketing budgets on
winning high-value customers back from competitors.... Our new
consumer segmentation model – Classic, Advanced or Premium
groupings – goes some way towards establishing the value to us of
each consumer customer and creating service propositions to meet
their specific requirements.... It is therefore vital that alongside measuring customer satisfaction and loyalty we measure some key
employee indicators – such as motivation, learning and training, and
satisfaction against the competencies and capabilities required to
achieve our strategies.

(Telecommunications company, where the business unit
is responsible for consumer products and services)

- The need to target individual customers in order to meet strategic
marketing goals and to build loyalty based on personalized service and
offerings, thereby improving key financial performance measures:

Our vision is to be (the country's) best bank, helping customers
achieve their financial goals. The bank has initiated 'Big Five' objec-

tives for planning and measuring its financial performance and internal and external relationships, hence establishing the vision in the core values of its business drivers.... Moving from traditional mass marketing we have the ability through our IT to manage our database of customers by tracking their behaviour, characteristics and requirements. As a result, we can specifically target individuals and manage a relationship with them through targeted offerings, with the ability to measure response, share of wallet and lifetime value. This in turn helps our bottom-line financials, and loops around to assist further in creating better products and services, committed staff and loyal customers.

(Trading bank business unit responsible for consumer markets)

- The need to configure process-based performance measures that reflect the possibilities of an increasingly IT-mediated environment when building closer relationships with customers:

All areas will increasingly rely on IT, either to distil information or disseminate it. The internal acceptance of this by all staff is crucial to the success of the company. Even if e-commerce directly with the end-user is still some way in the future, we need to be ready for this. We need to know what type of person will purchase a computer directly from the web, and what processes they went through to make this decision. We need to have the internal systems in place to handle not only the financial transaction, but also the ability to capture all the detail we require about the customer before, during and after the transaction. We need to foster in the internal team a desire to be totally service-focused – for both internal and external customers.

(Computer company)

Our senior executives have accountabilities in achieving shareholder growth through defined targets in both revenue and EVA (Economic Value Added) performance.... The philosophies of customer value and loyalty programmes are predominately marketing initiatives that complement our financial measures and have in the last year come to the forefront of integrated organizational management. As an example, we utilize the Balanced Scorecard in monthly financial packs with high level strategy-linked initiatives. Sales channels provide CVM (Customer Value Management) and target account plans to manage relationships, while in the consumer market we predominantly attempt to drive volume through database and tele-marketing-based approaches.... Customer Value Management and loyalty programmes will be driven by our customers' definition of values, and specified by individual customers through direct electronic linkages that will define the product and service, technical, experiential and functional attributes. We will eliminate the requirement to offer generic products and services with direct customer specification.

(Telecommunications company)

## CHANGE 2: INCREASING EMPHASIS ON SERVICE ASPECTS OF ALL PRODUCTS

The concept of a 'product' is well established. In their textbook, *Marketing*, Kotler et al. (2001) broadly define products as 'anything that can be offered to a market for attention, acquisition, use or consumption that might satisfy a want or need'.

Summing up Kotler et al: 'Thus, a product is more than a simple set of tangible features. Consumers tend to see products as complex bundles of benefits that satisfy their needs.' These writers' view is that these needs can be fulfilled at three levels:

1. *The core product:* provides the problem-solving services or core benefits that customers obtain when they buy a product.
2. *The actual product:* includes a product's parts, quality level, features, styling, brand name, packaging and any other attributes that are combined to deliver the core benefits.
3. *The augmented product:* includes any additional services or benefits, such as extended warranty, free installation, after-sales advice, and so on.

Is this approach sufficient today? Nearly two decades ago Levitt (1983) proposed that most competition takes place at the product augmentation level, where the goal is to go beyond satisfying customers. According to Levitt:

When the selling manufacturer of, say, computers implants a software diagnostic module inside his computers which automatically locates the source of failure or breakdown (as some now do), that seller has augmented the product beyond what was required or even expected by the buyer.

This approach is changing. By Levitt's broad definition a 'product' can fall anywhere along a continuum that ranges from a physical product (durable or non-durable) at one end to a 'pure' service at the other. The differences between these extremes have traditionally been explained by criteria such as intangibility, inseparability, variability and perishability. In reality, argued Kotler et al (2001), 'there are few so-called "pure" versions of either physical products or services ... most market offerings lie on a continuum between the two extremes ... and involve a combination of the two'. This is because the service sector now dominates Western and other developed economies, and the service component of products is increasingly used as the key point of differentiation or competitive advantage. As a result, it may be arbitrary where one now draws the line between what is a product and what is a service. What is more important is to focus on the value-creating processes of the business. More and more, this has more to do with the delivery of the (intangible) service than the (tangible) product.

Levitt (1983) argued that it was better to talk of 'tangibles' and 'intangibles' rather than 'goods' and 'services': 'All products have elements of tangibility and intangibility. Companies that sell tangible products invariably promise more than the tangible products themselves.' Thus, Kodak does not just market cameras (or film, or digital images): it also markets the promise of enduring memories. Volkswagen does not just market a retro-styled Beetle: it holds out the promise of 'serious fun'.

At the same time, said Levitt (1983), 'If tangible products must be intangibilized to add customer-getting appeal, then intangible products must be tangibilized' as a part of the process of 'managing the relationship' with the customer. For example, upon returning to his or her room later in the evening after a meal, a hotel patron finds a single-boxed serving of Belgian chocolate that has been carefully placed on the centre of the pillow at the head of the freshly turned-down bed.

## Beyond Augmentation

How much has changed since Levitt argued the importance of augmentation? As suggested by some of the executive comments from the first change above, one aspect of marketing today is the blurring of boundaries between what is a product and what is a service. While the distinction between goods and services was accepted twenty years ago as a way to get marketers more aware of the importance of the services sector, the distinction may no longer be useful. For example, Rust, Zahorik and Keningham (1996) challenged the dichotomy and suggested that service marketing, as opposed to services marketing, should not be confined to the service sector. Rather, all marketing strategy and practice should be viewed from a service marketing perspective.

Juttner and Wehrli (1994) argued that the value of either a product or a service is determined by the nature of the interactions between buyers and sellers and the complexity of these interactions leads to a higher 'density of values' being offered. Thus, firms need to focus not only on their product or service attribute-based benefits, but also on the means by which ralational benefits can be provided. In effect, for many companies that traditionally thought of themselves as makers of products, there is pressure now to focus on the value creating processes of the business, and increasingly this has more to do with the delivery of an (intangible) service than a (tangible) product. Nowadays it may be arbitrary – or irrelevant – where one draws the line between what is a product and what is a service.

Once a firm takes on a service orientation – and later in this section we will extend that to mean a 'solutions' orientation – then the management of both the internal and external relationships in an organization also become increasingly important. These relationships are identified by researchers such as Heskett, Sasser and Hart (1990) and Bitner (1995) in their description of the service delivery system; by Taher, Leigh and French (1996) in their argument that retailers should consider the 'total' retail patronage experience based on augmented services as a way to gain customer affection and store loyalty; by Rucci, Kirn and Quinn (1998) in their description of the employee–customer–profit chain in a retail setting; and by Schneider and Bower (1999) in their argument that retaining customers through the delivery of quality service may require relationship-building processes that recognize customers' needs for security, fairness and self-esteem. For example, upon picking up a car that has just been serviced by the dealership where the car was bought, the owner finds not only a detailed account of all work carried out, and a final price that is the same as that estimated earlier that day when the car was brought in, but also a vehicle that has been groomed and washed free of charge – together with a personal note of thanks signed by the salesperson who sold the customer the car in the first place. Most important, all work on the car has been completed correctly.

## The Importance of Information Technologies

Information technology is likely to be a facilitating factor where it is used to instil intelligence and capabilities in products in order to enhance their functionality and purpose. Some argue this instilled IT is becoming the most important aspect in the competitiveness of the organization, whether the 'product' is an automobile, an elevator or a pizza delivery service. It is possible to create intelligence and capabilities in mundane items such as a toaster or a washing machine. What results are 'intelligent' products that the buyer 'experiences', and it is this personal experience that may matter most to the value of the relationship between the buyer and the end product or service.

For example, in the automobile industry, Bouvard, Cornet and Rowland (2001) argued that 'vehicles are now being transformed by a wireless revolution' that will impact upon the 'front-seat' market, the 'back-seat' market and the market for 'engine and other mechanical applications'. IT-enabled diagnostic tools can now aid the driver in the everyday use of their vehicle, including:

- *To tailor engine output to the driver's abilities*. A careless driver finds an engine-management system automatically cuts in to reduce engine power output. A more skilled driver is allowed use of the vehicle's full power output.
- *To apply emergency braking that compensates for the driver's limitations*. Sensors record every movement of the brake pedal, thereby tracking the driver's normal braking style and usage. By continuously comparing data the system instantly recognizes when brakes are suddenly used with greater speed and force than normal. By linking with other computer-controlled systems monitoring vehicle speed, brake and tyre wear together with weather conditions, the car's brake-assist system instantly cuts in to build up maximum braking pressure. This is more effective than the driver is likely to achieve, thereby cutting down on braking distance.
- *To create a 'network vehicle' and provide distance servicing*. The car company may use global positioning system satellite technology, and a hands-free, voice-activated cellular phone that is integrated into the car's entire electronics system to link the driver and the vehicle with the car company's global on-line service center. This provides one-to-one services such as route advice, remote diagnostics, remote door unlocking, and so on. Another possible application is for developing traffic conditions on the road ahead to be automatically relayed back to the driver, and alternative routes suggested via the cars in-board navigation system.

In other words, diagnostic systems provide solutions to problems, possibly even before the driver might be aware of them. According to Stewart (1998), the decision to provide this depends on two main criteria: will it add value and will customers pay for it? Stewart suggested: 'the first element of knowledge-product strategy is definitional: begin by teasing out what knowledge and capabilities customers are buying.... Next, explore the ways this knowledge can be packaged.' As we will see when we consider the fifth change, going beyond augmentation can be described in two words: *increased personalization*.

## Providing Solutions

The automotive example above illustrates that it is becoming increasingly arbitrary where one draws the line between what is a goods and what is a service company. What is relevant is thinking in different ways to deliver superior value by providing solutions to everyday problems and needs, and by incorporating information technologies where appropriate. Work in these areas is well underway, both inside and outside the automobile industry, as firms grapple with the question of what business they are in. For example, in 2000 IBM and Motorola announced a deal to speed up technology that would deliver internet access, navigation, e-mail and emergency assistance to drivers in their vehicles (*New Zealand Herald*, 2000). Said IBM's director of automotive solutions: 'This is a very large opportunity because we believe that the vehicle is no longer an island of isolation from the outside world.'

In the trucking industry, Luciat-Labry, Rosenberg and Wilsby (2002), who work for McKinsey, recommend to their clients that:

> To capture more value, truck makers, like many companies before them must sell solutions. But to do so, these truck makers will have to think of their customers and products in new ways.... Each segment has distinct needs. The larger truck fleets, for instance, want telematics systems that provide vehicle-tracking tools to manage routes and to service vehicles remotely. Smaller operators, which tend to have less technical support and less systematic maintenance schedules, want onboard tools to diagnose failures, as well as 'infotainment' services to attract drivers.

What is at issue here is not that cars or trucks have these IT capabilities. Rather, the issue is that the designers, engineers and marketers in companies as diverse as vehicle and computer manufacturers all work together, and regard these developments as essential means to two ends: vehicles that are designed and built with continuously improved quality and performance characteristics for the individual owner/driver, and vehicles that systematically and unobtrusively help to ensure that the driver remains physically and emotionally 'connected' with what otherwise might become just another 'appliance'. This is consistent with the argument that what the customer 'experiences' as a result of a company providing problem-solving solutions, will increasingly matter in the building and maintaining of relationships.

McKinsey executives Foote et al. (2001) recommend four ways companies can think about providing solutions:

- *Build value propositions for customer outcomes:* 'In developing solutions, managers start with a desired outcome for a customer – an outcome that could encompass a range of needs.'
- *Include strange bedfellows:* 'Suppliers, distributors, customers, and ... even direct competitors may have an important role to play in providing products, services, skills, market knowledge, and customer relationships.'
- *Choose your customers:* 'The best customers for solutions may not be existing customers for products.... In the end, the solutions provider might decide to walk away from some of the oldest, biggest, or most prestigious customers it has.'
- *Guarantee delivered value:* 'Guarantees require solutions providers to assume risks normally borne by the customer.... Sometimes these risks are market risks. More often, the risks deal with organizational performance: the solutions provider guarantees that many parts of many different organizations will work together effectively.'

## CHANGE 3: ORGANIZATIONAL TRANSFORMATION

As we saw in Chapter 6, the degree to which organizations are responding to how IT developments may be changing the 'competitive landscape' is well documented. Downes and Mui (1998) said that succeeding at these early stages of IT development may require substantial changes to the organization:

> As technology moves from its position as a defining element of the back office to a disruptive force in the marketplace, the problem now faced by most organizations is that there is rarely anyone, much less an organization, with the mandate and the resources to help senior management treat digital technology strategically.

How have we got to this position of technology as a 'destructive force', and what are the marketing and market research implications? Writing a decade ago, Tapscott and Caston (1993) identified three major shifts away from the original reliance on mainframe computers. These shifts are similar to Venkatraman's (1994) 'organizational transformation' shifts:

- *From personal to work-group computing:* at the local, work-group level of the firm, as stand-alone personal computers became linked to each other, such networking systems allowed for greater streamlining of work-processes, and hence the possibility of both faster turnaround times and a reduction in errors.
- *From system islands to integrated systems:* here, the local 'islands of technology' began to be linked electronically – for example, R&D, purchasing, manufacturing, warehousing, logistics, marketing, selling, servicing etc. – as companies downsized and flattened their structures to achieve faster information flows, greater teamwork and speedier decision-making. Companies also began to install decision support systems that allowed executives to access vital information in a range of forms – numbers, graphics, pictures, video clips, and so on – from a variety of disparate systems and locations, increasingly in 'real-time' and, most critically, in a format tailor-made for each executive.
- *From internal to inter-enterprise computing:* not only were firms becoming 'wired' internally, but their computer and communications systems began to stretch outwards to link them electronically and systemically with other players in their industry value system: suppliers, distribution channels, customers and even competitors.

More recently, Davis (1998) suggested organizational transformation has evolved through five stages, beginning in the 1960s: first, the initial automation of clerical functions via centralized computing; second, followed by the development of management reporting systems; third, followed by the growth of desktop computing; fourth, leading to the rise in intra-enterprise data management and inter-enterprise communications; and, fifth and more recently, the emergence of what he termed 'customer integration' through the Internet. We can label this shift as:

- *From asynchronous to synchronous real-time interactions:* previously, the interactions between a company and its end-customers had been largely unidirectional, with products channelled through multi-stage distribution systems (wholesalers, retailers, agents, and so forth), and with communications broadcast via an array of targeted (but essentially mass) media. The emerging global, digital economy creates opportunities for continuous two-way links (with respect to products, services, information, processes, and so on) between companies and their individual customers, suppliers and other partners.

The overall rubric for this latest transformation can broadly be termed e-business, as we will examine in Chapter 9. At a number of levels, the combination of increasing computer information processing power and high-speed telecommunications is driving fundamental changes in organizations (Waters, 1999). At one level, it involves rethinking how organizations relate to their customers and suppliers, in particular. In the process, traditional arrangements are likely to change, as we saw earlier with respect to 'intelligent cars', or in Chapter 3, with respect to auto companies and their Tier 1 suppliers. At another level, as we will examine in Chapter 9, what might be termed e-business, e-commerce and m-commerce (mobile commerce) all affect the ways firms are structured and run. Issues such as specialist functions and organizational hierarchies take on new meaning, if they really mean anything at all.

What is emerging is the 'networked organization' (Achrol, 1997), 'distinguished from a simple network of exchange linkages by the density, multiplexity, and reciprocity of ties and a shared value system defining membership roles and responsibilities'. Conklin and Tapp (2000b) identified such organization forms as 'value webs', which are different from the traditional value chain:

A chain implies a unidirectional exchange along a distinct flow, whereas a web suggests interconnectedness and the multidirectional, multilevel relationships that can lead to better and faster innovations... If the initial producer of the components knows the needs of the ultimate user of its products, it will be able to design better products. If there is a free exchange of information and communication, all parties benefit from decreased development times, assured market acceptance and continual, planned future offerings.

Examples of inter-networked organizational forms include:

- *Internal networks*, for example, global auto or software R&D networks linked electronically to progress development on a 24/7 basis.
- *Virtually integrated (modular) networks*, for example, Dell.
- *Vertical market or channel networks*, for example, Amazon.com.
- *Virtual 'marketspace' networks*, for example, eBay.
- *Intermarket or concentric networks*, for example, Japanese Keiretsu networks.

- *Strategic alliance networks*, for example, the airline industry's OneWorld vs. Star Alliance.

Conklin and Tapp (2000b) said the automobile industry was moving toward networking structures. As we saw in Chapter 3, manufacturers are pushing greater responsibility for research, design, development and testing to a smaller number of Tier 1 suppliers. It may be the Tier 1 supplier who develops a new component, based on its greater understanding of both the technologies underpinning it and the needs of the driver who is the end user of it. In supplying the main assembler with such innovations the Tier 1 suppliers become systems integrators, in that by combining the innovations of their own Tier 2 or 3 suppliers, they help the entire value web to gain an extra competitive advantage. On that basis, competition increasingly is between networks of companies, not between the individual companies.

Another way to consider networked companies is from a power perspective. Hacki and Lighton (2001) termed them 'economic webs':

> Economic webs are the creatures of a Darwinian struggle in which several companies vie to establish a user base for their particular technologies. The technology that current users embrace becomes the 'standard' and thereby the choice of most new users. Thus, Microsoft's Windows operating software 'places it at the centre of an "economic web" composed of companies that produce Windows-based software applications and related services'. The sheer weight of the market preference for the platform – rather than any alliance, agreement, or inducement offered by the platform's proprietor – is the source of its influence over the economic web's existing members and of its ability to attract new ones.

This stimulates further demand by creating more applications, thereby reinforcing Microsoft's position. Claimed Hacki and Lighton (2001): 'winning companies (such as Microsoft) do it; losing companies (Apple Computer) do not'.

Power can also come from another set of factors, as exemplified by an increasing number of retail groups worldwide. This is the next major change facing marketers, especially those in fast-moving consumer goods (FMCG) companies.

## CHANGE 4: RETAILER POWER AND SYSTEMIC RELATIONSHIPS

Retailing has been growing in power for a couple of decades now, whether in the form of automobile mega-dealers, consumer electronics outlets,

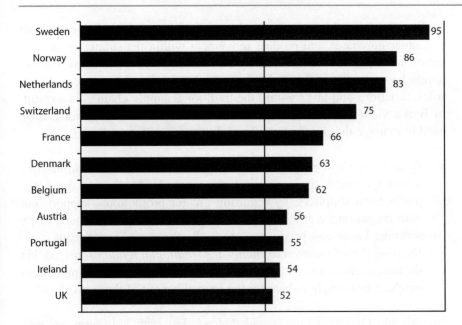

**Figure 7.2** Retail consolidation in Europe, market share of top three retailers

*Source:* supplied by A. C. Nielsen

grocery supermarket chains, home furnishing depots, or toy warehouses. The growth and concentration of retail power into fewer hands has changed the nature of the relationships between suppliers and retailers. As the CEO of Procter & Gamble said nearly 15 years ago: 'The major retailers around the world are moving toward cooperative alliances with a select few suppliers. We must be one of them' (*Business Week*, 1989). A major reason behind Unilever's recent decision to focus its efforts on 'power' brands, as we saw in Chapter 4, would have been in order to balance the growth of retail power (Figure 7.2).

In regions as diverse as Europe (Figure 7.2), North America and parts of the Pacific Basin, a small number of supermarket chains have gradually come to dominate their respective markets. In doing so they have become increasingly competent and sophisticated in the development of their marketing strategies, including own-branding and retail positioning. This is leading to retailers becoming increasingly dominant in their relationships with what they term their 'suppliers'. In a study of the major supermarket groups in the United Kingdom, Brookes (1995) identified several major shifts by leading chains such as J. Sainsbury, Marks & Spencer and Tesco, and the impact of these shifts on suppliers.

According to Burt (2000), increased scale – largely from acquisitions –

leading to greater buying power; the availability of information on both consumer purchases and product movement within the supply chain; and the ownership of this information by the retailers, are factors whose combination has meant that major retail groups have been able to 'reconfigure roles, functions and tasks within the traditional supply chain'. As a result, in Burt's view, this combination of scale and information power can be used to manage the distribution channel in either of two ways:

- *By using scale to reinforce existing adversarial trading relationships,* where the emphasis is on price, for example, by forcing down the prices from suppliers; by requiring greater promotional support, but with no guarantee any savings will be passed on to consumers; or by sourcing lower-cost producers, especially for stores' own brands.
- *By using the information to change the traditional relationships* 'so that the unique skills and competencies of the retailer and the manufacturer base can be brought to bear for the mutual benefit of those involved'.

Buzzell and Ortmeyer (1995) said that retailers with long-term perspectives are likely to seek to build long-term 'cooperative partnerships' as opposed to 'adversarial relationships' with their suppliers. Even while doing this, the increasingly powerful retail groups know they now have the capability to impose what may be termed their 'systemic power' over their suppliers, where systemic power is defined as the power that one party has to effect the whole 'system' of the other (Brookes, 1995). Systemic power can also be either coercive or cooperative in nature and in practice it is likely to be a combination of the two. The belief in the strategic importance of systemic power is consistent with the argument that effective supply chain management, and in particular the logistics component to ensure continuity of supply, is essential to success.

To ensure continuous supply, 'programme' buying on a global scale is now the norm for many leading retail groups, a trend which is set to continue (Figure 7.3). To ensure 'transparency' of suppliers' trading terms, retailers expect to probe their suppliers' cost structures and to suggest ways to reduce costs, and then ask that a substantial proportion of the savings be passed on to them. Given the importance of just-in-time delivery, retailers expect to be kept regularly informed and to be involved in all stages of quality assurance. They therefore also expect to impose standards at every stage between, from, for example, when a particular fruit or vegetable produce is planted to when it is placed on the supermarket shelves. They may want direct involvement with their suppliers' R&D activities, and they may ask for exclusive rights to new products when it suits their purpose.

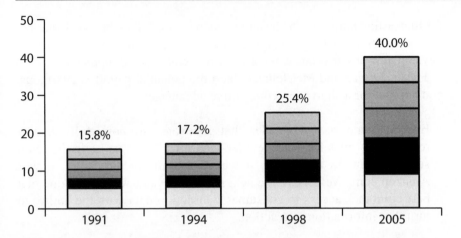

**Figure 7.3** Forecast of European retailer concentration: expected share of the top five food retailers in Europe in 2005

*Source:* M+M Eurodata/IGD Grocery Retailing, 2002

They expect their key suppliers to be current category leaders and builders, and new category seekers and developers, where growth is for the benefit of both parties.

To ensure systemic relationships actually work, retailers 'reach back' into their suppliers' research and development, production and processing, logistics and distribution, merchandising, marketing and servicing expertise, processes and systems, in order to ensure compatibility, compliance and cost control. A key to this integration is the sharing of data and the modelling that may ensue. This provides both partners with 'learning loops' that aid in progressively lowering costs throughout the value system. Those suppliers who can meet their major retailer customers' systemic requirements, by regarding expertise in information technologies as part of their core capabilities, are also likely to achieve preferred-supplier status, similar to the auto industry's Tier 1 suppliers.

In a study of 32 leading retailers, Fisher, Raman and McClelland (2000) said their focus was on offering 'the right product in the right place at the right time for the right price', in other words the traditional 4Ps. To achieve this 'rocket science retailing' they saw four areas as critical: improving forecasting; improving supply-chain speed; improving inventory planning processes; and improving the capture and maintenance of sales data through point-of-sale (POS) systems. However, the real key to leading retailers' success, say Fisher, Raman and McClelland, is the successful collaboration between left-brain technical planners and right-brain intuitive buyers and merchandisers. Whereas the planner typically focuses on historical sales data for forecasting purposes, the buyer and merchandiser look beyond historical data in order to identify changing patterns in consumer demand, and to develop new products and categories in cooperation with suppliers.

Fisher, Raman and McClelland claim the potential payoff is enormous, and not just for a short-term competitive advantage:

> Every decade sees a retailer that innovates so powerfully that it rewrites the rules for other retailers and for all companies in the retail supply chain. In the 1980s, it was Wal-Mart. In the 1990s, it was Amazon.com. We believe the next retail innovator will be the one that best combines access to consumer transaction data with the ability to turn that information into action.

As a result, supplying manufacturers have had to place increased attention on capabilities to do with brand, category, key account and promotional management. And while suppliers are re-developing relationships with major retailers, some are also building closer relationships with their end-consumers. Information technologies are at the forefront of this process as well. For example, some packaged goods companies are setting up home pages and cooperating with particular retailers through their Internet home shopping arrangements, all in order to participate in the increasing 'one-to-one' dialogue and delivery that is taking place. This issue represents the next change that is affecting marketing practice.

## CHANGE 5: INTERACTIVE MEDIA AND MASS CUSTOMIZATION

The issues examined in the previous section highlight a critical strategic issue facing marketers. For the last half century, consumer marketing in particular was practised largely on the basis of masses: mass markets, mass production and mass advertising. This left marketers in a quandary, however: they had little direct contact with their end customers. Most of the one-to-one interactions took place at the retail level, and therefore manufacturers could not tell directly what customers were buying, and why. The customer feedback was basically indirect, and customers were generally treated as 'averages'. The *Economist* (1999b) said that a fundamental change is now underway: 'This is a move away from mass marketing, which starts with a product and finds customers to buy it, towards an information-led, one-to-one marketing, which may ultimately sell each individual a customized product.'

Two drivers of change appear to be, first, the increased fragmentation of broadcast and other mass media, and, second, the digital revolution leading to the convergence of four IT streams: computers, consumer electronics, telecommunications and software. In this digital world, as computers link with televisions, mobile phones, cameras and various other forms of interactive communications devices, information merges with the products and services, as was seen earlier.

The application of information technologies is having a major impact in building individual relationships through electronic interactions. These include:

- new interactive possibilities, from local CD-ROM kiosks to the global Internet
- ever increasing computer processing power at ever reducing costs
- developments in master databases and complex decision support systems
- expanding collaborative networking arrangements with suppliers and other stakeholders in the new value systems.

IT-based interactivity has several crucial characteristics: the ability to address an individual; the ability to gather and remember the response of the individual; and the ability to address the individual once more in a way that takes into account their particular response (Deighton, 1996b). When interactive communications are matched to agile operations and manufacturing, such as in the computer industry (Kraemer, Dedrick and Yamashiro, 2000), one effect is the possibility of *any thing, in any way, at any time, and any where*, as earlier predicted by McKenna (1991).

In the process, firms become two things: one-to-one marketers, whereby information is elicited from each customer with respect to individual needs, preferences and other characteristics; and mass customizers, whereby the customer is provided with personalized goods or services (Pine, Rogers and Dorf, 1999). Rather than continuing to mass produce and mass market for increasingly elusive 'average' consumers, or segments of 'average' consumers, some consumer goods manufacturers are now starting to target individual customers. This involves using their new-found agile research, manufacturing and marketing capabilities to design, develop, build, deliver and service products, services and messages to 'fit' the specific requirements of individual customers. A feature of this agile manufacturing and marketing is that the flexibility moves the centre of value away from the 'hardware' technology (the product and service), and towards the combined software and networking possibilities (Port, 1999), including improved customer acquisition (Hoffman and Novak, 2000) and improved relationship building and loyalty (Hart et al., 1999). Mass customization also calls for a 'transformed company', claimed Pine, Victor and Boynton (1993).

According to a confidential accounting firm's report into financial service providers, and as shown to the authors, changing the fundamentals of relationship management can yield various bottom line results, including:

- A competitive advantage through increased understanding with existing customers.
- Increased revenues from improved targeting and holding on to high-value customers, and higher cross-sell success through better profiling of customer needs and product or service profitability.
- Reduced marketing and support costs through increased one-to-one interactions with high-value customers, more automation of standardized interactions, and better targeting and tracking of customer development, marketing and servicing costs.

Electronic retailing (e-tailing), such as the Amazon bookstore, offers a glimpse of the latest relationship marketing efforts via the intersection of interactive media and mass customization through manufacturing and operations. The research, modelling and individual customer relationship building possibilities of the likes of Amazon.com are limited only by the firm's internal resources, goals and imagination; its capacity to process and use the vast amounts of continuous data available to it; and the amount of time the share market will allow it to start making a financial return.

Whatever the current mixed signals and mixed results, as noted by Port (1999): 'A Copernician revolution of sorts is under way. Executives used to imagine their companies as the centre of a solar system orbited by suppliers and customers. The Internet is changing that – dramatically. Now the customer is becoming the centre of the entire business universe.' The Chair of Chrysler said to *Business Week* that 'For the first time, the customer is going to control the retail system' (Armstrong et al., 1998). And, as Prahalad and Ramaswamy (2000) argue:

Customers are fundamentally changing the dynamics of the marketplace. The market has become a forum in which consumers play an active role in creating and competing for value. The distinguishing feature of this new marketplace is that the consumers become a new source of competence for the corporation.

In the process, companies are finding it necessary to incorporate all six dimensions of relationship marketing.

## INTEGRATING THE FIVE CHANGES

To conclude the section, an example from the car industry is used to illustrate the integration of the five trends. None of the issues listed below are beyond the realm of what is currently possible, particularly from an auto assembly perspective (Alford, Sackett and Nelder, 2000). The example focuses on how a buyer, dealer and manufacturer interact, and illustrates how all six facets of relationship marketing are crucial to the creation of value.

The example starts with a driver wishing to replace his or her vehicle, and the initial stage of need arousal and search effort illustrated here is condensed simply for the sake of brevity. Thus, based on first hearing of a new vehicle via television and magazine advertising, or by a direct mail offer or a telephone solicitation from the dealer or the manufacturer, the customer begins an on-line search service from a home computer and pulls down comparative information on a number of competitive makes. A complete listing of local dealers selling the make that is considered most appropriate is requested, and the nearest dealer is e-mailed for a car to be delivered to the customer's home for a test drive.

Assuming the test drive is satisfactory, the customer visits the dealer to discuss the financial arrangements and the specific requirements and attributes of the vehicle. This negotiating process could also be done electronically. The sales consultant electronically orders the car to suit the customer's requirements, and confirms the exact date and time when the car will be built and delivered to the customer's home. All the parts and components are electronically ordered from the factory's preferred suppliers and arrive just in time for assembly. The car is built and delivered exactly as promised.

When the car is delivered, the customer is issued with a 'smart' card that has the capacity to act as a keyless entry system, thereby triggering the in-car functionality discussed earlier in this chapter. It can also store information both about the car and the driver. At various times the driver may access an electronic forum set up on the Internet by the manufacturer, and from which the driver may request information or assistance. Using this same forum, and with the approval of the customer, at regular interviews he or she may be asked for details of satisfaction and dissatisfaction, including future buying intentions. Car and driver details are 'tracked' and emerging patterns determined and assessed. Potential problems may be pre-empted by either the manufacturer or dealer sending an e-mail message to inform the customer when preventative maintenance work is due. When paying for any repair work, customers may use their main credit card, which has been issued by a bank in conjunction with the automobile manufacturer. Or, they may use the 'smart' card which has a similar arrangement between the bank and manufacturer.

The car company may use global positioning system satellite technology and a hands-free, voice-activated cellular phone, integrated into the car's electronics system, to link the driver and the vehicle with the company's global on-line service centre. For a fixed service fee the driver anywhere anytime can call the service centre staff to obtain real-time and one-to-one services, such as route advice, remote diagnostics and remote door unlocking, as discussed earlier.

At some stage (perhaps after three or four years, at some specific mileage level, or as the car's financing term nears its end), the customer is personally invited by either the dealer or the manufacturer to trade-in the car for a new one. The new vehicle may be better suited to the customer's changed personal, household, lifestyle or driving characteristics (which are identified though the electronic 'tracking' process).

Why should an automobile manufacturer wish to spend the funds needed to install such a system? In a presentation to Australian business and government leaders, Scott McNealy, the Chair and CEO of Sun Microsystems, said that while today's new cars have many microprocessors in them, they are not yet connected to the Internet: 'Would it not have been useful for Ford to have on-line access to every car and to know about their tyre pressures?' (Pamatatau, 2000).

In this example, the customer is impacted at an early stage by traditional media advertising (transaction marketing). Then he/she begins an electronic relationship with the company (e-marketing). Currently, most new car buyers still visit a dealership to negotiate the final contractual details (interaction marketing). Over time they may be targeted by the dealer and/or manufacturer both personally and electronically (thereby maintaining an ongoing interaction, database and e-marketing relationship). This relationship is developed in the context of the relationships that exist between the manufacturer, dealers, and other partners such as suppliers and the financial service organization managing the customer's credit card relationship (network marketing). It is also developed in the context of the collaboration that occurs between the sales, finance and service processes within the dealer organization, and the collaboration between marketing, research and development and other processes within the auto company, where the sharing of customer information is crucial in order for the company to realize its value-creating purposes (internal relationship marketing). Overall, this is but one example of how both transaction and relationship marketing might be practised. Most importantly, to paraphrase Levitt, the auto manufacturer has not moved out of the automobile business and into the transportation business, but out of the automobile business and into the personal transportation solutions business.

The effects of the five changes are summarized in Table 7.1. The table shows that the changes not only have an impact on relationship marketing, but also on marketing practice with a transactional emphasis. An important issue for companies is that if they are to embrace the six facets of relationship marketing, will this require a transformation of their organizational status quo, or will firms be able to achieve this by mainly reinforcing, or perhaps enhancing, their status quo? In fact, what are firms currently doing with respect to these three possibilities? And whichever possibility they choose, what are the issues they might face with respect to the processes of managing change? These issues will be examined more closely in Chapter 9.

**Table 7.1** Key underlying characteristics of changing marketing practices

| Change | Transactional marketing characteristics | Relationship marketing characteristics |
|---|---|---|
| 1. Service aspects of all products | • Emphasis on product or service benefits.<br>• Focus on managing and improving product/service uses and experiences. | • Emphasis on product/service interdependencies.<br>• Emphasis on managing and improving product/service uses, experiences and relationships with supplier. |
| 2. Financial accountability, loyalty and customer value management | • Focus on measures of financial control, in particular.<br>• Focus on internal measures, especially. | • Focus on a balanced set of strategic, operational and organizational measures of performance, advantage and improvement, in particular.<br>• Focus on both internal and external measures. |
| 3. Organizational transformation | • Focus on internal functional specializations and coordination.<br>• Competition is between companies. | • Focus on internal and external networks and 'boundaryless' processes of interdependencies.<br>• Competition is between inter-networks of organizations. |

**Table 7.1**  continued

| Change | Transactional marketing characteristics | Relationship marketing characteristics |
|---|---|---|
| 3. Organizational transformation (continued) | • Organization structure ensures control and coordination.<br>• Customer is the focus of the firm's value creating activities. | • Information sharing facilitates commitment and cooperation.<br>• Customer plays an active role in creating and competing for value. |
| 4. Retailers and systemic relationships | • Mainly adversarial interactions between retailer and suppliers, with power balanced through the equalization of each party's respective scale and scope.<br>• Short-term series of transactions for longer-term competitive advantage. | • Increasing 'systemic' relationship building and sharing of expertise and interdependencies throughout the industry value system, facilitated by pervasive use of information technologies.<br>• Continuous relationship building for long-term mutual advantage. |
| 5. Interactive media and mass customization | • Focus on one-way communication to aggregates of target customers. | • Focus on integration of interactive communications with individual customers and the mass customization possibilities in operations and/or manufacturing. |

# CHAPTER 8

# Pluralism in Marketing Practice

## CHAPTER INTRODUCTION

This chapter discusses in detail the research work conducted by the Contemporary Marketing Practice (CMP) group. This work has a number of distinctive features: the connection that has been built between theory and practice, the wide-ranging nature of the research and the international context in which it has been conducted, and, not least, the quality of the findings that have emerged.

The work of the CMP group has introduced a new realization and understanding of not just the theory but also the practice of marketing. This has opened up many new opportunities for further research and for the continued development of the domain of marketing.

## CHALLENGING THE PARADIGM

At first glance it does seem rather extraordinary that the concept of relationship marketing should have been so widely studied, extensively written about, much discussed, frequently implemented by managers, and yet so little researched. Surprisingly little empirical research, generating field-based findings, has been conducted (Mattsson, 1997). The original CMP work (Brodie et al., 1997) represented a significant step forward in developing a researchable framework to test the tenets of relationship marketing. Earlier chapters considered the background to relationship marketing, so perhaps the notion of marketing by focusing on the relationship and interaction with the customer, and with other stakeholders, is not so surprising after all. Yet the area has generated prodigious interest, not least from the academic perspective.

There are still many issues requiring further insight and clarification before the claim for a paradigm shift can be made. Even the term relationship marketing is open to multiple interpretations, as it has passed through the hands of numerous, if well-intentioned, academic spin-doctors to arrive

at the feet of managers as another buzzword to be used to imply significance, but with no real understanding of meaning (Nevin, 1995). Relationship marketing could mean the use of a database, or a wider application of
IT to manage the customer base, or even a type of sales technique
(Coviello, Brodie and Munro, 1997). It is now more widely accepted and
used at a more strategic, stakeholder level. In terms of transactional
marketing one major stakeholder was identified: the customer who buys
the product. As the field has developed so this has enlarged to incorporate
six (Christopher, Payne and Ballantyne, 1991), ten (Morgan and Hunt,
1994) or even 30 distinct types of relationships (Gummesson, 1999). How
many are enough, and how does this help managers in the course of their
marketing endeavours?

Egan (2000) identifies a number of areas of similar conceptual overload
and lack of clarity that are regarded as almost axiomatic, with only selec-
tive and limited research to justify them. An interesting area concerns the
economic rationale that underlies relationship marketing. This is the
contrast between the cost of acquiring customers as against the benefits of
retaining them. Contingent upon this is the notion of lifetime profitability,
which assumes an ongoing income stream from the retained customer.
While there is some research that demonstrates the value of customer
retention, and the increase in customer lifetime profitability from more
effectively managing the customer over the life cycle (Reichheld, 1996),
there remain considerable difficulties in demonstrating the outcome of
transactional versus relational strategies. Assumptions surrounding the
customer value and lifetime, and the basis for the allocation of sales and
marketing costs, make these variables difficult to calculate. A sales visit
that results in an order may be just another transaction demonstrating the
persuasive skills of a sales professional, or a further demonstration of the
attitudinal commitment of both parties to one another. Or it could be both.

There is research, however, that clearly demonstrates that not all
customers are the same in terms of profitability (Cooper and Kaplan,
1991). There are examples of companies who have developed costing
systems that enable them to estimate – sufficiently accurately for management purposes – the profitability of individual customers and accounts.
However, a greater understanding of this area and the development of suitable managerial techniques would represent a substantial benefit.

Another area that Egan (2000) questions is the response of the customer
targeted with relationship marketing strategies. If we, as a supplier, actively
change the way that we work with a customer, does this mean that the
customer will in turn respond? Do customers actually want a relationship
with us (Brown, 1998)? The terms 'relationship' and 'loyalty' may be used

by the buyer, but it remains very questionable as to whether these are terms that sellers would apply to the exchange they have just experienced. The experience of General Motors discussed in an earlier chapter suggests that customers are hard bargainers: the removal of interest-free credit caused a rapid drop in sales. Such customers seem unlikely candidates to develop a relationship with the seller, since they seem to be doing well enough without one.

Perhaps customers are now so value driven, information rich and conscious of choice that they have no need or desire to make an emotional or psychological commitment to the seller. As an example, the bank of one of the authors, and an Internet company from which he once bought a case of wine, seem to regard their transactions as an opportunity to communicate with him by direct mail, e-mail and even the telephone. Apparently the relationship has developed to such an extent they feel able to address him by his first name.

The proposal that a paradigm shift in the domain of marketing has occurred was challenged in the introduction. This now further proposes that more empirical research is required to develop and substantiate the concepts that are collectively referred to as relationship marketing.

## THE ROLE OF RESEARCH

Yet, despite the lack of research to justify the concepts, arguments, models and frameworks put forward, there is an intuitive feeling that it must be correct to focus on developing relationships with customers rather than developing still more products, in a world already cluttered with me-too lookalikes. However, there is a significant gap between the thinking of great and profound thoughts, and the generation of sustainable competitive advantage by a business.

Schon (1983) puts forward a convincing argument for a dialogue between managers with problems, and academics and researchers with the skills and capabilities to resolve them, arguing that an easy dialogue and interaction between theory and practice leads to development of the field. Yet there are some academics who argue that conducting research with managers is unlikely to lead to significant conceptual and theoretical development. After all, managers don't know what they don't know, so how can new knowledge be generated (Wilkinson, 2002)? It would be wrong, indeed dangerous, to suggest that re-thinking and new perspectives relevant to the field are inappropriate. However, marketing is not like physics. It does not exist in a vacuum as an independent researchable phenomenon: it exists only because people interact in some way with each other to fulfil their needs.

Inherent within the research approach that is used by the CMP group is an ongoing correspondence with managers and practitioners of marketing, while firmly maintaining a strong basis of theory and conceptual development. The CMP group represents a broad church of research traditions; the researchers are not academic and methodological dogmatists, but more problem-driven pragmatists.

Within the field of marketing research, traditions have tended to crystallize between the North American approach, which is positivistic and theory testing, and the European approach, which tends to be more qualitative and inductive, seeking to develop theory as well as to test it (Wensley, 1995). The CMP group are of the view that each research tradition can contribute to understanding, and that the nature of the research question and the insight required are intrinsic to the design of the research methodology (see Figure 8.1).

By using multiple research methods and a variety of approaches to data collection it is possible to develop a wide pool of data that can give greater insight and understanding (Carson and Coviello, 1996).

## THE CONTEMPORARY MARKETING PRACTICE STUDY

This stream of research originated at the University of Auckland in the mid-1990s. Two seminal papers were published in 1997 which initiated interest in the work of what has now become known as the CMP group (Brodie et al., 1997; Coviello, Brodie and Munro, 1997). From New Zealand the research expanded to Canada and subsequently to the USA, South America and many European countries as well as into Asia and Africa. In line with the group's principle of pluralistic research co-workers

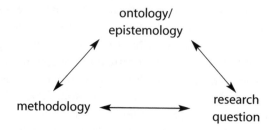

**Figure 8.1** Elements of a research strategy

are encouraged to use the output of the group and the research instruments, consistent with the research protocol to ensure comparability, and to develop these further in line with their own particular areas of interest and research. A considerable database of output, both quantitative and qualitative, is being developed, which will enable longitudinal studies to be conducted. This has been further enhanced by Ph.D. theses building on the original work of the group to expand and develop the concepts and ideas.

The objectives of the CMP group are:

- To profile the contemporary marketing practices of different types of firms competing in different market and sector contexts, in an international forum.
- To develop an understanding of how firms relate to their markets in a manner that integrates both traditional and more modern views of marketing, and incorporates an understanding of both the antecedents and consequences of different practices.

The strength of the original work lies in the review of the literature as the foundation for the development of research tools and researchable propositions. Chapter 2 discussed the three main schools of thought that are generally accepted within the field (Sheth and Parvatiyar, 2000b). But, as Brodie et al. (1997) comment in one of their original papers, 'marketing has resulted in a plethora of conceptual and empirical research, and a number of books discussing the topic'. The literature review analyzed in detail six streams of research, with three objectives in mind (Coviello et al., 1997):

1. Integrate both normative and positive literatures, in an effort to develop a conceptual framework that can be used for future investigation of marketing practice.
2. Synthesize the Scandinavian-based European school of marketing thought with that of the North American school, recognizing that each has developed its own emphases and traditions over time.
3. Focus on issues relevant to the practice of marketing (rather than the theory of marketing).

This represented a successful attempt to draw together the disparate and diffuse bodies of thought in the area and, most importantly, with the aim of taking this into the area of practice. Detailed content analysis enabled two main themes to be identified – relational and managerial – which were then further classified in terms of 12 dimensions (see Chapter 2). These 12 dimensions were iterated against the literature in order to ensure that they were as representative as possible of the streams of thought. Further analysis of the themes and dimensions enabled two marketing perspectives – transactional and relational – to be identified, together with four distinct types of marketing.

It was also apparent that IT was assuming a much more important role within organizations, consistent with the increasingly ubiquitous presence of IT tools. The much wider availability of the Internet to business from the early to mid-1990s gave further prominence to the role of IT, together with considerable speculation as to its value and application for marketing purposes. It was therefore appropriate to assess this against the framework already identified. In the process of this review the original twelve dimensions were distilled down to nine (Coviello et al., 2000), and a further type of marketing was characterized (Coviello, Milley and Marcolin, 2001).

The two perspectives and five types, or practices as they are now known, of marketing resulting from this work (Brodie et al., 1997; Coviello et al., 2001; and Coviello et al., 2002) are:

Transactional:
1. Transaction marketing (TM) – managing the marketing mix to attract and satisfy customers.

Relational:
2. Database marketing (DM) – using technology-based tools to target and retain customers.
3. Interaction marketing (IM) – developing interpersonal relationships between individual customers and sellers.
4. Network marketing (NM) – positioning the firm in a connected set of inter-firm relationships.
5. E-marketing (EM) – the use of interactive technologies to create and mediate dialogues between the firm and identified customers.

This work has helped to provide a valuable link between the theory and practice of marketing (see Figure 8.2). Marketing has stood accused of being an academic discipline attempting to be a business function (Webster, 1992). By building the linkages between theory and practice, this is at least a positive step towards providing managers with a basis on which they may judge their marketing strategy, and also provides a link to further theory development.

In attempting to represent the marketing domain in this way, this highlights several interesting questions. First, as within the perspective of relationship marketing, there can be more than one interpretation and

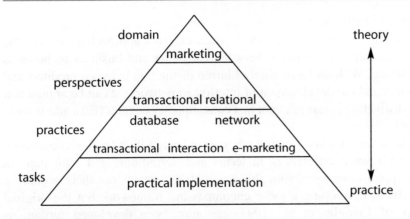

**Figure 8.2** The marketing domain hierarchy

understanding of what constitutes a marketing practice. Coviello et al. (2001) investigated this and identified several alternative interpretations of what constitutes marketing practice (see Table 8.1).

The ubiquity of IT applications, and the wider adoption of the Internet and other interactive media, has stimulated a more recent development of these types of classifications in an attempt to reflect current practice. Each of the schemes has different implications. For example, Day (1998) links the classification scheme he has developed to organizational structure. The classification of Hagel (1999) emphasizes the role of communication not only to and from customers, but also between customers. Iacobucci and

**Table 8.1** Classification schemes of marketing practice (Coviello et al., 2001)

| Recent frameworks | Traditional marketing mix | Augmented marketing mix | Information technology driven | Interpersonal interaction | Inter-firm interaction |
|---|---|---|---|---|---|
| Coviello, Brodie and Munro (1997) | Transaction marketing | Database marketing | | Interaction marketing | Network marketing |
| Day (1998) | Traditional | Augmented | Fully interactive | | Fully interactive |
| Hagel (1999) | Mass marketing | Direct marketing | Collaboration marketing | | Collaboration marketing |
| Iacobucci and Hibberd (1999) | | Business to consumer | Business to consumer | Interpersonal commercial | Business marketing |

Hibberd (1999) maintain the distinction between communications with individual consumers and with businesses. This approach maintains the conventional differentiation between consumer and business to business marketing. With an increasingly blurred distinction between products and services and the development of interlinked networks it can be argued that this distinction is less relevant in a contemporary context (Fern and Brown, 1984).

These various classification schemes indicate a high level of consistency but with some differences in terms and definitions, and with gaps in conceptual coverage. From this it could be argued that there would be benefit in developing a more encompassing framework but the original work of Coviello et al. (1997) has now been developed further, as published in the *Journal of Marketing* (Coviello et al., 2002), and can be considered as an 'established conceptualisation of marketing practice' (Brady, Saren and Tzokas, 2002b).

The CMP framework has been developed into a questionnaire that has been validated and subsequently used extensively around the world. This has provided a rigorous and consistent basis for co-researchers to generate data and compare their findings. Consistent with the pluralistic approach of the group, individual researchers have also included additional sets of questions with the core instrument in order to integrate their own research interests. The research framework has helped to answer a question originally posed by Webster (1992), concerning the relative emphasis given to transactional and relational perspectives under different market conditions. The findings of the CMP research study are discussed below.

## CONTEMPORARY MARKETING PRACTICE FINDINGS

### Early Results

The first results to be published using the CMP questionnaire were from work conducted in New Zealand. While it could be argued that the results generated are not necessarily transferable to other environments, the sample of 134 firms, with supporting case study data, provided a robust set of results. All firms participating in the survey were analyzed against the original four marketing practices that had been identified at this stage. The degree to which they expressed each of these marketing practices was rated as low, medium or high. These results are presented in Table 8.2.

These early results gave substance to the proposition voiced by Webster (1992), and much speculated upon by others, that transactional and relational marketing are not mutually exclusive. As the table demonstrates, most organizations practise most types of marketing.

A feature of the contemporary marketing practice work is the way in which this aspect of multiple practices has been investigated. Further analysis of the statistical data can be conducted in two main ways. First, by considering 'cross tabulations' and investigating the correlation between one practice and another. If a correlation can be demonstrated then this suggests that the practices concerned are conducted concurrently. An alternative technique is to apply a clustering analysis, whereby those practices that demonstrate the lowest level of variation from a mean can be grouped together. This type of analysis indicates the range of most common combinations giving further additional insight. Examples of this are discussed later.

These early results were subjected to analysis by cross tabulation and correlation. This helped to give a much more comprehensive understanding of the relationships between the various marketing practices. These can be expressed diagrammatically, as in Figure 8.3.

Figure 8.3 shows the range of correlations between each of the marketing practices. These are labelled as positive, negative or no association, depending on the 'r' value. The r value refers to the coefficient of correlation and is a figure that expresses the degree to which one variable increases in magnitude when compared to another variable, giving either a positive correlation, in which both increase in tune with each other, or a negative correlation, whereby as one becomes greater the other decreases. From a natural sciences perspective, r values often need to be much higher before an association between variables is claimed. For example, there is a very strong, positive correlation between body height and navel height. Hence, such a strong relationship exists between the two that one is almost a predictor of the other. Such high r values are much less frequently found in the social sciences. This is because there are many other variables that are not as discrete, and cannot be controlled and measured as in the case of

**Table 8.2** Comparison of index values by marketing type

| Index value | Transaction | Database | Interaction | Network |
|---|---|---|---|---|
| Low | 19 | 30 | 13 | 34 |
| Medium | 55 | 49 | 37 | 35 |
| High | 26 | 21 | 50 | 31 |
| Total | 100 | 100 | 100 | 100 |

a scientific experiment. Consequently association can be inferred with lower r values, as indicated in Figure 8.3.

When these results are considered, together with the original data from the questionnaires, it can quite clearly be seen that TM and DM are strongly associated. As are DM and IM, and IM and NM. There is a strong negative association between TM and IM. What this means is that those firms that practise TM are very unlikely to practise IM at the same time. Overall then, where these positive associations are noted this indicates that these types of marketing are practised together.

Good research will answer some questions, but raise others. Interesting issues that arise from this initial research conducted in New Zealand concern whether or not the patterns of marketing practice observed there are similar to, or different from, practices in other countries. Another important point also raised in the marketing literature is whether or not different types of practices are associated with particular types of businesses or industries (Gronroos, 1990b; Easton, 1992; Hakansson and Snehota, 1995; Low, 1996). Could it be that financial services firms usually practise DM, for example? If the contents of one of the author's letterboxes are anything to go by, this would appear to be the case. Do manufacturers of industrial components – part of integrated manufacturing networks – practise IM and NM, or should they put more emphasis on this in future? The former head of purchasing at General Motors, Jose Ignacio Lopez de Arriortua, is said to have been so tough on his suppliers that even today there is a lingering resentment towards

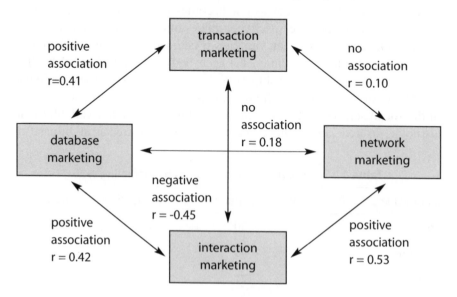

**Figure 8.3** Transactional and relational marketing correlations

the company (Anon., 1998), thus emphasizing the difficulties in the transition from one practice to another. Further research has helped to throw light on some of these questions, and pose further interesting ones.

## INTERNATIONAL COMPARISONS

The original CMP work was conducted in New Zealand, a country that shares many cultural ties with the UK. In addition, both these countries enjoy a developed and growing economy and a stable political situation. As advanced economy nations they share similar cultural dimensions, as described by Hofstede (1980); these include the dimensions of individualism, power distance and uncertainty avoidance. Hence comparisons between these two countries would be of considerable interest as a test of the international validity of the CMP framework.

Data was collected from a total of 132 firms in the year 2000 (48 NZ, 84 UK). Results were subsequently reported in 2001 and later in 2003 (Coviello et al., 2001, 2003). Similar research protocols were applied so that the results would be as comparable as possible. The results from the study are noted in Table 8.3.

Overall, these results demonstrate a broad level of comparability in the types of marketing practice between these two countries. In addition, relatively high levels of IM and NM are demonstrated, particularly at the high index level, which would suggest the level of importance that is now being placed on marketing relationships. Also of interest are the relatively low scores at the high index level for the other marketing practices. So far as EM is concerned, this shows the lowest overall level of practice, despite the business press rhetoric concerning the topic of e-business, and the perception of a dynamic shift as IT is adopted for marketing purposes. This is a subject that will be discussed further elsewhere in this book.

**Table 8.3** New Zealand and the UK: comparison of index values (% of firms)

| Index level | Transaction NZ | UK | Database NZ | UK | E-marketing NZ | UK | Interaction NZ | UK | Network NZ | UK |
|---|---|---|---|---|---|---|---|---|---|---|
| Low | 0 | 9 | 0 | 5 | 13 | 51 | 0 | 12 | 0 | 14 |
| Medium | 81 | 73 | 79 | 84 | 79 | 42 | 48 | 42 | 58 | 55 |
| High | 19 | 18 | 21 | 11 | 8 | 7 | 52 | 46 | 42 | 31 |
| Total | 100 | 100 | 100 | 100 | 100 | 100 | 100 | 100 | 100 | 100 |

There is also an interesting difference between the extent to which EM is practised when comparing New Zealand and the UK. Over half the UK firms report EM at a low level of practice, while the great majority of New Zealand firms practise EM to a greater extent. Compared with New Zealand the UK has a higher proportion of larger firms, which may reflect greater organizational flexibility on the part of small firms in their more rapid response to business trends. Despite these conjectures, however, these results overall would not support the suggestion that there has been a wholesale adoption of e-techniques in the paradigmatic sense of a shift in practice. Jacques Nasser, former CEO of Ford, attempted a transformation to an e-business model that eventually cost him his job. According to an industry analyst: 'Nasser's been the primary architect of a failed transformation of Ford from its core automotive heritage to some expansive consumer-centric organization, which we think employees, suppliers and investors have found to varying degrees to be somewhat incomprehensible' (Isidore, 2001). Many firms still practise TM, but the role of relationships is underlined by both these findings and comments.

Further studies have gone on to demonstrate similar comparability between countries using, for example, data from USA, Canada, Finland and Sweden (Coviello et al., 2002). In terms of cultural comparability, however, using Hofstede's classification as a basis for comparison (Hofstede, 1980), these are all similar. As with other areas of investigation, such as market orientation, the extent to which the results can be generalized may be limited to the fact that these are culturally similar countries, and advanced, developed economies (Kohli, Jaworski and Kumar, 1993).

In order to develop the reach of the framework, various studies have been undertaken of Argentina (Pels, Brodie and Johnston, 2003; Pels and Brodie, 2001; Palmer and Pels, 2003) in comparison with developed economies. Argentina has undergone considerable political and economic change since the early 1990s, when the economy was privatized and deregulated and democratic elections were introduced. There were dramatic economic improvements as the inflation rate fell to virtually zero from a figure of 4924 per cent in 1989. At the same time GNP increased substantially, reaching its highest recorded level of 8.5 per cent in 1994. The economy slowed in the mid to late 1990s as important export markets declined, leading to a loss of confidence in the economy. This culminated in the currency crisis of late 2001/early 2002 when the peg of the peso against the dollar was removed. This initiated a sudden recession. Argentina may therefore be described as a transition economy, with lower levels of affluence and relatively low standards of living for most of the population (Pels and Brodie, 2001). All the studies mentioned here were conducted prior to the most recent and most severe economic problems.

Table 8.4 shows the results of a study comparing New Zealand and the USA with Argentina. Once again, the values are expressed as an index for reasons of clarity. The study encompassed 284 firms (NZ 122; USA 79; Argentina 83).

What these results suggest is that in Argentina there is a somewhat lower use of TM, and less use of DM. By way of compensation there is a higher use of IM. It is proposed that this is due to the greater emphasis that is placed on face-to-face interaction in Argentina, a Latin country where relationships are intrinsic to business practice. The rather lower availability of IT tools may, however, account for the low extent to which DM is practised.

With the development of the Argentine economy there has been an influx of multinational corporations, and further analysis of the data demonstrated the role of such companies in influencing marketing practice. The further analysis conducted also showed that multinationals used a plurality of practices whereas locally owned firms emphasize IM.

The results also lead to speculation about the possibility of further research areas, particularly with respect to the evolution of marketing practice. There is a higher incidence of NM within the US sample, but in New Zealand there still appears to be a focus on TM. The relatively low levels of marketing practice in Argentine firms may suggest a continuum of marketing practice associated with economic and market development.

## PLURALISTIC MARKETING PRACTICE

Earlier in this chapter there was some discussion concerning the correlation between various types of marketing practice, and the way in which data could be interpreted in order to give further insight into the pluralistic nature of practice. The CMP work clearly suggests that firms

**Table 8.4** Marketing practices: international comparison (% of firms)

| Index level | Transaction | | | Database | | | Interaction | | | Network | | |
|---|---|---|---|---|---|---|---|---|---|---|---|---|
| | NZ | US | Arg | NZ | US | Arg | NZ | US | Arg | NZ | US | Arg |
| Low | 28 | 19 | 48 | 29 | 18 | 60 | 7 | 9 | 10 | 28 | 17 | 24 |
| Medium | 53 | 54 | 40 | 50 | 52 | 31 | 35 | 33 | 21 | 37 | 40 | 46 |
| High | 19 | 27 | 12 | 21 | 30 | 9 | 58 | 58 | 69 | 35 | 43 | 30 |
| Total | 100 | 100 | 100 | 100 | 100 | 100 | 100 | 100 | 100 | 100 | 100 | 100 |

do not necessarily or exclusively practise a particular style of market-ing but use a range of different marketing practices. This is explored in more detail.

The earlier work showing the correlation between the different marketing practices (see Figure 8.4) was enlarged upon following the derivation of the fifth marketing practice, EM. The correlations between the five practices of marketing, based on work in both the UK and New Zealand (Coviello et al., 2003), can be seen in Figure 8.4

These results provide confirmation of the earlier work, demonstrating a negative association between TM and IM, and as may be anticipated now, no association between TM and either NM or EM. DM has positive asso-ciations with the other four aspects of marketing. This raises some very interesting and as yet unresolved questions with regard to the role of IT in marketing. It may be that DM is an extension of TM, with the use of rela-tively simple and straightforward IT tools to intensify or extend transac-tional practice to the current or wider customer base. Perhaps DM acts as a bridge or linkage to the more sophisticated use of IT typified by EM. EM is itself associated with IM and NM, again suggesting that EM is practised alongside other relational-type practices.

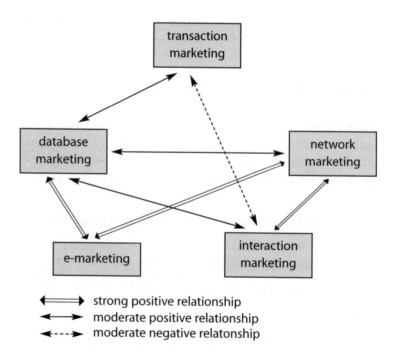

**Figure 8.4** Correlations between five marketing practices

One way in which these suggested relationships between marketing practices can be explored is to use the clustering technique referred to earlier. This is a type of statistical analysis that allows the various practices to be clustered on the basis of statistical similarities and differences between each practice. This was carried out using data from New Zealand and the UK, and builds on the correlation shown in Figure 8.4 discussed above. The results of a clustering analysis are given in Table 8.5.

When conducting the cluster analysis a small number of firms were excluded since their results did not conform to the general pattern. After excluding these outliers, the data from 124 firms was analyzed. The table shows that some practices are implemented concurrently and, based on these characteristics, each cluster has been labelled accordingly. The 'traditional transactional' and 'tradition relational' clusters are clearly distinguished by their scores, where the nearer the figure is to 1 demonstrates that the practice is exhibited to a high degree.

The 'transactional plus' cluster also shows quite clearly the predominance of TM and DM, where DM might be seen as a technological extension of TM. Of note here also is the relatively high score for IM. A subsequent review of the data and of the types of companies included in this cluster shows that a high proportion of them were business-to-business goods/services firms. This issue of the type of firm will be explored in the next

**Table 8.5** New Zealand and the UK: cluster analysis

| Cluster | 1 Traditional transactional | 2 Traditional relational | 3 Transactional plus | 4 Pluralistic |
|---|---|---|---|---|
| Transaction marketing | **.73** | .47 | **.68** | **.65** |
| Database marketing | .44 | .47 | **.67** | **.67** |
| E-marketing | .28 | .37 | .48 | **.63** |
| Interaction marketing | .38 | **.79** | .70 | **.79** |
| Network marketing | .36 | **.72** | .58 | **.84** |

section. Finally, there are a group of companies that practise all types of marketing to a similar extent. Of considerable interest here are the management processes that enable firms such as these to be apparently so diverse in their approach to their customer base.

As has been stated before, both New Zealand and the UK are culturally similar countries. When this type of analysis is repeated by comparing New Zealand, the USA and Argentina some differences emerge (Pels et al., 2003). The analysis discussed here was conducted using the four original marketing practices (see Table 8.6).

**Table 8.6** New Zealand, USA and Argentina: cluster analysis

| NZ and USA | Pluralistic | Relationship and network | Transactional |
|---|---|---|---|
| Transaction marketing | .71 | .60 | .73 |
| Database marketing | .76 | .62 | .64 |
| Interaction marketing | .84 | .77 | .64 |
| Network marketing | .80 | .69 | .57 |

| Argentina | Pluralistic | Relationship and network | Low marketing |
|---|---|---|---|
| Transaction marketing | .68 | .51 | .60 |
| Database marketing | .67 | .46 | .51 |
| Interaction marketing | .80 | .82 | .61 |
| Network marketing | .73 | .71 | .51 |

In conducting this cluster analysis the optimal solution was found by using three groups. As a technique clustering considers differences between groups and also within groups. In this example of the technique, the three groups solution gave the optimal average within group difference (Hair et al., 1998).

Again this analysis demonstrates pluralistic practice both in New Zealand and the USA and also in Argentina. Similarly we can also see what is termed a 'relationship and network' cluster. Interestingly, Argentina demonstrates a slightly higher score for IM, although substantially lower with respect to both DM and TM. The third cluster for New Zealand and the USA could be clearly identified as TM; for Argentina the third cluster was termed as 'low marketing', with this group of firms demonstrating a moderate approach to marketing.

The questionnaire instrument that is used also gathers data concerning the size, ownership and type of firm. This was also considered alongside this analysis. Argentina is a transition economy, but does have industries and firms that compete in a similar way to that seen in developed economies. When comparing the characteristics of the firms represented by the other two groups this showed that the 'relationship and network' cluster for Argentina was largely composed of locally owned, older firms. The 'low marketing' cluster was also locally owned but smaller in size. Using the additional available information a further analysis was conducted including ownership as one of the clustering criteria. This gave a five-cluster solution as optimal. When enhancing this solution with the additional details available concerning the characteristics of the Argentinian sample, considerable insight was gained. Each of these five clusters can be characterized according to a number of criteria, as illustrated in Figure 8.5, to give a series of archetypes of the types of firms and their marketing practices.

The clusters of archetypes have been labelled to reflect the marketing practice revealed by the analysis. The 'relational traditional' cluster has an above-average score for IM, but is below-average with respect to TM and DM. The 'transactional traditional' group has an above-average score for TM but is below-average with respect to the relational practices. The cluster labelled 'relational progressive' has above-average scores for all three relational aspects; DM, IM and NM. The final cluster has above-average scores for all marketing types and is termed 'pluralistic'.

Additional qualitative data has enabled insight to be gained into the marketing practice and attitude towards the market of these various archetypes (Pels and Brodie, 2001). This is a good example of how multiple data sources converge to give greater insight and understanding. One of the

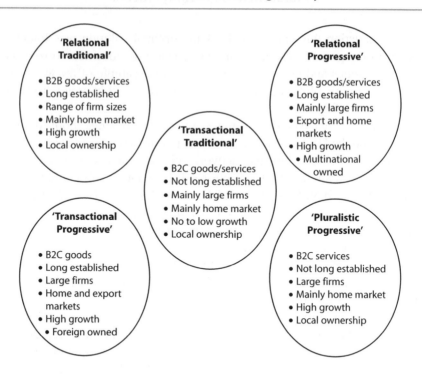

**Figure 8.5** Argentina: marketing practice and firm archetypes

most interesting issues arising from this analysis is the fact that some clusters are oriented to particular sectors, such as business-to-business (B2B) or business-to-consumer (B2C) goods and/or services. This is a further critical insight that has arisen from the CMP work in helping to understand how marketing practices vary by the type of business.

## MARKETING PRACTICE AND BUSINESS SECTOR

It is an axiomatic belief that the conventional 4Ps approach to marketing is primarily associated with consumer markets. The work of the IMP group and others has demonstrated the importance of relationships in business-to-business markets. There has developed a polarized and entrenched belief that transaction marketing relates to consumer markets, and that this framework can be extended and developed by the use of relationship marketing. Concepts of business-to-business marketing have been developed from those of consumer marketing, and further adapted in the light of the growing awareness of the importance of relationships and relationship marketing.

The Argentinian work seen in Figure 8.5 demonstrates that the business sector does relate to or influence marketing practices. However, it should be remembered that Argentina is a transitional economy, where the context of the marketplace is very different, and a proportion of firms do not necessarily successfully practise marketing as a strategic commitment. It is therefore interesting to investigate this further, and review whether these axiomatic beliefs are supported in practice. The opportunity statistically to analyze the data using a clustering technique enables firms that practise particular types of marketing to be grouped together. By then analyzing the data further, in order to understand which particular types of firms are predominant in each category, a further step is taken towards answering this question (Coviello et al., 2003).

Table 8.7, which considers this point with respect to developed economies, shows the analysis conducted with aggregated data from New Zealand and the UK. As was seen earlier, both economies have similar profiles of marketing practice. When the clusters are cross-tabulated against the business sectors in which the responding firms operate, then a clear picture emerges. It can be seen that the belief that consumer-oriented businesses are transactionally oriented and business-to-business companies are relational is supported to some extent.

However, over half the firms in the sample did not conform to this neat categorization. There are as many consumer goods firms engaged in 'pluralistic' practices as there are in 'traditional transactional', and almost as many consumer services firms fall in the 'transactional plus' cluster as in the 'traditional transactional' cluster alone. Firms selling business-to-business goods dominate in the 'transactional plus' cluster, and half the firms in the 'pluralistic' cluster are business-to-business service firms.

As can be seen from this data it is possible to make some broad generalizations as to how particular types of firms practise marketing, but this is by no means a 'one size fits all' solution. It would be inappropriate to rely on this generalization for a particular firm, for which a different type of practice or practices may be just as appropriate. This is supported by further data from a study of 308 firms in the USA, Canada, Finland, Sweden and New Zealand (Coviello et al., 2002).

Table 8.8 shows the results of this study with a three-cluster analysis (transactional, pluralistic, relational) together with the scores within each of those categories for the four original marketing practices. The higher the score, up to a maximum of 1, the greater the extent to which the practice is exhibited. In addition, the profile of firm types within each of those clusters is also shown.

**Table 8.7** Firm types profiled by cluster

| | | Traditional transactional (n=18) | Traditional relational (n=34) | Transactional 'plus' (n=34) | Pluralistic (n=38) |
|---|---|---|---|---|---|
| Consumer goods | % | 44 | 6 | 15 | 21 |
| | No. of firms | 8 | 2 | 5 | 8 |
| Consumer services | % | 39 | 9 | 17 | 8 |
| | No. of firms | 7 | 3 | 6 | 8 |
| B2B goods | % | 6 | 38 | 42 | 21 |
| | No. of firms | 1 | 13 | 14 | 8 |
| B2B service | % | 11 | 47 | 26 | 50 |
| | No. of firms | 2 | 16 | 9 | 19 |

## BUYER AND SELLER INTERACTION

As the previous discussion suggests, sellers may approach a particular customer or market with a transactional or relational intent. There may be varying degrees of commitment to an ongoing relationship, and this could vary depending on circumstances and context. Similarly buyers may have a range of intentions and motivations. Many discussions about relationship marketing take place in the absence of the perspective of the buyer. Without reciprocity a relationship can hardly be said to exist, even if a transaction has taken place and intent exists only on behalf of one or other party.

Also apparent from the discussion so far is that firms rarely adopt one particular marketing practice, but a range of practices. This will result in a range of alternatives available to the market, and hence suppliers should be able to engage successfully with different types of customers and their needs. This argues against the idea of a continuum of relationships with transactions at one pole and relationships at the other (Gronroos, 1991), with consumer goods firms practising transactional marketing based around the manipulation of the marketing mix, and business-to-business firms adopting a relational style. The research presented so far suggests that most firms adopt a range of marketing practices, and therefore deal with a range of different needs in the marketplace.

As the CMP research has demonstrated, there is overlap and diffusion between marketing practices and types of customers, in which case static

**Table 8.8** International comparison: marketing practice by business sector

| Cluster | TM score | DM score | IM score | NM score | Consumer goods | Consumer services | B2B goods | B2B services |
|---|---|---|---|---|---|---|---|---|
| Transactional 103 firms | **.81** | .63 | .48 | 39 | 41 | 35 | 27 | |
| Pluralistic (107 firms) | **.85** | **.78** | **.82** | **.75** | 50 | 30 | 35 | 32 |
| Relational (98 firms) | .65 | .60 | **.79** | **.71** | 11 | 29 | 30 | 41 |
| Average index score (308 firms) | .79 | .68 | .75 | .64 | 100 | 100 | 100 | 100 |

Source: after Coviello et al., 2002

models of business and consumer buyer behaviour are less relevant. What is required is a dynamic model that more adequately represents what appears to be happening in the marketplace. This should take into account the fact that companies practise a range of different types of marketing, in order to address a range of customers. They do this in an environment which is increasingly challenging and competitive and they, and their customers, must respond to environmental and market signals in order to maintain and develop their position.

Such a model (see Figure 8.6) is proposed by Pels et al. (2000). This has a number of features that help to describe the complexity of buyer and seller interactions. First, of course, it considers the dyad – the two parties to the relationship. This is enhanced by incorporating the lessons learnt from the CMP research programme in particular, understanding that different types of offering are made concurrently by the seller, and that these have to match the buyer's needs for a transaction to result or for a relationship to be sustained. The model also takes into account the environment in which the interaction takes place, and the effect that this may have on each party's perceptions.

In the marketplace the buyer and seller 'meet', with the conjunction of the seller's offer proposition and its match with the buyer's need structure.

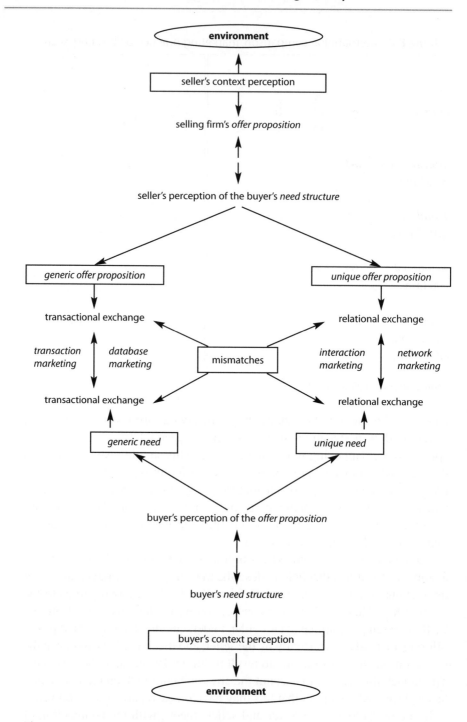

**Figure 8.6** The buyer–seller interaction model

The offer proposition represents not just the product but the enhancement of that product with service and customization features. It could now be argued that there is increasingly less distinction between the physical tangible product and the intangible service. One melds with the other in order to meet the buyer's needs and to compete successfully. The seller's perception of the buyer's needs may well differ from those of the buyers themselves. A buyer will interpret the seller's offer proposition against their own understanding of that offer and competitors' offers and their specific needs and requirements. Understandably, a gap may arise between the seller's offer proposition and the buyer's perception of that proposition.

The role of marketing is to bridge the gap between buyers and sellers, and hence the practices identified by the CMP group can be incorporated into this model. This view of the buyer/seller interaction has a number of advantages. First, it incorporates the views and perceptions of both buyers and sellers, and reflects the environment in which they operate. Depending on the effectiveness of the conjunction between buyer and seller, then a satisfactory exchange – either transactional or relational – may take place.

Although this model is theoretical, it more comprehensively addresses the range of variables that can affect the outcome of a buyer/seller interaction. From a practical perspective, managers need to appreciate that adopting a 'relationship marketing' approach may not be an answer to their problem, if it does not in turn solve a problem for their customer. Managers may need to manage a range of different marketing practices actively against their understanding of customer needs, and in addition realize that these may change and adapt as the environment and circumstances change. The uninformed adoption of a particular marketing practice is ill-advised and potentially detrimental. It could add cost and complexity to a business, over-service or even alienate current customers, and yet not appeal to a wider market.

## MANAGERIAL IMPLICATIONS

From these results it is now apparent that neither transactional nor relational marketing offers a complete explanation of marketing in practice. While certain types of firms may adopt particular marketing practices, it is still not clear as to what the contexts and circumstances are in which particular types of practice are appropriate. Nor has relational marketing overtaken and been substituted for transactional marketing. Companies and their managers need to be aware of – and actively to consider – how all aspects of marketing can contribute to their business. Transactional marketing, with its emphasis on the marketing mix, remains an important component of the suite of marketing tools.

No less important is the ability to build and manage relationships. This can be at the personal level through one-on-one relationships, with all the implications for organizational structure and personal qualities of staff that this implies. However, relationships at the organizational level, as represented by NM, are also likely to be of increasing importance in the future as retailers push back into supply chains and manufacturers, brand owners and other integrators organize and manage their own constellation of relationships. The implication that is apparent here is that, if the position of a firm within a network is not actively managed, abdicating this responsibility may well lead to loss of competitive advantage as differentiation reduces, and the drift to commodity status increases.

In the Introduction a sixth practice was mentioned – that of internal relationship marketing. While not formally identified as a marketing practice, its importance and significance in terms of the practical implementation of marketing has been noted (Millier and Palmer, 2000). As is discussed shortly, while IT can in some senses be seen as supporting or underpinning various marketing practices, internal relationship marketing could be seen as integral to them all, as illustrated in Figure I.2 in the Introduction. In Chapter 9 the role of internal relationship marketing is also discussed, and emphasis is placed on the important and essential part it plays in implementation.

The role of IT in supporting marketing is a complex one, and is discussed elsewhere in this book. With respect to the marketing practice, it would appear that DM and EM are in a sense supplementary to the more mainstream marketing practices. The technology tools available allow an extension and development of marketing practice, but it is unlikely that these marketing practices will stand alone, unaccompanied by other styles of marketing within a cluster. It may be that IT has a supporting or underpinning role to TM, IM and NM (see Figure 8.7).

This interpretation of DM as essentially a transactional activity automated by IT, supported by the findings to date, suggests that it should actually be regarded as a transactional perspective of marketing (Pels et al., 2000). There is ample evidence from the business world that DM, evidenced by direct mail and other forms of one-way communication, is essentially designed to gain customers and capture new business rather than to maintain a relationship. The presence of a name and address on a database, indicating that the customer has previously purchased, has no more influence on the type of communication than that. A financial services company could just as easily send a customer, who has already

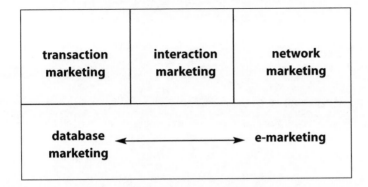

**Figure 8.7** Marketing practice and the underpinning role of IT

purchased a savings product, information about a loan. In such cases there is little intent to develop and enhance a relationship, but simply to lever the asset of the database in a 'transactional plus' sense.

For firms that practise a specific style of marketing, this would suggest that there is an opportunity to develop and expand their position in the marketplace by exploring alternative marketing practices. In expanding their suite of capabilities this also implies that they expand not just the customer base, but the types of customers with which they interact. There will be an increasing requirement for firms to offer a more comprehensive range of marketing solutions by developing a more comprehensive marketing approach. Concepts such as B2B, B2C and the marketing mix are still relevant but insufficient. These concepts were at one time building blocks to understanding, but are now barriers to progress as we enlarge and enrich our understanding of contemporary marketing practice.

## CHAPTER 9

# The Future of Marketing

## OBJECTIVES

As we have seen throughout this book, the extent to which information technologies are reshaping marketing practices has become the subject of some debate. What is perhaps most challenging for many marketers is that they are accommodating the impacts of IT developments at the same time as they grapple with the processes of adopting a more relational approach to their marketing practices. These two issues are not mutually exclusive. As Gummesson (2002) says, 'IT has a lot in common with RM', adding, 'Just like in RM, the heart of IT is relationships, networks and interaction.' In an examination of the literature on the impacts of information technologies on marketing, Coviello, Milley and Marcolin (2002) note that the Internet creates new opportunities for firms to engage in 'IT-enabled interactivity', that is, 'the creation of electronic dialogue with customers to allow for not only personalization but customization, and as such, enhanced customer relationships' (Deighton, 1996a).

How organizations – and marketers in particular – are responding to the possibility of IT-induced change is the subject of this final chapter. In this chapter, we proceed first by revisiting the 'profound impact that information technology (IT) is having on organizations' (Morton, 1991), and the possibility of a resulting 'underlying transformation' in organizations (Child and McGrath, 2001). Second, we examine the stream of study to do with the possible assimilation of IT-enabled interactivity, particularly the Internet, into these changes in marketing practice. This is important, for while Gummesson (2002) comments that 'the Internet is an electronic network of relationships', there is also a view that 'marketers are currently struggling to embrace IT' (Brady, Saren and Tzokas, 2002b). This raises a third issue, that of internal relationship marketing for, as Gummesson (2002) also notes: 'IT is a secondary enabler; the real enabler is the human being.' Fourth, we present empirical data from the CMP work to illustrate the extent to which firms are 'embracing' IT. In particular, we extend the work of Orlikowski (2000), by examining the perceptions of mid-level managers as to whether or not IT in marketing is reinforcing, enhancing or transforming their organizational status quo. We conclude by examining some management of change issues, in order to answer the question: 'How does one get from here to there?'.

## IT AND PREDICTIONS OF ORGANIZATIONAL TRANSFORMATION

Rockart (1988) and Cecil and Hall (1988) predicted that IT would become inextricably intertwined with business, moving from the back end of the business system to the front end (that is, from accounting to production to selling and marketing to servicing). They foresaw that IT would help link companies and their suppliers, distributors, resellers and customers into what might be termed 'seamless' networks of relationships and interactions throughout an industry's entire value system. In introducing the MIT study into the impacts of IT on the corporation decade ago, Morton (1991) listed six major ways that the nature of work was changing:

1. *Fundamental changes:* IT is enabling fundamental changes in the way work is done, in terms of production work (for example, robotics in factories, CAD/CAM tools for designers); coordinative work (for example, shared databases, JIT supply systems) and management work (for example, improved monitoring and control systems).
2. *Integrating functions:* IT is enabling the integration of business functions at all levels within and between organizations, such as within existing value systems; between existing value systems; and in the creation of new forms of electronic marketplaces or 'marketspaces'.
3. *Shifting competitive climate:* IT is causing shifts in the competitive climate in many industries, thereby increasing the degree of interrelatedness between companies, such as parts suppliers linked electronically with OEMs (original equipment manufacturers) for real-time design and manufacturing purposes.
4. *Presenting new opportunities:* IT presents new strategic opportunities for organizations that are reassessing their missions and operations, in terms of the extent to which firms 'automate' (for example, banks replacing outlets with ATMs); 'informate' (for example, as new forms of information become valued by-products of tasks or offerings); or 'transform' (for example, where entirely new forms of offerings are created, such as through the merging of IT).

5.  *Changing structures:* successful applications of IT will require changes in management and organizational structure, in that IT becomes an enabler of the re-creation (redefinition) of existing organizations (for example, the 'virtual' organization).
6.  *Challenging management of transformation:* a major challenge for management in the 1990s will be to lead their organizations through the transformation necessary to prosper in the globally competitive environment, depending on the goals of the change, the degree of change that is undertaken and the economic payoffs that are expected and realized as a result of the change.

## THE INTERNET, IT-ENABLED INTERACTIVITY AND ORGANIZATIONAL TRANSFORMATION

What Morton (1991) and others did not foresee was the coming of the Internet, which in essence is but a more recent stage in the development of IT-enabled interactivity, as we have seen over several chapters. Morton had also predicted that a challenge for managers in the 1990s would be to lead their organizations through the IT-enabled transformation process. This would depend on both the degree of change that each company would deem to be necessary, and the expected payoffs. While there may be agreement with the argument that as new IT developments evolve, 'basic assumptions about corporate organization will be overturned' (Hagel and Singer, 1999), there are also uncertainties about the full extent of IT's impacts (Evans and Wurster, 1997). For example, as firms shift from a physical to an information-intensive economy, the 'structural implications are not yet clear' (Child and McGrath, 2001). As Malone and Laubacher (1998) put it, 'what is lagging behind technology is our imagination'.

Given Morton's (1991) challenge to managers to lead organizations through IT-induced transformation processes, and the uncertainties over the impacts of IT on organizations overall, we now turn to the possible impacts of IT-enabled interactivity on marketing. As McKenna (1991) posits: 'Marketing evolves as technology evolves.'

Tedlow (1990) suggested that marketing up until then had evolved through three stages: from fragmentation to mass marketing to segmentation marketing. We saw this in Chapter 3, when we examined how General Motors grew to be one of the world's great marketing corporations, based on its early understanding of segmenting its five car divisions. We might term this a 'mass-class' strategy, overtaking Ford's 'mass' strategy, and constituting an auto industry inflection point. It occurred in the late 1920s and, even with the growth of increasingly sophisticated marketing research, targeting and positioning approaches, and the rise of mass communications through television, marketers in the early 1990s still had little direct contact with their end-customers and few opportunities for customization.

Technological developments, especially the Internet, have the potential to change that, with the *Economist* (1999b) considering IT-enabled interactivity to be a fundamental shift: 'This is a move away from mass marketing, which starts with a product and finds customers to buy it, towards an information-led, one-to-one marketing, which may ultimately sell each individual a customized product'. The empowerment of supply chains by means of the Internet enables businesses to respond in real time to customer requirements, as exemplified by the Dell business model. The shift is already happening, as we move from differentiation to customization and product push to market pull, synchronized through the network by substituting inventory and time with information, while simultaneously providing higher levels of service at lower cost.

As we saw in Chapter 6, three aspects make the Internet distinct: it is pervasive; it is interactive in a variety of formats; and it is a new medium, with characteristics different from the physical world (Ward and Peppard, 2002). Accordingly, early proponents of the Internet believed that the added value to customers of shopping electronically, and engaging in IT-enabled dialogue, was bound into the combination of products and services that were being offered simultaneously (Deighton, 1996a; Taher, Leigh and French, 1996), and therefore bypassed the limitations of physical space and time (Ranchhod, Gurau and Hackney, 2000). As a result, says Quinn (2001), the Internet has 'changed the experience of the customer'. Thus, marketers are increasingly concerned about issues such as the extent to which enhanced Web interactivity design is 'an important driver of enhanced on-line relationships' (Merrilees, 2002).

With respect to relationship marketing, Gummesson (2002) explains that: 'IT would not be given a prominent place in RM if it were only a matter of technology and faster data processing. The interactive role of the customer, as well as customer power, grows.' Prahalad and Ramaswamy (2000) agree, saying that dialogue via the Internet is becoming 'a dialogue of equals. Companies no longer have a monopoly on – or even an advantage in – information access.'

The Internet is also changing the 'experience' of those who market goods and services. For example, by using technologies such as interactive communications, electronic networks and sophisticated software, firms are looking to find new ways to build closer relationships with their customers and with their employees, suppliers and other players in what Ward and Peppard (2002) say is the 'information-defined transaction space'. However, as Gummesson (2002) argues, 'IT is a secondary enabler; the real enabler is the human being.'

## DIFFERING VIEWS ON THE EXTENT OF IT IMPACTS ON MARKETING PRACTICES

We also saw in Chapter 6 that there are several differing views on the impact of the Internet on marketing: it changes everything; it is a tool; it is a new channel; it offers a balance of opportunities. (Coviello, Milley and Marcolin, 2001). To which we added a fifth: it is 'one of the great pieces of infrastructural constructions in history' (Hall, 1998).

In providing an overview of the Internet, Cairncross (2000) was of the view that:

It is not simply a new distribution channel, or a new way to communicate. It is many other things: a marketplace, an information system, a tool for manufacturing goods and services. It makes a difference to a whole range of things that managers do every day, from locating a new supplier to coordinating a project to collecting and managing customer data. Each of these, in turn, affects corporate life in many different ways. The changes that the Internet brings are simply more pervasive and varied than anything that has gone before.... At the root of the change is a dramatic fall in the cost of handling and transmitting information.

Another feature is that more data can be gathered and utilized far more readily than in the traditional commercial environment. As the *Economist* (2000c) noted, now:

Everything can be recorded: not just every transaction, but which web pages a customer visits, how long he spends there and what banner ad he clicks on'. What is termed 'tacit' knowledge (Wind and Mahajan, 2000) about customers is now more accessible owing to advances in IT, for example, specific customers' shopping and information search patterns, interests and activities, payment transactions and chatroom discussion comments are all available from on-line-based research and data-mining techniques. This can produce a formidable array of data that makes possible one-to-one marketing – directing sales pitches at particular individuals – and 'mass customisation' – changing product specifications, for instance for jeans or computers, to match individual orders to the individual customer's preferences.

Companies are thus beginning to learn that the Web can be used at a number of levels. For example, from a marketing perspective it can be used as another transactional channel to the market (I offer you something – you buy), and from a research perspective it can also be thought of as another transactional channel to the market (I ask you a question – you respond). However, the Internet offers parties the opportunity to move the interaction to a higher plane. (We converse. We learn. We exchange. We collaborate. We change.)

The possibility of a transformation requires active compliance from the customers and possible shifts in regulatory authorities' attitudes toward the collection and use of confidential information. It may also require a major shift in how organizations manage their internal interaction processes to build and maintain external relationships with customers.

Given these differing views, it is perhaps not surprising that Day (1996) warns: 'Does interactivity represent the greatest marketing opportunity of all time or 101 ways to lose money?', while Jap and Mohr (2002) caution: 'establishing successful B2B on-line strategies can be tough and complicated'.

## THE INTERNET AND B2B RELATIONSHIPS

The interactivity potential of the Internet is seen as particularly well-suited for building business-to-business (B2B) relationships (Bauer, Grether and Leach, 2002; Dowling, 2002). Jap and Mohr (2002) say that IT can help provide value-added services and improve relationship building through the technologies' capabilities for improving processes such as reaching customers, providing customer service and information sharing. The view of Sawhney and Kaplan (2000) is that in a B2B context, where the focus may be on cost savings, the Internet can also help improve the efficiency and effectiveness of operations and processes, such as 'just-in-time' access to data.

That the impact of the Internet is most felt in B2B conditions is perhaps not surprising. In summing up a major review of the Internet after the bubble burst, the *Economist* (2001c) said:

The spectacular bursting of the Internet bubble has led some to question the very importance of the net. Eighteen months ago, it was said that this was the greatest change since the Industrial Revolution two centuries ago, and thus that it would have a greater effect on productivity and management than did electricity and the telephone in the first quarter of the 20th century. Executives queued up to attend e-business conferences in order to learn how to bring the magic of the web to their companies, and companies vied to produce the best soundbites. 'E-business or out of business' was one of the favourites.

The *Economist* (2001c) cautioned that, while the early hype of the Internet was greatly exaggerated, so too has been the later disparagements, for: 'Where e-business has had a genuine and sometimes powerful effect in the transformation of established companies, even as the headlines blared about the bust of first B2C and then B2B firms, these older giants have been quietly taking to new technology and the Internet with a new purpose.'

Coltman et al. (2001) say there are a number of reasons for established firms to be less interested currently in selling on-line to consumers than in using the Internet to interact with their suppliers and their large buyers, for example:

- With their available computers, networks and bandwidth, larger companies are already better equipped to communicate electronically.
- Already using existing electronic forms of interactions, such as fax and EDI, means it is relatively easy for firms to then transfer to the Internet.
- Applications such as supply chain management mean both greater efficiencies and reduced costs.
- The savings from on-line procurement impact directly on bottom-line results.
- The Internet allows for both closer relationships and new forms of relationships with business partners, such as through shared databases or remote diagnostic and servicing facilities.

More recently, both interest and investment in the Internet by companies has continued, though at a slower level, and with more realistic expectations. As Mullaney (2003) notes:

It's now more apparent the Internet is connecting farflung people and businesses more tightly than ever. It is helping companies slash costs. It is speeding the pace of innovation and jacking up productivity. And even some of those harebrained business models are working.... In the eight years since the Web went commercial, it already has shaken up many industries. Music fans sharing 35 billion song files annually are battering the recording industry. Predation by dot-coms such as Expedia Inc. – now the top leisure-travel agency, on-line or off – helped shutter 13 per cent of traditional travel-agency locations last year. Powerhouse Dell Computer Corp. has muscled its way to industry dominance by building its sales and manufacturing around the Internet. The choice facing Dell's rivals, from Gateway Inc. to Hewlett-Packard Co., is simple: adopt many of Dell's net-efficient methods or exit the business.'

In other words, as shown above by Mullaney (2003), and as we will examine later in the chapter, IT-enabled interactivity is now being adopted at all the three levels proposed by Orlikowski (2000):

- to reinforce the status quo (for example, by slashing costs)
- to enhance the status quo (for example, by speeding the pace of innovation)
- transforming the status quo (for example, the harebrained business models).

However, as Mullaney also says, given the external tensions such as the Gulf War and acts of terrorism, and the continuing economic uncertainties, a feature of today's business investments in IT is the degree of selectivity:

> For the next year, don't expect to see many of the big, brassy e-business schemes of old. These have been flushed away, along with the other excesses of the dot-com boom. Instead, companies have spent the last three years figuring out what really works and what delivers a return – quickly. Now, they're breaking up e-business tasks into bite-size pieces.

Said one Silicon Valley venture capitalist to *Business Week*: 'Runaway tech projects don't work. You need the revolution by 1000 small cuts, not one big dramatic change' (Mullaney, 2003). So perhaps Malone and Laubacher's earlier argument that 'what is lagging behind technology is our imagination' has become, 'what is moving ahead of technology is our pragmatism'.

## IT-ENABLED INTERACTIVITY AND CRM

An example of this new-found pragmatism is the introduction of customer relationship management (CRM). CRM is premised on the notion that the customer should be placed at the centre of business management, and to succeed and profit firms need to learn from, and proactively respond to, what their customers require.

According to Dowling (2002), CRM has its origins in two unrelated places. One place was the USA and, in Dowling's view, it is largely driven by IT: 'Under the direction of marketers, information technology and statistical algorithms were developed to increase the efficiency and effectiveness of selling what a company makes. CRM systems such as call centres, websites, customer service and support teams, and loyalty programs are used to manage the relationship with customers.' Flores and Briggs (2001) agree: 'The most critical feature of any CRM solution is the ability to transform customer data, collected from a wide variety of sources, into the type of detailed customer information around which a company can organize its enterprise and build its customer relationships.'

The other place was in business-to-business marketing in Scandinavia and Northern Europe, with a strong advocacy from the IMP (Industrial Marketing and Purchasing) Group which 'has been instrumental in developing our understanding about the nature and effects of building long-term, trust-based relationships with customers.... They may be based as much on the structural ties between companies as they are on personal relationships among managers' (Dowling, 2002). Under these circumstances, IT is largely used to support, rather than drive, a company's relationship building efforts.

Dowling (2002) considers that CRM 'is a seductive marketing strategy'. Increasingly however, there are a number of serious questions being raised about CRM. First, Dowling queries whether many customers actually want a relationship with most products or services they buy. Second, Dowling and Uncles (1997) and Reinartz and Kumar (2002) provide evidence that undermines many of the key assumptions underpinning the reasons for investing in loyalty programmes. These include the assumptions, for example, that the costs of serving loyal customers are less, that loyal customers are less price sensitive, and that loyal customers spend more with the company. Third, James (2002) cites evidence that shows, despite the market currently growing at some 30 per cent a year, that most CRM projects will be viewed as failures, the main reason being that 'the highly paid professionals who are supposed to use CRM in their day-to-day work aren't using it'. James further argues that salespeople in particular are reluctant to enter all the details they have on their customers and contacts into a database that will be assessed and used by others: 'They wanted to know where the value was for them as salespeople.'

In other words, while many companies may be investing large sums of money in IT to build better relationships with their most valued customers, their efforts may be thwarted by their failure, first, to build better internal relationships and support and, second, to manage successfully the change processes for making the programmes work. We can examine each of these two issues in turn.

## INTERNAL RELATIONSHIP MARKETING

As firms recognize that employees are increasingly a core competency of the firm, and therefore part of the differentiation processes of adding value, so too the importance of internal marketing is receiving more attention. While much of the work on internal marketing has centred on issues to do with improving service delivery to customers, the concept of internal marketing is still relatively unexplored. For example, Clark (2000) recommends that more empirical work be done to gain a better understanding of the dimensions and workings of the internal marketing model first proposed by Varey (1985).

Gummesson (2002) agrees, and argues that, while creating a network of relationships both inside and outside the firm constitutes a firm's core marketing activities, as yet 'there is no marketing theory treating the internal market mechanisms'. This is despite the fact that, in his explanation of 30 relationships of marketing (the 30Rs), he identifies six possible internal 'nano relationships'.

If there is no marketing theory 'treating the internal market mechanisms', one reason may be that it is not prevalent, even in what were considered the leading marketing-oriented corporations. Gummesson (2002) cites Lee Iacocca's first impressions when he took over the ailing Chrysler Corporation some two decades ago (Iacocca, 1984):

> Nobody at Chrysler seemed to understand that interaction among different functions in a company is absolutely critical. People in engineering and manufacturing almost have to be sleeping together. These guys were not even flirting.... The manufacturing guys would build cars without even checking with the sales guys. They just built them, stuck them in a yard, and then hoped that somebody would take them out of there. We ended up with a huge inventory and a financial nightmare.

Has much changed? When Lou Gerstner took over as chairman and CEO of IBM in 1993 he found a very similar situation. However, he also quickly understood that a company like IBM needed a high degree of internal coordination because it comprised a four-way matrix: geography, product, customer, and solutions. What he found inside the matrix (Gerstner, 2002) was:

> a culture of 'no' – a multiphased conflict in which units competed with one another, hid things from one another, and wanted to control access to their territory from other IBMers – the foot soldiers were IBM staff people. Instead of facilitating coordination, they manned the barricades and protected the borders.... For example, huge staffs spent countless hours debating and managing transfer pricing terms between IBM units instead of facilitating a seamless transfer of products to customers.... Research-and-development units would hide projects they were working on, so other parts of the company would not learn of them and try to take advantage of their knowledge.

Early on Gerstner agreed with some key executives that IBM's future had to be based on providing a kind of service that meant it 'would literally take over and act on behalf of the customers in all aspects of information technology – from building systems to defining architectures to actually managing the computers and running them for the customers'. The problem was, 'despite the powerful logic – that this services-led model was IBM's unique competitive advantage – the culture of IBM would fight it'.

The reason was that, traditionally, services had been treated as an adjunct to the main product business: 'IBM's services were completely tied to products – more specifically, products bearing IBM logos.' However, Gerstner realized that if services were truly to address customers' needs they had to have the flexibility to recommend solutions from competitors. Moving to this approach was not easy:

> Throughout those critical early days, it seemed there was a crisis a week between services and some other IBM unit. Many of our brand executives or sales leaders went ballistic every time the services unit proposed a product solution that incorporated a competitor's product. On more than one occasion I found one of these people in my office, railing against the renegades from services. My answer was always the same: 'You need to invest the resources necessary to work with the services team to ensure they understand the competitive advantages of your products. View them as a distribution channel for your products. Your competitors do!'

How successful was Gerstner in instilling a greater sense of internal relationship marketing, and in moving IBM toward a solutions-providing company? As we saw in Chapter 6, a major factor behind Hewlett-Packard's 2001 acquisition of Compaq was its perceived need to create a solutions company of a scale that would enable it compete against the resurgent IBM. In 1992, the year before Gerstner joined IBM, services accounted for 23 per cent of the company's total revenues of US$64.5 billion. In 2001, the final full year before he left, services accounted for 41 per cent of IBM's total revenues of approximately US$86 billion. Much of this growth was due to Gerstner's efforts to create an integrated company, where internal relationship marketing played a vital part, even though he never used the phrase in his book.

Clark (2000) notes that there are two aspects concerned with internal marketing. First, staff need to work together across functional boundaries to ensure the company's purpose, strategy and objectives are served. Second, every employee has a dual role to do with being both an internal supplier and an internal customer, and therefore the delivery of internal customer service is essential if what Heskett et al. (1994) term the 'service –profit chain' is to work: 'Value is created by satisfied, loyal and productive employees. Employee satisfaction, in turn results primarily from high-quality support services and policies that enable employees to deliver results to customers'. Increasingly, some of these 'high-quality support services' are based on information technologies.

## IT AND INTERNAL RELATIONSHIP MARKETING

Bitner, Brown and Meuter (2000) argue that increasingly information technologies are influencing how service encounters, in particular, can be both changed and improved through the use of technology. For example, technology provides a way for information about a customer to be stored and accessed readily by a service employee. This therefore enhances the value of an interaction between the service employee and a customer, in that the employee has a better understanding of a customer's past dealings with the organization, and may be better equipped to provide more flexible, customized service and recover from service failures (Tax and Brown, 1998). At the other extreme, technology may replace employees altogether, as is the case with, say, ATM machines or self-scanning devices in supermarkets. According to Bitner et al. (2000), however, there are potential pitfalls:

Infusing technology into an existing operation requires extensive adaptation on the part of employees, customers, and the company as a whole.

The financial benefits to the firm are hard to quantify, making the original investment hard to justify. For employees, recruitment and extensive training must emphasize the importance of the new role of technology. Many employees may feel threatened by the technology and fear for the loss of their jobs. Because of this, the technology may be incorporated only reluctantly into the service encounter by employees.

What Bitner et al. did not mention here was that senior managers may also feel threatened by technology, and this can affect the infusion of technologies into organizations, as we will see shortly.

## MANAGING CHANGE PROCESSES

We can consider the organizational implications of new IT initiatives by drawing upon management of change theories (Broadbent and Weill, 1999; Heracleous and Barrett, 2001). Porter and Millar (1985) warned that the issue was not whether or not IT would have a significant impact on organizations, but

> rather the question is when and how this impact would strike. Companies that anticipate the power of information technology will be in control of events. Companies that do not respond will be forced to accept changes that others initiate and will find themselves at a competitive disadvantage.

A few years later, Morton (1991) was warning: 'Today's senior executives just aren't comfortable with the new technologies. They feel threatened and therefore do not use them to their full potential.'

Whether this attitude prevails today is a useful starting point when considering management of change processes. For example, the Shaw and Stone (1988) framework for the stages of an IT development, as adapted by Palmer and Brookes (2002), is given in Table 9.1. This model shows that the first phase is primarily used for direct mail, and as an initiating step to gaining experience in the application of IT for marketing purposes. Although the framework was originally developed before the introduction of the Internet and associated opportunities for e-marketing, this framework stands comparison with the positioning of database marketing in Phase 1 and CRM in Phase 4. It also suggests that the progression of the innovation is consistent with the earlier organization transformation arguments.

The introduction of any innovation is inherently risky, particularly with technology-based tools (Christensen, 1997). Day (1999a) argues that

**Table 9.1** Marketing and IT: development phases

|                  | Phase 1        | Phase 2              | Phase 3                              | Phase 4                              |
| ---------------- | -------------- | -------------------- | ----------------------------------- | ----------------------------------- |
| Characterization | Mystery lists  | Buyer databases      | Coordinated customer communications | Customer relationship management    |
| Application      | Direct mail    | Direct mail          | Planning and resource allocation tool | Fully integrated tool for strategic and tactical planning |
|                  |                | Telemarketing        |                                     |                                     |
|                  |                | Sales support        | Integrated communication            |                                     |

Source: Palmer and Brookes, 2002

change programmes therefore are essential if organizations are to remain market-driven. However, one possible problem is that some developments in engineering and manufacturing may not be market-driven (Scully, 1996), but precede developments in marketing. For example, as McKenna (1991) observed:

> In a world of mass manufacturing the counterpart was mass marketing. In a world of flexible manufacturing, the counterpart is flexible marketing. The technology comes first, the ability to market follows. The technology embodies the adaptability, programmability, and customisability; now comes marketing that delivers on those qualities.

This adoption process may not happen easily. Day (1996) observes that incumbent firms may be slow to migrate to electronic commerce because they fall into a number of 'traps': they cannot see beyond the limitations of early applications and so defer participation; they fear that by moving too quickly they may choose the wrong technology; they are concerned that existing revenue streams or relationships with some key customers will be put at risk; and they do not have the perseverance to overcome early setbacks in the process of implementation. Christensen and Bower (1996) also show that 'disruptive' innovations are often *not* taken up by the incumbent firms in an industry. Rather, they may *intensify* their commitments to conventional technology while starving efforts to commercialize new technologies – even while the new technologies are gaining ground in the market. One reason is that firms pay too much attention to what their current customers say they want, and this can stymie their introduction of new solutions.

Another possible problem, as Ward and Peppard (2002) note, is that: 'IT has no inherent value – the mere purchase of IT does not confer any benefits to the organization; these benefits must be unlocked.' As a result,

> investments are often made in technology without understanding or analyzing the nature of the activities the technology is supposed to support – either strategically or operationally.... For example, over the last few years, many organizations have built websites without sufficient thought to the rationale behind the decision.

This is an argument echoed by Rifkin and Kurtzman (2002) who, citing Barnes and Noble, say that too many websites are disconnected from the firm's existing channels, and therefore too many 'e-business efforts become technology plays rather than business moves'.

Downes and Mui (1998) warned of a further problem:

> As technology moves from its position as a defining element of the back office to a disruptive force in the marketplace, the problem now faced by most organizations is that there is rarely anyone, much less an organization, with the mandate and the resources to help senior management treat digital technology strategically.... Succeeding at these early stages of digital strategy development requires substantial changes to the organization. In particular, it requires a new attitude toward technology itself. You can't build a wired organization if you still believe ... that technology is essentially a tool to implement strategy rather than the basis of forming strategy.

Many organizations also carry the burden that their IT leaders, such as the chief information officer (CIO), are expected to lead on technical issues while also attempting to stay abreast of their firm's business strategy (Broadbent and Weill, 1999; Rifkin and Kurtzman, 2002).

Finally, another possible problem has to do with the sheer number of internal organizational barriers to change. Fletcher and Wright (1995), for example, and Desai, Fletcher and Wright (1998), looked into the barriers to the successful implementation of IT, with particular emphasis on the financial services, retail and travel sectors. They identified the following barriers, here ranked in order of importance:

1. high cost of development
2. highly fragmented systems
3. data quality

4. account-based customer records
5. no clear database marketing strategy
6. lack of company-wide marketing orientation
7. lack of direct marketing specialists
8. fragmented sales and marketing organization
9. lack of board-level backing
10. poor agency relations
11. poor relationships betweens marketing and IT.

All these barriers have internal marketing implications if internal change is to be successful. Not surprisingly, Saunders and Chan (2002) say an organization 'framework' is needed to reduce both intra- and inter-departmental disparities.

In discussing the successful implementation of innovation, Poolton and Barclay (1998) list six criteria for success that might be elements in such a framework:

- top management support for innovation
- long-term strategy with an innovation focus
- long-term commitment to major projects
- flexibility and responsiveness to change
- top management acceptance of risk
- support for an entrepreneurial culture.

All these criteria also have internal marketing implications.

Concerns such as these may help explain why Gerstner at IBM played a similar coaching role in terms of mediating between the sales/marketing and service functions. They also help explain why Bill Gates relinquished his position as CEO of Microsoft in 2002 in order to concentrate on a new function somewhat grandly titled 'Chief Software Architect', and which allows him to tackle both market-led and technology-driven issues. Schlender (2002) says Gates' new role 'plays to perhaps his greatest skill – that uncanny ability to foresee how emerging software technologies can be woven together and parlayed into must-have "industry standard" products, which, in turn, reinforce demand for other software from Microsoft and its allies'. In other words, Gates has placed himself at the technical forefront of Microsoft in order to ensure that internal and external relationship marketing efforts are in place to prevent the company being caught out by unforeseen inflection points. And if he is successful, as Schlender predicts, 'competitors will have to live in a world even more dominated by Microsoft'.

## THE CMP STUDY OF MANAGERS' PERCEPTIONS OF THE ROLES OF IT

The above discussions suggest it is useful to consider not just the extent to which firms are incorporating IT-enabled interactivity into their current marketing operations, but also what managers think about the role of IT in their organization as a whole. In particular, the CMP group became interested in understanding the extent to which IT is used to reinforce, enhance or transform the status quo. According to Orlikowski (2000), each role reflects a different level of IT integration in the organization. For example, when IT is used to support/preserve current marketing efforts reinforces the status quo; when IT is used to extend/improve existing marketing efforts it enhances the status quo; and when IT is used to redefine/drive the marketing efforts it transforms the status quo.

Furthermore, Orlikowski (2000) states, 'my empirical data did not capture the richness of users' affective connections with technologies. Understanding these attachments and meanings could offer richer explanations for the range of structural responses enacted by users as they engage with technology in practice.' While emotions can affect how different groups in organizations interpret and respond to radical change, as yet there has been little systematic research into the combined cognitive–affective reactions to radical change by middle managers (Huy, 2002), particularly in the context of the impact of IT on marketing practices.

Based on the results from our UK and New Zealand studies, where this research issue has been first explored, it appears that a majority of firms, regardless of the industry type, currently regard IT in a reinforcing capacity, as shown in Table 9.2. The table also shows that consumer goods, consumer services and B2B services companies are more heavily weighted toward the use of IT in reinforcing or enhancing roles, while B2B Goods firms are slightly more heavily weighted toward the use of IT in a transforming role.

While B2B goods firms showed the greatest incidence of using IT for transformational purposes, within other industries there is also likely to be a small number of firms doing so, even in the face of the general conservatism or reluctance of the majority.

Although Orlikowski (2000) cautions that the three categories of organizational change may not be comprehensive or exhaustive, the results from our study show that managers can both relate their own firm to one of the three categories, and explain clearly and succinctly the roles of IT within that category. Our current study also shows that managers are able to express a range of cognitive–affective responses that tend to be similar

**Table 9.2** Use of IT in organizations: number of firms (%)

|  | Reinforce | Enhance | Transform | Total | % |
|---|---|---|---|---|---|
| Consumer goods | 6 | 5 | 2 | 13 | 14 |
|  | (46) | (39) | (15) | 100 % |  |
| Consumer services | 11 | 6 | 2 | 19 | 21 |
|  | (58) | (32) | (10) | 100 % |  |
| B2B goods | 11 | 3 | 8 | 22 | 24 |
|  | (50) | (14) | (36) | 100 % |  |
| B2B services | 17 | 14 | 6 | 37 | 41 |
|  | (46) | (38) | (16) | 100 % |  |
| Total | 45 | 28 | 18 | 91 | 100 % |
| % | 49% | 31% | 20% | 100 % |  |

within a category, and that are different in content and intent from the other categories. This is illustrated by the examples that follow.

## Reinforcing the status quo

According to Orlikowski (2000), these companies use IT to retain their existing ways of doing things; consequently, IT represents no discernible change in processes, and results in the preservation of the structural status quo. Firms also show little integration of IT into their ongoing work practices. Orlikowski uses phrases such as 'users having limited understanding and/or being skeptical of the technological properties available to them' and, 'institutional conditions that included a rigid career hierarchy, individualistic incentives and task assignments, and a competitive culture'.

The managers' responses in the CMP study appear to be consistent with Orlikowski's views. For example, the firm may be seen as lacking in strategic support, and failing in IT understanding, foresight and commitment by senior management. For some, the firm may be seen as 'anti-IT'. The largely cautious, reactive and ad hoc changes tend to be seen in the context of internal organizational shortcomings and possible obstacles to implementation, such as inadequate training and financing. There is little integration of IT into ongoing work practices, with few discernible changes in processes, and without clear goals and longer-term perspectives. For some managers, investing in IT may be seen as possibly diverting their firm away from the critical task of maintaining personal business and customer relationships.

These conclusions are illustrated by the managers' discourse comments, as demonstrated below:

- 'Selling cars is a personal transaction and nothing will ever replace that, in fact over the past 12–18 months there are moves away from IT-related marketing activities as these have proved to be singularly unsuccessfully' (consumer durable goods).
- 'IT is not funded to provide an adequate service to existing users and in a much-maligned Department, initiatives are soured in the face of e-mail or network problems that recur too often and are only reactively addressed. The management outside the Department have little faith, and less finance to consider changing the situation even if there was some inclination to do so' (consumer durable goods).
- 'Marketing/Sales team is technophobic. Advances are forced on them by finance and acquisitions departments' (consumer services).
- 'Website used as an on-line brochure but follow-up carried out via traditional (phone) methods. E-mail used extensively but often just to arrange meetings and most messages are printed. Database is used for information storage and reporting but only generates the same reports as used over previous years' (consumer services).
- 'The CEO of the company wants to exploit IT to promote his organi-zation and has brought in to various (supplier) companies to further develop this strategy. However he is too busy to consistently carry through his strategy, so only has an average deliverable. His existing IT Manager is 'momentum driven' and has not championed the exploitation of IT to enhance/expand our market share' (consumer services).
- 'The introduction of new network system has replaced the old paper-based system that was then entered into a central database. No training has been given on how to use information that is stored in database for "coal-face" applications' (B2B goods).

## Enhancing the status quo

According to Orlikowski (2000), while there may be a full understand-ing of their technology at hand, these companies use IT to augment, improve or refine their existing work processes, and this can result in both a reinforcement and an enhancement of the status quo.

The managers' responses in the current study appear to be consistent with Orlikowski's views. For example, the IT emphasis is seen to be more tactical than strategic, and designed to increase efficiencies or improve, supplement or extend the firm's current offerings, but not fundamentally change them. There is more likely to be an integration of IT into ongoing work practices, particularly through greater integration and sharing of existing data sets. There may be some discernible changes in processes or practices, but no new ones started. IT initiatives may also be undertaken with the intention to improve current customer relationships, but not to change their nature or to instigate new ones. Overall, the firm is seen as 'pro-IT', but on a limited-use, limited-scale and limited-budget basis.

These conclusions are illustrated by the following managers' comments:

- 'The investment banking industry uses IT primarily to ensure front office has fast access to market and latest information. In terms of marketing, the ongoing development of a client relationship management system will enhance the status quo' (consumer services).
- 'We are one of the few companies in our industry to have a website. We generate about 5 per cent of our leads from our website. This website gives our customers instant access to our product catalogue. We are in the process of getting a CRM package up and running so that we can better utilize our time and take advantage of our leads. In our in-house design department new products are developed and proofs, etc. are e-mailed and instantly accessible. This cuts an enormous amount of time out of the design process' (B2B goods).
- 'IT is currently used to provide customers with more efficient communication via the Internet – sharing knowledge, quotations, distribution status, etc., adding to personalized service and helping to build relationships. It also improves on marketing efforts by providing cost-efficient ways of delivering useful information to customers in real time' (B2B services).
- 'We are an IT-based company – financial and supply chain software – and so we are heavily reliant on technology. However it doesn't drive the business in the sense of setting goals. The technology fits our solutions' (B2B services).

## Transforming the status quo

According to Orlikowski (2000), these companies treat IT as a philosophy and use IT to alter substantially their existing ways of doing business. There may be much improvisation and experimentation, and adapting/customizing IT tools and data content. Users tend to be more knowledgeable about technology, are motivated to use it in recasting work practices, and are supported by institutional conditions and resources, including a more cooperative culture.

Again, the managers' responses in the current study appear to be consistent with Orlikowski's views. For example, the firm is seen to be proactive, innovative, strategic and confident in its approach, with the customer or market as the focus. Transformational change is the goal, and the change process is likely to be more inclusive and integrative, and involve inter-functional and inter-firm collaboration. The firm may be prepared to invest in experiments, with the changes seen as on-going and aimed at a longer-term gain based on current and new relationship building. IT may be a means by which the firm accepts the competitive challenges and opportunities to change 'the rules of the game'. The firm may take a more global/networking perspective, and is seen to be 'IT-optimistic', within an actively supportive organizational culture.

These conclusions are illustrated by the following managers' comments:

- 'We are the first company in the world with an "early adopter" programme that is testing a connection between CRM package (X) and our financial package called (Y)' (consumer packaged goods).
- 'Our company is working as a test project for (two major telecommunications companies) in B2B supply chain management projects, described by both companies as e-procurement' (B2B goods).
- 'We have reached a level for an IT-enabled business transformation, i.e. we have integrated systems within the company that facilitate cross-functional cooperation and we pursue inter-enterprise computing. We have excellent e-services in place and will implement customers on-line this year' (B2B goods).
- 'Our corporate is attempting to exit the commodity market (high competition, downward pricing spiral, shrinking market) and add value to its product by developing (IT-based) management systems which will be offered to transport companies as a management tool' (B2B goods).
- 'Technology has enabled our business (small firm) to reach new international markets in an economic way. This let us transform our marketing programme' (B2B goods).
- 'Using IT gives our knowledge "form", i.e. turns verbal or intangible concepts or ideas into a visual and understandable picture. In short, IT transforms our communication and knowledge into a tangible understanding for our clients' (B2B services).

## HAS THE INTERNET REALLY CHANGED EVERYTHING?

The results of this study suggest that no one view prevails. For some firms, the Internet may have changed everything; for some it may be a tool and a channel; for others, IT-enabled interactivity may mean that while the 'rules of the game' are changed: the context is critical. Consistent with Brady, Saren and Tzokas (2002), the evidence from this study shows that only a small proportion of firms consider themselves to be high users of technology, and few see themselves as having reached a higher level of IT-enabled business transformation.

Nevertheless, the managers in our study appear able to categorize their own firm's investments in IT according to the three categories identified by Orlikowski (2000), and, as summarized in Table 9.3, the organization's intentions with regard to IT, the nature and purpose of IT investment, and organizational characteristics are different for each category. Furthermore, managers clearly demonstrate various cognitive–affective responses to the organization's approach to IT and the role IT takes. These responses may range from expressions of apparent disappointment, pessimism and scepticism concerning their firm's investments in IT for reinforcement purposes, to expressions of anticipation, optimism and confidence concerning their firm's investments in IT for transformation purposes. This latter group, in particular, appear to be proceeding on the basis of what Lynn, Monroe and Paulson (1996) term a 'probe and learn process', and with the full support of their organizations.

## MANAGERIAL IMPLICATIONS

IT appears to offer a range of opportunities for all types of firms attempting to build closer relationships in their respective marketplaces, and in a variety of ways. While half the firms in our study currently use IT as reinforcement tools, this could be considered the start of a longer-term process of change. It may also mean missed opportunities, especially if some firms now have customers or other stakeholders who are more 'technology-ready' and willing to interact through IT in order to enhance or even transform the relationships they have with others. The step-up to the enhancing stage does not appear to be great, as evidenced by the one-third of the firms currently using IT for this purpose, and by the findings from a related question showing virtually all firms anticipate they will be heavier users of IT in the future. For example, while fewer than 25 per cent of firms currently

**Table 9.3** Suggested organizational issues

| Key issues | Reinforce the status quo | Enhance the status quo | Transform the status quo |
|---|---|---|---|
| Organization's strategic intent/ purpose | – Unlikely to 'drive' the IT initiatives<br>– 'Inside-in' thinking<br>– Short term gain horizon with little long term thinking<br>– Tactical mind-set<br>– Reactive/ad hoc thinking<br>– May be some concern that going 'IT-interactive' will inhibit close personal relationships. | – May 'drive' some IT initiatives<br>– 'Inside-out' thinking<br>– Short term gain horizon but may be some long term view<br>– Mainly tactical mindset<br>– Limited proactivity in thinking<br>– May be an attitude that going 'IT-interactive' will help in customer relationship building. | – Likely to 'drive' the IT initiatives<br>– 'Outside-in' thinking<br>– Long term gain horizon through short term gains<br>– Strategic 'change the rules' mindset<br>– 'First-mover' advantage thinking<br>– Strong attitude that 'IT-interactivity' will enhance existing relationships and help in creating new ones. |
| Nature/ purpose of the IT initiatives | – May be 'imposed' on marketing<br>– Likely to be replacing/updating existing (outlived) function or process<br>– Are likely to be treated in isolation of other IT initiatives and data sets/functions/ processes<br>– As an add-on to existing ways of operating. | – Likely to involve marketing input<br>– Likely to be enhancing a current function or process<br>– May be seen as way to enable greater integration of current IT initiatives and data sets/ functions/processes<br>– To facilitate incremental improvements. | – Likely to be jointly led by marketing<br>– Likely to be extending a current function or process, or creating a new one<br>– Likely to be seen as a way to more fully integrate/change current IT initiatives and data sets/ functions/processes<br>– To drive desired transformational change. |

**Table 9.3** continued

| Key issues | Reinforce the status quo | Enhance the status quo | Transform the status quo |
|---|---|---|---|
| Nature/ purpose of the IT initiatives (continued) | – Strictly existing 'state-of-knowledge' IT<br>Unclear how IT initiatives are likely to be appraised. | – To be 'up with the play' with current IT, and possibly even emerging IT<br>– IT initiatives likely to be appraised mostly in terms of cost/efficiency gains. | – To be at forefront of emerging information technologies<br>– IT initiatives likely to be appraised in both cost/efficiency and competitive gain/market/ relationship building terms. |
| Organizational characteristics | – Leadership support of IT may range from guarded to hostile, and be inadequately resourced<br>– 'Risk-avoidance' culture<br>– Any current IT setbacks may justify a halt to future initiatives. | – Leadership is likely to be pro-IT, but on a limited-use scale, including the resourcing<br>– 'Risk-management' culture<br>– Unclear how much any current IT setbacks may affect future initiatives. | – Leadership support of IT is likely to be that of encouragement, and to provide necessary resourcing<br>– 'Opportunity/change seeking' culture<br>– Any IT setbacks are likely to be seen as part of the learning/ advancement process. |

see themselves as high users of technology, when asked to consider their use of technologies in five years' time this proportion increases to nearly 45 per cent. How many of these firms will be using IT for transformational purposes is not known, but the results do suggest that IT is likely to play an increasingly important role in marketing practices in the future. It is also likely that managers do not necessarily need to proceed to IT extremes in order to plan, and incorporate, greater IT integration and increased sophistication into their development of enhanced relationship capabilities. What is rather more of a critical issue is the extent of senior management commitment and overall organizational support.

Relatively few firms now use IT to transform their current marketing practices, and the results suggest this may be a function of their situational needs or contextual 'fit'. However, a risk for firms competing against those who are at the transformational stage now is that they may be denied future relationship building opportunities. For example, their more innovative competitors may already be 'locking in' key customers and suppliers through proprietary electronic networking arrangements, such as global supply chain management systems.

## INTERNAL RELATIONSHIP MANAGEMENT AND CHANGE MANAGEMENT

The issue of change management underlies many of the findings. Huy (2002) argues that middle managers are critical to the success of organizational change, by being personally committed to championing the change and by attending to the emotional reactions and concerns of others, especially subordinates. The responses in this study suggest that mid-level managers are likely to be more emotionally attuned to – and supportive of – IT-related change that is more transformational in character. By contrast, many firms may have sound strategic, financial or other reasons for currently investing in IT for reinforcement or enhancement purposes. How to ensure that middle management champion these changes may be a critical issue that senior managers themselves need to champion. For example, they could encourage their managers to view limited IT-enabled interactivity as a basis for 'changing the rules' longer-term, as opposed to tools for saving costs or improving efficiencies short-term.

The issue of internal change management could be considered integral to the wider internal relationship marketing function within a firm. While internal relationship marketing is a relatively undeveloped construct, as Gummesson (2002) suggests, perhaps more firms should focus on their internal 'network of relationships and projects' if IT changes such as IT-enabled interactivity are to be smoothly implemented. Jap and Mohr (2002) agree: in their view, 'e-commerce technologies cannot be successfully leveraged without considering the organizational relationships in which the technologies are being embedded'.

Perhaps the defining marketing challenges over the next few years will therefore be:

1. *External:* in order to deliver value to customers and other parties, the challenge will be how firms can structure their external relationship marketing practices on the basis of the five drivers of change discussed in Chapter 7.
2. *Internal:* in order to ensure that value is both created and readied for market entry and delivery, the challenge will be having IT-enabled inter-activity initiatives that are successful, and instilling the concomitant internal relationship marketing practices.

Marketing challenges and practices have got more demanding, more complex and more paradoxical as we move into a new era of 'doing business'. Through our examination of various discourses, we have considered how many of the world's greatest, and not so great, companies have attempted to change. We have examined how executives in our CMP studies are trying to 'make sense' of what is happening in their organizations and in their markets. And we have also proposed various frameworks, models and principles that we trust our readers may find helpful as they also try to make sense of what is happening both 'in there' and 'out there'. We wish you the best of success.

# REFERENCES

Aaker, D. A. (1996) *Building Strong Brands*, New York: Free Press.

Abernathy, W. J., Clark, K. B. and Kantrow, A. M. (1981) The new industrial competition, *Harvard Business Review*, Sep–Oct: 68–79.

Achrol, R. S. (1991) Evolution of the marketing organization: new forms for turbulent environments, *Journal of Marketing*, **55**, Oct: 77–93.

Achrol, R. S. (1997) Changes in the theory of interorganizational relationship marketing: toward a network paradigm, *Journal of the Academy of Marketing Science*, **25**(1): 56–71.

Aijo, T. S. (1996) The theoretical and philosophical underpinnings of relationship marketing, *European Journal of Marketing*, **30**(2): 8–18.

Alford, D., Sackett, P. and Nelder, G. (2000) Mass customization – an auto perspective, *International Journal of Production Economics*, **65**: 99–110.

Allee, V. (2000) Reconfiguring the value network, *Journal of Business Strategy*, Jul–Aug: 36–39.

Ambrosini, V. (2002) Resource-based view of the firm, in Jenkins, M. and Ambrosini, V. (eds), *Strategic Management; A Multi-Perspective Approach*, 132–152. Basingstoke: Palgrave.

Anderson, J. C. and Narus, J. A. (1995) Capturing the value of supplementary services, *Harvard Business Review*, Jan–Feb: 75–83.

Anderson, J. C. and Narus, J. A. (1998) Business marketing: understanding what customers value, *Harvard Business Review*, Nov–Dec: 53–65.

Anderson, J. C. and Narus, J. A. (1999) *Business Market Management*, Upper Saddle River, NJ: Prentice-Hall.

Anon. (1998) Germans let Lopez off with monetary fine, *Purchasing*, 8 Oct.

Armstrong, L., Miller, K. L., Peterson, T. and Woodruff, D. (1998) A new era for auto quality, *Business Week*, 22 Oct.

Arndt, M. (2001) Eli Lilly: life after Prozac, *Business Week*, 23 Jul.

*Automotive News* (2001) GM's Lutz: still pushing for higher market share, 12 Dec (http://www.autonews.com/printStory.cms?newsId=1158).

*Autoweek* (2001) Interview with Bob Lutz, General Motors newly appointed Vice Chairman of Product, *Autoweek* online (www.autoweek .com/cat_print.mv?port_code=autoweek&cat_code=carnews&loc_cod e=&content_code_09403554&1277563089)

Bain, J. S. (1951) Relation of profit rate to industry concentration, *Quarterly Journal of Economics*, **65**(3): 293–324.

Ball, D. (2002a) Unilever net increases by 68 per cent, aided by stress on big brands, *Wall Street Journal*, 3 Oct, B.2.

Ball, D. (2002b) Is Unilever putting best foods forward?, *Wall Street Journal*, 4 Dec, B.3.

Ball, J. and Miller, S. (2001) German auto titans battle for supremacy, *Asian Wall Street Journal*, 27 Feb, N.1, 8.

Ballantyne, D. (1994) Relationship marketing: designing a way forward from concept to practice, *Second International Colloquium in Relationship Marketing*, Cranfield School of Management.

Bartram, P. (2000) Brand power, *Management Accounting*, Jun: 17–18.

Barry, A. (2000) Strange market, *Barron's*, 21 Feb: 29–34.

Bauer, H. H., Grether, M. and Leach, M. (2002) Customer relations through the internet, *Journal of Relationship Marketing*, 1(2): 39–55.

Beam, A. and Port, O. (1985) The filmless camera is here, but will it sell?, *Business Week*, 15 Apr: 79–80.

Bear, S., Benson-Armer, R. and Hall, J. (2000) Performance leadership: making value happen, *Ivey Business Journal*, May–Jun: 51–57.

Beck, E. (2000) Hungry Unilever faces a full plate, *Asian Wall Street Journal*, 1 Jun: 2.

Bekier, M. M., Bogardus, A. J. and Oldham, T. (2001) Why mergers fail, *McKinsey Quarterly*, 4: 6–9.

Bennett, R. and Cooper, R. (1981) The misuse of marketing: an American tragedy, *Business Horizons*, Nov–Dec: 51–60.

Berry, L. (1983) Relationship marketing, in Berry, L. L., Shostack, G. L. and Upah, G. D. (eds), *Emerging Perspectives in Services Marketing*, Chicago: AMA.

Berry, L. (1995) Relationship marketing of services – growing interest, emerging perspectives, *Journal of the Academy of Marketing Science*, 23(4): 236–245.

Berry, L. (2000) Cultivating service brand equity, *Journal of the Academy of Marketing Science*, 28(1): 128–137.

Berthon, P., Holbrook, M. B. and Hulbert, J. M. (2000) Beyond market orientation: a conceptualization of market evolution, *Journal of Interactive Marketing*, 14(3) Summer: 50–66.

Bidlake, S. (2000) Unilever's new direction, *AdAge International*, Jun, 3: 15.

Bitner, M. J. (1995) Building service relationships: it's all about promises, *Journal of the Academy of Marketing Science*, 23(4): 246–251.

Bitner, M. J., Brown, S. W. and Meuter, M. L. (2000) Technology infusion in service encounters, *Journal of the Academy of Marketing Science*, 28(1): 138–149.

Blaikie, N. (1993) *Approaches To Social Enquiry*, Oxford: Blackwell.

Blois, K. J. (1996) Relationship marketing in organizational markets: when is it appropriate?, *Journal of Marketing Management*, **12**: 161–173.

Borden, N. H. (1964) The concept of the marketing mix, *Journal of Advertising Research* (June): 2–7.

Boulton, R. E. S., Libert, B. D. and Samek, S. M. (2000) A business model for the new economy, *Journal of Business Strategy*, Jul–Aug: 29–35.

Bouvard, F., Cornet, A. and Rowland, P. J. (2001) The road ahead for telematics, *McKinsey Quarterly*, no. 2 (www.mckinseyquarterly.com/article_page.asp?tk=317583:1034:2&ar=1034&L2=2&L3=38)

Bovel, D. and Martha, J. (2000) From supply chain to value net, *Journal of Business* Strategy, Jul–Aug: 24–28.

Bower, J. (2001) Not all M and As are alike – and that matters, *Harvard Business Review*, Mar: 92–101.

Brady, M., Saren, M. and Tzokas, N. (2002a) Integrating information technology into marketing practice – the IT reality of contemporary marketing, *Journal of Marketing Management*, **18**(5–6): 555–577.

Brady, M., Saren, M. and Tzokas, N. (2002b) Integrating information technology into marketing, *Journal of Marketing Management*, **18**: 1–23.

Brandenburger, B. J. and Nalebuff, A. M. (1996) *Co-opetition*, New York: Doubleday.

Broadbent, M. and Weill, P. (1999) The implications for information technology infrastructure for business process redesign, *MIS Quarterly*, **23**(2): 159–182.

Brodie, R. J., Coviello, N. E., Brookes, R. W. and Little, V. (1997) Towards a paradigm shift in marketing? An examination of current marketing practices, *Journal of Marketing Management*, **13**: 383–406.

Brookes, R. W. (1995) Recent changes in the retailing of fresh produce: strategic implications for fresh produce suppliers, *Journal of Business Research*, **32**(2), Feb: 149–161.

Brown, S. (1996) Art or science: fifty years of marketing debate, *Journal of Marketing Management*, **12**: 243–267.

Brown, S. (1998) *Postmodern Marketing*, London: Thomson Business Press.

Bryman, A. (1988) *Quantity and Quality in Social Research*, London: Routledge.

Burck, C. (1981) How GM stays ahead, *Fortune*, 9 Mar: 48–56.

Burck, C. (1983) Will success spoil General Motors?, *Fortune*, 22 Aug: 94–104.

Burrows, P. (1999) Can Compaq catch up?, *Business Week*, 3 May: 124–127.

Burt, S. L. (2000) The strategic role of retail brands in British grocery retailing, *European Journal of Marketing*, **34**(8): 875–890.

Burt, T. (1999) The best or one of the rest?, *Financial Times*, 7 Sep: 23.

Burt, T. and Tait, N. (2000) Chrysler to slash supplier costs by $6bn, *Financial Times*, 8 Dec: 21.

*Business Week* (1980) US autos: losing a big segment of the market – forever, 24 Mar: 78–88.

*Business Week* (1984) GM moves into a new gear, 16 Jul: 70–75.

*Business Week* (1989) Stalking the new consumer, interview with John Smale, CEO, Procter & Gamble, 28 Aug: 36–41.

Buttle, F. (ed.) (1996) *Relationship Marketing, Theory and Practice*, London: Paul Chapman.

Buzzell, R. D. and Ortmeyer, G. (1995) Channel partnerships streamline distribution, *Sloan Management Review*, Spring: 85–95.

Bylinsky, G. (1983) The race to the automatic factory, *Fortune*, 21 Feb: 52–64.

Bylinsky, G. (1994) The digital factory, *Fortune*, 14 Nov: 56–65.

Cairncross, F. (2000) Inside the machine. *Economist E-Management Survey*, 11 Nov: 1–31.

Carlzon, J. (1989) *Moments of Truth*, New York: Harper Collins.

Carson, D. J. and Coviello, N. E. (1996) Qualitative research issues at the marketing/entrepreneurship interface, *Marketing Intelligence and Planning*, **14**(6): 51–58.

Carson, R. (1962) *Silent Spring*, London: Penguin.

Cartwright, S. D. and Oliver, R. W. (2000) Untangling the value web, *Journal of Business Strategy,* Jan–Feb: 22–27.

Caulkin, S. (2002) Four moves to live long and prosper, *Herald*, 25 Sep, D.1.

Cecil, J. and Hall, E. (1988) When IT really matters to business strategy, *McKinsey Quarterly*, Autumn: 2–26.

Chalmers, A. F. (1982) *What Is This Thing Called Science?*, Buckingham: Open University Press.

Child, J. and McGrath, R. G. (2001) Organizations unfettered: organizational form in an information-intensive economy, *Academy of Management Journal*, **44**(6): 1135–1148.

Christensen, C. (1997) *Innovators' Dilemma: Why Great Companies Fail*, New York: Harper Collins.

Christensen. C. and Bower, J. (1996) Customer power, strategic investment, and the failure of leading firms, *Strategic Management Journal*, **17**: 197–218.

Christopher, M. G. (1996) From brand values to customer values, *Journal of Marketing Practice*, **2**(1): 55–66.

Christopher, M., Payne, A. and Ballantyne, D. (1991) *Relationship Marketing,* Oxford: Butterworth-Heinemann.

Clark, M. (2000) Customer service, people and processes, in *Marketing Management: A Relationship Marketing Perspective,* 210–227, London: Macmillan.

Coltman, T., Devinney. T. M., Latukefu, A. and Midgley, D. F. (2001) E-business: revolution, evolution or hype?, *California Management Review,* **44**(1): 57–84.

Colvin, G. (2000) The wrath of Wall Street, *Fortune,* 16 Oct: 147–149.

Conklin, D. and Tapp, L (2000a) The creative web: a new model for managing innovation, *Ivey Business Journal,* May–Jun: 60–68.

Conklin, D. and Tapp, L. (2000b) The creative web, in Chowdhury, S. (ed.) *Management 21C: Someday We'll All Manage This Way,* Harlow: Prentice Hall.

Cooper R., Kaplin R. S. (1991) Profit priorities from activity-based costing, *Harvard Business Review,* **69**(3), May–Jun: 130–135.

Coviello, N. E., Brodie, R. J., Brookes, R. W. and Collins, B. (1997) From transaction to relationship marketing: an investigation of market perceptions and practices, *Fifth International Colloquium in Relationship Marketing,* Cranfield University, Nov 1997.

Coviello, N. E., Brodie, R. J., Brookes, R. and Palmer, R. A. (2001) The role of e-marketing in contemporary marketing practice, in *Conference Proceedings, 9th International Colloquium on Relationship Marketing,* John Molson School of Business, Concordia University, Montreal, Sep.

Coviello, N. E., Brodie, R. J., Brookes, R. and Palmer, R. A. (2003) The role of e-marketing in contemporary marketing practice, *Journal of Marketing Management,* **18**, forthcoming.

Coviello, N. E., Brodie, R. J., Danaher, P. J. and Johnston, W. J. (2002) How firms relate to their markets: an empirical examination of contemporary marketing practices, *Journal of Marketing,* **66**(3): 33–46.

Coviello, N. E., Brodie, R. J. and Munro, H. J. (1997) Understanding contemporary marketing: development of a classification scheme, *Journal of Marketing Management,* **13**: 501–552.

Coviello, N. E., Brodie R. J. and Munro, H. J. (2000) An investigation of marketing practice by firm size, *Journal of Business Venturing,* **15**(5–6): 523–545.

Coviello, N. E., Milley, R. and Marcolin, B. (2001) Understanding IT-enabled interactivity in contemporary marketing, *Journal of Interactive Marketing,* **15**(4): 18–33.

Cramer, J. (2003) The dotcom boom begins, *Time,* 31 Mar, A56.

Cusumano, M. (1988) Manufacturing innovation: lessons from the Japanese auto industry, *Sloan Management Review*, Fall: 29–39.

Darling, S. (1998) Marketing going to get personal, *NZ Herald*, 9 July: D6.

Davis, T. (1998) Effective supply chain management, *Sloan Management Review*, **34**, Summer: 35–46.

Day, G. (1996) The future of interactive marketing, *Harvard Business Review*, Nov–Dec: 151–162.

Day, G. (1998) Organizing for interactivity, *Journal of Interactive Marketing*, **12**(1): 47–53.

Day, G. (1999a) *The Market Driven Organization*, New York: Free Press.

Day, G. (1999b) Creating a market-driven organization, *Sloan Management Review*, Fall: 11–22.

Day, G. S. and Montgomery, D. B. (1999) Charting new directions for marketing, *Journal of Marketing*, **63** (Special Issue): 3–13.

Day, S. (2002) McDonald's cuts forecast and will close 175 outlets, *New York Times*, 9 Nov.

Day, S. (2003) McDonald's strives to regain ground, *New York Times*, 3 Mar.

De Vincentis, J. R. and Kotcher, L. K. (1995) Packaged goods salesforce – beyond efficiency, *McKinsey Quarterly*, **1**: 72–85.

Deighton, J. (1996a) The future of interactive marketing, *Harvard Business Review*, Mar–Apr: 133–141.

Deighton, J. (1996b) The future of interactive marketing, *Harvard Business Review*, Nov–Dec: 151–162.

Dempsey, P. (2000) Collaboration chain, *Electronic Times*, London, 11 Dec.

Demsetz, H. (1973) Industry structure, market rivalry and public policy, *Journal of Law and Economics*, **16**: 1–9.

Desai, C., Fletcher, K. and Wright, G. (1998) Barriers to successful implementation of database marketing: a cross industry study, *International Journal of Information Management*, **4**: 265–276.

Dignam, C. (2002) Choosing the winners in the brand value game, *Financial Times*, 5 Aug: 12–13.

Dowling, G. (2002) Customer relationship management: in B2B markets, often less is more, *California Management Review*, **44**(3), Spring: 87–104.

Dowling, G. R. and Uncles, M. (1997) Do customer loyalty programs really work?, *Sloan Management Review*, Summer: 71–82.

Downes, L. and Mui, C. (1998) *Unleashing the Killer App*, Boston: Harvard Business School Press.

Doyle, P. (2000) *Value-Based Marketing*, London: John Wiley.

Easton, G. (1992) Industrial networks: a review, in B. Axelsson and G. Easton (eds), *Industrial Networks: A New View of Reality*, 32–37, London: Routledge.

*Economist* (1998a) Mercedes goes to motown, 9 May: 15.

*Economist* (1998b) The decline and fall of General Motors, 10 Oct: 65–67.

*Economist* (1999a) Rosen cavalier, 24 Apr: 70.

*Economist* (1999b) Direct hit, 9 Jan: 57–59.

*Economist* (2000a) Shrinking to grow, 26 Feb: 75–76.

*Economist* (2000b) A Finnish fable, 14 Oct: 93–97.

*Economist* (2000c) Dotty about dot.commerce? E-commerce survey, 26 Feb: 1–38.

*Economist* (2001a) Shareholder value, corporate finance survey, 27 Jan: 13–15.

*Economist* (2001b) Hewlett-Packard and Compaq: sheltering from the storm, 8 Sep: 65–66.

*Economist* (2001c) Older, wiser, webbier, 30 Jun: 10.

*Economist* (2002) Fast food in America: not so fast, 7 Dec: 65.

*Economist* (2002) Rescue mission, 5 Jan (http://www.economist.com/people/PrinterFriendly.cfm?Story-ID=922497).

*Economist* (2002) Storm clouds over Detroit, 16 Nov: 55–56.

*Economist* (2003a) Rising above the sludge, 5 Apr: 61–63.

*Economist* (2003b) Ahold out, 1 Mar: 12.

*Economist* (2003c) Hewlett-Packard: a good deal after all?, 19 Apr: 53.

Egan, J. (2000) *Challenging the Relationship Marketing Paradigm*, Middlesex University Discussion Series No. 15, London: Middlesex University Press.

Eggert, A. and Stieff, J. (1999) What constitutes a relationship? Towards a conceptualisation of relationship marketing' s central construct, in McLoughlin, D. and Horan, C. (eds), *Proceedings of the 15th Annual IMP Conference*, University College, Dublin.

Eisenberg, D. (2002) Can McDonald's shape up?, *Time*, 30 Sep: 42–45.

Elkind, P. (1997) Blood feud, *Fortune*, 14 Apr: 46–56.

Elkind, P. (2001) Why Mary Meeker went wrong, *Fortune*, 14 May: 98–106.

Ellison, S. (2002) Unilever's results turn around on gains from sale of businesses, *Wall Street Journal*, 15 Feb: B6.

Elofson, G. and Robinson, W. N. (1998) Creating a custom mass-production channel on the internet, *Communications of the ACM*, **41**(3): 56–62.

Evans, P. and Wurster, T. R. (1997) Strategy and the new economics of information, *Harvard Business Review*, Sep–Oct: 71–82.

Fairclough, N. (1992) *Discourse and Social Change*, Cambridge, MA: Polity Press.

Fairclough, N. (1995) *Critical Discourse Analysis*, New York: Longman.

Farrell, C. (2002) Needed: 21st century accounting rules, *Business Week*, 22 Mar.

Fern, E. F. and Brown, J. R. (1984) The industrial/consumer marketing dichotomy: a case of insufficient justification, *Journal of Marketing*, **48**, Spring: 68–77.

Fisher, M. L., Raman, A. and McClelland, A. S. (2000) Rocket science retailing is almost here, *Harvard Business Review*, Jul–Aug: 115–124.

FitzGerald, N. (1999) How and why Unilever favours power brands, *AdAge*, 11 Oct: 14.

Flax, S. (1985) Can Chrysler keep rolling along?, *Fortune*, 7 Jan: 44–49.

Fletcher, K. and Wright, G. (1995) Organizational, strategic and technical barriers to successful implementation of database marketing, *International Journal of Information Management*, **15**(2): 115–126.

Flores, L. and Briggs, R. (2001) Beyond data gathering: implications of CRM systems to market research, in *Proceedings of ESOMAR 2001 Annual Congress*, Rome, 169–189.

Foote, N., Galbraith, J., Hope, Q. and Miller, D. (2001) Making solutions the answer, *McKinsey Quarterly*, **3**: 84–93.

Ford, D. (ed.) (1998) *Managing Business Relationships,* Chichester: John Wiley.

Fournier, S., Dobscha, S. and Mick, D. G. (1998) Preventing the premature death of relationship marketing, *Harvard Business Review*, Jan–Feb: 42–51.

Frick, K. A. and Torres, A. (2002) Learning from high-tech deals, *McKinsey Quarterly*, **1**: 113–123.

Gardner, N. (2000) Financial services can be trusted to play dirty, *Sunday Times*, 2 Apr.

Gates, B. (1999) *Business @ The Speed of Thought*, Victoria: Viking.

Gengler, B. (2001) So, what's next Bill?, interview with Bill Gates, reprinted in *Infotech Weekly*, **514**, 4 Nov: 13–14.

Gerstner, L. V. (2002) *Who Says Elephants Can't Dance? Inside IBM's Historic Turnaround,* Australia: Harper Collins.

Ghazvinian, J. and Miller K. L. (2002) Hold the fries, from *Newsweek*, and reported in *Herald*, 26 Dec, C1–2.

Ghosh, M. and John, G. (1999) Governance value analysis and marketing strategy, *Journal of Marketing*, **63**: 131–145.

Ghosh, S. (1998) Making business sense of the internet, *Harvard Business Review*, Mar–Apr: 126–135.

Gleick, J. (1987) *Chaos – Making a New Science*, Harmondsworth: Penguin.

Goodstein, L. D. and Butz, H. E. (1998) Customer value: the linchpin of organizational change, *Organizational Dynamics*, Summer: 21–33.

Goulian, C. and Mersereau, A. (2000) Performance measurement: implementing a corporate scorecard, *Ivey Business Journal*, Sep–Oct: 48–53.

Greene, J. (2003) Is Small Biz Microsoft's next big thing?, *Business Week*, 10 Apr (http://www.businessweek.com/print/smallbiz/content/apr2003/sb200304101194sb014.htm).

Greenwald, J. (2000) J'adore content, *Time*, 26 Jun: 28–29.

Grinyer, P. H., Mayes, D. G. and McKiernan, P. (1988) *Sharpbenders*, Oxford: Blackwell.

Gronroos, C. (1990a) Relationship approach to marketing in service contexts: the marketing and organizational behaviour interface, *Journal of Business Research*, **20**: 3–11.

Gronroos, C. (1990b) The marketing strategy continuum: towards a marketing concept for the 1990s, *Swedish School of Economics and Business Administration Working Papers*, 201.

Gronroos, C. (1991) The marketing strategy continuum: towards a marketing concept for the 1990s, *Management Decision*, **1**: 7–13.

Gronroos, C. (2000) *Service Management and Marketing*, 2nd edn, Chichester: Wiley.

Grossman, L. (2003) How the web was spun, *Time*, 21 Mar, A54.

Guilford, D. (2001) Car guys take charge at GM, *Automotive News*, 17 Dec (http://www.autonews.com/printStory.cms?newsId=1181).

Gulati, R. and Garino, J. (2000) Getting the right mix of bricks and clicks, *Harvard Business Review*, May–Jun: 107–114.

Gulati, R., Nohria, N. and Zaheer, A. (2000) Strategic networks, *Strategic Management Journal*, **21**: 203–215.

Gummesson, E. (1987) The new marketing – developing long-term interactive relationships, *Long Range Planning*, **20**(4): 10–20.

Gummesson, E. (1999) *Total Relationship Marketing – Rethinking Marketing Management: From 4Ps to 30Rs*, Oxford: Butterworth Heinemann.

Gummesson, E. (2002) Relationship marketing in the new economy, *Journal of Relationship Marketing*, **1**(1): 37–57.

Gummesson, E. (2003) *Total Relationship Marketing*, 2nd edn, Oxford: Butterworth Heinemann.

Gutermann, U., Hartung, S., Looser, U., von der Ohe, C. H. and Zielke, A. E. (2000) Building a growth model for machinery manufacturers, *McKinsey Automotive and Assembly Research*, 1–7 (https://autoassembly.mckinsey.com/insights/research/fuelinggrowth.asp).

Hacki, R. and Lighton, J. (2001) The future of the networked company, *McKinsey Quarterly*, **3**: 26–39.

Haeckel, S. H., (1998) Net gain: exploring markets through virtual communities, *Journal of Interactive Marketing*, **13**(1): 55–65.

Hagel, J. (1999) Net gain: expanding markets through virtual communities, *Journal of Interactive Marketing*, **12**(1): 63–71.

Hagel, J. and Singer, M. (1999) Unbundling the corporation, *Harvard Business Review*, Mar–Apr: 133–141.

Hair, J. F., Anderson, R. E., Tatham, R. L. and Black, W. C. (1998) *Multivariate Data Analysis*, Englewood Cliffs, NJ: Prentice Hall.

Hakansson, H. and Snehota, I. (1995) *Developing Relationships in Business Networks*, London: Routledge.

Hakim, D. (2001) A type B chief guides GM on a course to revival, *New York Times*, 25 Nov (http://www.nytimes.com/2001/11/25/business/25GMGM.html).

Hakim, D. (2003a) Steel supplier is threatening to drop GM, *New York Times*, 6 Feb (http://www.nytimes.com/200302/07/business/07AUTO.html).

Hakim, D. (2003b) Long road ahead for Ford, *New York Times*, 14 Mar (http://www.nytimes.com/2003/03/14/business/14AUTO.html).

Hall, P. (1998) *Cities in Civilization*, London: Phoenix.

Hamel, G. and Prahalad, C. K. (1994a) *Competing for the Future*, Boston, MA: Harvard Business School Press.

Hamel G. and Prahalad, C. K. (1994b) Competing for the future, *Harvard Business Review*, Jul–Aug: 122–128.

Hamel, G. (1998) Strategy innovation and the quest for value, *Sloan Management Review*, Winter: 7–14.

Harre, R (1970) *The Principles of Scientific Thinking*, London: Macmillan.

Hart, S., Smith, A., Sparks, L. and Tzokas, N. (1999) Are loyalty schemes a manifestation of relationship marketing?, *Journal of Marketing Management*, **15**: 541–562.

*Harvard Business Review*, Jan–Feb: 84–93.

Hayes, N. S. and Ball, D. (2003) Unilever's net profit rises 16 per cent on reorganization successes, *Wall Street Journal*, 14 Feb, B.5.

Hayward, C. (2002) Efficiency driver, *Financial Manangement*, May: 26–27.

Hendrickson, M., Heffernan, W. D., Howard, P. H. and Heffernan, J. B. (2001) Consolidation in food retailing and dairy, *British Food Journal*, **103**(10): 715–728.

Henry, D. (2002) Mergers: why most big deals don't pay off, *Business Week*, 14 Oct: 70–75.

Heracleous, L. and Barrett, M. (2001) Organizational change as discourse: communicative actions and deep structures in the context of IT implementation, *Academy of Management Journal*, **44**(4): 755–778.

*Herald* (2000) IBM targets on-line drivers, 11 Jan, C5.

*Herald* (2001) Chrysler chief confronts mammoth repair job, 8 Feb, C7.

*Herald* (2003) VW sees sharp fall in earnings, 14 Mar, C7.

Heskett, J. L. (1994) Comment made in *The Lifetime Value of Customers: People, Service, Success*, A video production of the Harvard Business School, Boston, MA: HBS Management Productions.

Heskett, J. L., Jones, T. O., Loveman, G. W., Sasser, Jr., W. E. and Schlesinger, L. A. (1994) Putting the service-profit chain to work, *Harvard Business Review*, Mar–Apr: 164–174.

Heskett, J. L., Sasser, W. E. and Hart, C. W. L. (1990) *Service Breakthroughs: Changing the Rules of the Game*, Free Press.

Himelstein, L. and Galuszka, P. (1999) P & G gives birth to a web baby, *Business Week*, 27 Sep: 85–86.

Hirschman, E. C. (1986) Humanistic enquiry in marketing research: philosophy, method and criteria, *Journal of Marketing Research*, **23**, Aug: 237–249.

Hoffman, D. L., Novak, T. P. (2000) How to acquire customers on the web, *Harvard Business Review*, May–Jun: 179–188.

Hofstede, G. (1980) *Culture's Consequences: International Differences in Work Related Values*, Beverly Hills: Sage Publications.

Holm, D. B., Eriksson, K. and Johanson, J. (1999) Creating value through mutual commitment business relationships, *Strategic Management Journal*, **20**: 467–486.

Hutt, M. D. and Speh, T. W. (2001) *Business Marketing Management*, Orlando, FL: Harcourt.

Huy, Q. N. (2002) Emotional balancing of organizational continuity and radical change: the contribution of middle managers, *Administrative Science Quarterly*, **47** (Mar): 31–69.

Iacobucci, D. and Hibberd, J. (1999) Towards an encompassing theory of business marketing relationships (BMRs) and interpersonal commercial relationships (ICRs): an empirical generalization, *Journal of Interactive Marketing*, **13**(3): 13–33.

Iacocca, L. (1984) *Iacocca: an Autobiography*, New York: Bantam Books.

Isidore, C. (2001) Nasser out as Ford CEO (online) (http://money.cnn.com/2001/10/30/ceos/ford).

Jackson, B. B. (1985) Build customer relationships that last, *Harvard Business Review*, **62**(6): 120–128.

James, G. (1997) IT fiascoes and how to avoid them, *Datamation*, Nov: 84–88.

James, G. (2002) Underwhelmed: a much-hyped sales tool turns out to be a letdown, *Red Herring*, July 12, 2002 (http://www.redherring.com/

insider/2002/0712/underwhelmed071202.html).

Jap, S. D. and Mohr, J. J. (2002) Leveraging internet technologies in B2B relationships, *California Management Review*, **44**(4) Summer: 24–38.

Jick, T.D. (1979) Mixing qualitative and quantitative methods: triangulation in action, *Administrative Science Quarterly*, **24**: 602–610.

Johnson, G. and Scholes, K. (2002) *Exploring Corporate Strategy*, London: Prentice-Hall.

*Journal of Business Strategies*, **18**(2): 177–190.

*Just-auto.com* (2002) USA: GM restructures vehicle development, 1 Feb (http://just-auto.com/news_detail.asp?art=37140&dm=yes).

Juttner, U. and Wehrli, H. P. (1994) Relationship marketing from a value system perspective, *International Journal of Service Industry Management*, **5**(5): 54–73.

Kaplan, R. and Norton, D. (1992) The balanced scorecard: measures that drive performance, *Harvard Business Review*, Jan–Feb: 71–79.

Kaplan, R. and Norton, D. (1993) Putting the balanced scorecard to work, *Harvard Business Review*, Sep–Oct: 134–142.

Kaplan, R. and Norton, D. (1996a) Using the balanced scorecard as a strategic management system, *Harvard Business Review*, Jan–Feb: 75–85.

Kaplan, R. and Norton, D. (1996b) Linking the balanced scorecard to strategy, *California Management Review*, **39**(1), Fall: 53–79.

Kaplan, R. and Norton, D. (2000) Having trouble with your strategy? Then map it, *Harvard Business Review*, Sep–Oct: 167–176.

Kaplan, S. and Sawhney, M. (2000) E-hubs: the new B2B marketplaces, *Harvard Business Review*, May–Jun: 97–106.

Keller, M. (2002) quoted in *Globe and Mail*, 22 Feb, B-20.

Kerstetter, J. (2003) The Linux uprising, *Business Week*, 3 Mar (www.businessweek.com/print/magazine/content/03_09/b3822601_tc102.html?tc&sub=03Linux)

Kerwin, K. (1996) Not your father's Corvette, *Business Week*, 23 Dec: 35.

Kerwin, K. (1999) Reviving GM, *Business Week*, 1 Feb: 50–55.

Kim, W. C. and Mauborgne, R. (1997) Value innovation: the strategic logic of high growth, *Harvard Business Review*, Jan–Feb.

Kim, W. C. and Mauborgne, R. (1999) Strategy, value innovation, and the knowledge economy, *Sloan Management Review*, Spring: 41–54.

Kinsella, R. (2002) Unilever defends world view, *Financial Management*, Jun: 6.

Kirkpatrick, D. (1997) Houston, we have some problems, *Fortune*, 23 Jun: 50–51.

Kirkpatrick, D. (1999) Eckhard's gone but the PC rocks on, *Fortune*, 24 May: 83–87.

Kisiel, R. (1997) Chrysler: suppliers hit savings goal early, *Automotive News*, 5 May: 6.

Kohli, A. K., Jaworski, B. J. and Kumar A. (1993) MARKOR: A measure of market orientation, *Journal of Marketing Research*, **30**, Nov: 467–477.

Kotler, P. (1991) Philip Kotler explores the new marketing paradigm, *Marketing Sciences Institute Review*, Spring.

Kotler, P., Armstrong, G., Brown, L. and Adam, S. (1998) *Marketing*, 4th edn, Sydney: Prentice Hall.

Kraemer, K. L., Dedrick, J. and Yamashiro, S. (2000) Refining and extending the business model with information technology: Dell Computer Corporation, *The Information Society*, **16**(1) Jan–Mar: 5–21.

Kranz, R. and Connelly, M. (2003) Chrysler alters product plans, *Automotive News*, 17 Mar (http://www.autonews.com/printStory.cms?articleId= 42919).

Kuhn, T. S. (1970) *The Structure of Scientific Revolutions*, Chicago: Chicago University Press.

Kumar, N. (1996) The power of trust in manufacturer–retailer relationships, *Harvard Business Review*, Nov–Dec: 92–106.

Lapidus, G. and Cuttler, J. (2003) Global automobiles and auto parts, in presentation to World Economic Forum, Davos, 30 Jan, Goldman Sachs Equity Research, New York.

Leonhardt, D. (1998) McDonald's: can it regain its golden touch?, *Business Week*, Mar 9: 44–49.

Levitt, T. (1983) *The Marketing Imagination*, New York: Free Press.

Levy, S. (2003) Mosaic – the idea that changed the world, *New Zealand Herald*, 17 Apr, C13.

Lipe, M. G. and Salterio, S. E. (2000) The balanced scorecard: judgmental effects of common and unique performance measures, *Accounting Review*, **75**(3), Jul: 283–298.

Lippman, S. A. and Rumelt, R. P. (1982) Uncertain imitability; an analysis of interfirm differences in efficiency under competition, *Bell Journal of Economics*, **13**(2): 418–438.

Lohr, S. (2003a) IBM says earnings to fall short of estimates, *New York Times*, 9 Apr (http://www.nytimes.com/2002/04/09/technology/ 09BLUE.html).

Lohr, S. (2003b) Profits up at IBM, *New York Times*, 15 Apr (http://www. nytimes.com/2002/04/15/technology/15PLAC.html).

Loomis, C. (1993) Dinosaurs?, *Fortune*, 3 May: 28–34.

Loomis, C. (2001) The 15 per cent delusion, *Fortune*, 5 Feb: 44–59.

Low, B. (1996) Long term relationships in industrial marketing, *Industrial Marketing Management*, **25**: 23–35.

Luciat-Labry, J., Rosenberg, J. H. and Wilsby, L. (2002) *A Full-Service Pit Stop* (http://www.mckinseyquarterly.com/article_page.asp?tk=317583: 1159:2&ar=1159&L2=2&L3=38).

Lynn, G. S., Monroe, J. G. and Paulson, A. S. (1996) Marketing and discontinous innovation: the probe and learn process, *California Management Review*, **28**(3): 8–37 (Spring).

Magretta, J. (2002) *What Management Is*, Free Press: New York.

Mahadevan, B. (2000) Business models for internet-based e-commerce, *California Management Review*, **42**(2) Summer: 55–69.

Malone, T. W. and Laubacher, R. J. (1998) The dawn of the e-lance economy, *Harvard Business Review*, Sep–Oct: 145–52.

Mandel, M. J. and Hof, R. D. (2001) Rethinking the internet (Special Report), *Business Week*, 26 Mar: 43–61.

Mapleston, P. (1993) World car highlights shifts in supplier relationships, *Modern Plastics International*, Oct: 46–49.

Marcolin, B. and Gaulin, B. (2001) Changing the e-commerce value chain: a modular approach, *Ivey Business Journal*, Jul–Aug: 23–28.

Mattsson, L-G. (1997) Relationship marketing and the markets-as-networks approach – a comparative analysis of two evolving streams of research, *Journal of Marketing Management*, **13**(5): 447–461.

McDonald, M. and Dunbar, I. (1998) *Market Segmentation: How To Do It, How To Profit From It,* Oxford: Palgrave.

McKenna, R. (1991) Marketing is everything, *Harvard Business Review*, Jan–Feb: 65–79.

McWhirter (1997) GM gets to hit the road, *Time*, 14 Apr: 44–48.

McWilliams, G. (1998) Power play, *Business Week*, 9 Feb: 34–41.

Mendonca, L. and McCallum, G. D. (1995) Battling for the wallet, *McKinsey Quarterly*, **2**: 76–92.

Merrilees, W. (2002) Interactivity design as the key to managing customer relations in e-commerce, *Journal of Relationship Marketing*, **1**(3/4): 111–125.

Miller, S. (1999) How GM's German unit went from prodigy to problem child, *Asian Wall Street Journal*, 27 Mar, N-6.

Millier, P. and Palmer, R. A. (2000) *Nuts, Bolts and Magetrons – A Practical Guide to Industrial Marketing*, Chichester: John Wiley.

Millman, G. J. (2000) Desperately seeking synergy, *Financial Executive*, Mar–Apr: 12–17.

Mintzberg, H. (1998) *The Strategy Safari: A Guided Tour Through the Wilds of Strategic Management,* Free Press.

Mitchell, R. (1986) How Ford hit the Bulls-Eye with Taurus, *Business Week*, 30 Jun: 47–48.

Moorman, C. and Rust, R. (1999) The role of marketing, *Journal of Marketing*, **63** (Special Edition): 180–197.

Morgan, R. M. and Hunt, S. D. (1994) The commitment-trust theory of relationship marketing, *Journal of Marketing*, **58**, Jul: 20–38.

Morris, M. H., Brunyee, J. and Page, M. (1998) Relationship marketing in practice, *Industrial Marketing Management*, 27: 359–371.

Morton M. S. ed. (1991) *The Corporation of the 1990s: Information Technology and Organizational Transformation*, New York: Oxford University Press.

Mullaney, T. J. (2003) The e-biz surprise, *Business Week*, 12 May.

Muller, J. (1999) Your turn, Mr Holden, *Business Week*, 6 Dec: 64, A2, A6.

Nevin, J. R. (1995) Relationship marketing and distribution Channels: Exploring Fundamental Issues, *Journal of the Academy of Marketing Science*, **23**(4): 327–334.

*New York Times* (2003) Intel issues warning on sales, 7 Mar (http://www.nytimes.com/2003/03/07/technology/07CHIP.html).

*New Zealand Herald* (1999) Internet changes the corporate landscape, Apr 21, E6.

*New Zealand Herald* (2003) Innovative Saab, 23 Apr, F1.

Nilsson, R. (1999) Perspectives-retailing: confronting the challenges that face bricks-and-mortar stores, *Harvard Business Review*, Jul–Aug: 166–168.

Normann, R. and Ramirez, R. (1993) From value chain to value constellation: designing interactive strategy, *Harvard Business Review*, Jul–Aug: 65–77.

Norris, F. and Sorkin A. R. (2001) Wall Street finds fault with computer merger, *New York Times*, 5 Sep (http://www.nytimes.com/2001/09/05/technology/05PLAC.html?).

O' Brien, T. L. (2003) P & G to acquire German hair-care concern for $5.8 billion, *New York Times*, 18 Mar (http://www.nytimes.com/2003/03/18/business/18CND-Proc.html).

Oliver, R. L. (1999) Whence consumer loyalty?, *Journal of Marketing* (Special Edition) **63**: 33–44.

Orlikowski, W. J. (2000) Using technology and constituting structures: a practice lens for studying technology in organizations, *Organizational Science*, **11**(4): 404–428.

Ostle, D. (2003) Opel set to take over Saab's sales operations in Europe, *Automotive News Europe*, 24 Mar (http:///europe.autonews.com/printStory.cms?articleId=52434).

Palmer, A. J. (1996) Relationship marketing: a universal paradigm or management fad, *The Learning Organisation*, **3**(3): 18–25.

Palmer, R. and Brookes, R. (2002) Incremental innovation: a case study analysis, *Journal of Database Marketing*, **10**(1): 71–83.

Palmer, R. A. (2001) A theoretical model of relationship marketing in market maturity, unpublished PhD thesis, Cranfield University, UK.

Palmer, R. A. and Pels, J. (2003) *Marketing Practice and Market Orientation: An Exploratory International Study*, forthcoming.

Pamatatau, R. (2000) Getting the world online, *NZ InfoTech Weekly*, 1 Oct: 13.

Parasuraman, A. (1997) Reflections of gaining competitive advantage through customer value, *Journal of the Academy of Marketing Science*, **25**(2): 154–161.

Park, A. (2003) Rick Wagoner's game plan, *Business Week*, 10 Feb: 44–50.

Payne, A. and Holt, S. (1999) A review of the 'value' literature and implications for relationship marketing, *Australasian Marketing Journal*, **7**(1), 41–51.

Pels, J., Brodie, R. J. and Johnston, W J. (2003) Benchmarking business to business marketing practices in emerging and developed economies: Argentina compared to the USA and New Zealand, *Journal of Business and Industrial Marketing*, forthcoming.

Pels, J., Coviello, N. and Brodie, R. (1999) Transactions versus relationships? The risk of missing the real issues, in McLoughlin, D. and Horan, C., *Proceedings of the 15th Annual IMP Conference*, University College, Dublin.

Pels, J., Coviello, N.and Brodie, R. (2000) Integrating transactional and relational marketing exchange: a pluralistic perspective, *Journal of Marketing Theory and Practice*, **8**(3): 11–20.

Pels. J. and Brodie, R. J. (2001) Profiling marketing practice in a transition economy: the Argentine case, in *Proceedings of the 30th EMAC Conference*, Bergen, Norway, May.

Peters, T. and Austin, N. (1985) *A Passion for Excellence*, 4, Collins: London.

Peterson, R. A., Balasubramanian, S. and Bronnenberg, B. J. (1997) Exploring the implications of the internet for consumer markets, *Journal of the Academy of Marketing Science*, **25**(4): 329–346.

Piercy, N. F. (1998a) *Market-Led Strategic Change*, Oxford: Butterworth Heinemann.

Piercy, N. F. (1998b) Marketing implementation, *Journal of the Academy of Marketing Science*, **26**(3): 222–236.

Pine, B. J., Rogers, M. and Dorf, B. (1999) Is your company ready for one-to-one marketing?, *Harvard Business Review*, Jan–Feb: 151–160.

Pine, B. J., Victor, B. and Boynton, A. C. (1993) Making mass customization work, *Harvard Business Review*, Sep–Oct: 108–119.

Polanyi, M. (1966) *The Tacit Dimension*, New York: Doubleday.

Poolton, J. and Barclay, I. (1998) New product development from past research to future applications, *Industrial Marketing Management*, **27**: 197–212.

Porretto, J. (2003) Car industry's top 10 trendsetters, *NZ Herald*, 22–23 Mar: F3.

Port, O. (1999) Customers move into the driver's seat, *Business Week*, 4 Oct: 58–60.

Porter, M. (1980) *Competitive Strategy*, New York: Free Press.

Porter, M. (1985) *Competitive Advantage: Creating and Sustaining Superior Performance*, New York: Free Press.

Porter, M. (1996) What is strategy?, *Harvard Business Review*, Nov–Dec: 61–78.

Porter, M. (2001). Strategy and the internet. *Harvard Business Review*, **79**(3): 63–78.

Porter, M. E. and Millar, V. E. (1985) How information gives you competitive advantage, *Harvard Business Review*, Jul–Aug: 149–160.

Prahalad, C. K. and Hamel, G. (1990) The core competencies of the corporation, *Harvard Business Review*, **68**(3): 79–91.

Prahalad, C. K. and Ramaswamy, V. (2000) Co-opting customer competence. *Harvard Business Review*, Jan–Feb: 79–87.

Puffer, S. M. (1999) Global executive: Intel's Andrew Grove on competitiveness, *Academy of Management Review*, **13**(1): 15–24.

Quinn, C. (1999) How leading-edge companies are marketing, selling, and fulfilling over the internet, *Journal of Interactive Marketing*, **13**(4): 39–50.

Quinn, C. (2001) How leading-edge companies are marketing, selling, and fulfilling over the internet, in *Internet Marketing: Readings and Online Resources*, ed. P. Richardson, 23–34, New York: McGraw-Hill Irwin.

Ramirez, R. (1999) Value co-production: intellectual origins and implications for practice and research, *Strategic Management Journal*, 20: 49–65.

Ranchhod, A., Gurau, C. and Hackney, R. (2000) Marketing and the internet: observations with the biotechnology sector, *International Journal of Physical Distribution and Logistics Management*, **30**(7–8).

Rayport, J. F. and Sviokla, J. J. (1995) Exploiting the virtual value chain, *Harvard Business Review*, Nov–Dec: 75–85.

Reichheld, F. F. (1996) *The Loyalty Effect: The Hidden Forces Behind Growth, Profits and Lasting Value*, Boston MA: Harvard Business School Press.

Reichheld, F. F. and Sasser, W. E. (1990) Zero defections: quality comes to services, *Harvard Business Review*, **67**(5): 105–111.

Reinartz, W. and Kumar, V. (2002) The mismanagement of customer loyalty, *Harvard Business Review*, Jul: 4–12.

Reuters (1999) Internet changes the corporate landscape, *New Zealand Herald*, 21 Apr, E6.

Revell, J. (2002) GM's slow leak, *Fortune*, 28 Oct: 59–65.

Rich, J.T. (1999) The growth imperative, *Journal of Business Strategy*, Mar–Apr: 27–31.

Rifkin, G. and Kurtzman, J. (2002) Is your e-business plan radical enough?, *MIT Sloan Management Review*, Spring: 91–95.

Rockart, J. (1988) The line takes leadership – IS management in a wired society, *Sloan Management Review*, Summer: 57–64.

Rodin, R. (1999) *Free, Perfect and Now*, New York: Simon and Schuster.

Roos, D. and Altshuler, A. (1984) *The Future of the Automobile: The Report of MIT's International Automobile Program*, London: George Allen and Unwin Inc.

Rossant, J (2003) Shoring up Suez, *Business Week*, European edition, 17 Mar: 26–27.

Rossiter, J. R. (2001) What is marketing knowledge?, *Marketing Theory*, **1**(1): 9–26.

Roth, D. (1998) New-media nightmare, *Fortune*, 22 Jun: 141–144.

Rothstein, E. (2001) The unforeseen disruption of moving ahead, *New York Times*, 22 Dec (www.nytimes.com/2001/12/22/arts/22TECH.html?)

Rucci, A. J., Kirn, S. P. and Quinn, R. T. (1998) The employee-customer-profit chain, *Harvard Business Review*, Jan–Feb: 82–97.

Rust, R. T. and Varki, S. (1996) Rising from the ashes of advertising, *Journal of Business Research*, **37**: 173–178.

Rust, R. T., Zahorik, A. J. and Keningham, T. T. (1996) *Service Marketing*, New York: Harper Collins.

Rust, R. T., Ziethaml, V. A. and Lemon, K. N. (2000) *Driving Customer Equity: How Customer Lifetime Value is Reshaping Corporate Strategy*, New York: Free Press.

Saren, M. J. and Tzokas, N. X. (1997) Some dangerous axioms of relationship marketing, *Fifth International Colloquium in Relationship Marketing*, Cranfield School of Management.

Saunders, C. and Chan, Y. E. (2002) Rapid-growth firms: the challenge of managing information technology, *Ivey Business Journal*, Jan–Feb: 63–67.

Sawhney, M. and Kaplan, S. (2000) B2B e-commerce hubs: towards a taxonomy of business models, *Harvard Business Review*, May–Jun.

Schefter, J. (1996) *All Corvettes Are Red*, New York: Simon and Schuster.

Schlender, B. (2002) Gates@Work, *Fortune*, 8 Jul: 56–68.

Schneider, B. and Bower, D. (1999) Understanding customer delight and outrage, *Sloan Management Review*, Fall: 35–45.

Schon, D. A. (1983) *The Reflective Practitioner*, New York: Basic Books.

Schonberger, R. J. (1982) *Japanese Manufacturing Techniques*, New York: Macmillan.

Schultz, D. E. (1996) The inevitability of integrated communications, *Journal of Business Research*, **37**: 139–146.

Scully, J. I. (1996) Machines made of words: the influence of engineering metaphor on marketing thought and practice, *Journal of Macromarketing*, Fall: 70–83.

Senge, P. M. and Carstedt, G. (2001) Innovating our way to the next industrial revolution, *MIT Sloan Management Review*, Winter: 24–38.

Shaw, R. (1998) *Improving Market Effectiveness*, London: Economist Books.

Shaw, R. and Stone, M. (1988) *Database Marketing*, Aldershot: Gower.

Sheth, J. N. (1995) Searching for a definition of relationship marketing, *Third International Colloquium in Relationship Marketing*, Melbourne.

Sheth, J. N., Gardner, D. M. and Garrett, D. E. (1988) *Marketing Theory: Evolution and Evaluation*, New York: Wiley.

Sheth, J. N. and Parvatiyar, A. (2000a) Relationship marketing in consumer markets, in Sheth and Parvatiyar (eds), *Handbook of Relationship Marketing*, Thousand Oaks, CA: Sage Publications.

Sheth, J. N. and Parvatiyar, A. (2000b) *Handbook of Relationship Marketing*, London: Sage Publications.

Sheth, J. N. and Sisodia, R. S. (1999) Revisiting marketing's generalizations, *Journal of Academy of Marketing Science*, **27**(1): 71–87.

Simison, R. and Blumenstein, R. (1997) Cadillac, Lincoln try to reclaim their status as kings of the road, *Asian Wall Street Journal*, Jul 4–5: 8.

Simon, H. (1957) *Models of Man*, New York: Wiley.

Simpson, B. (2003) A twist in the tale of GTO Tiger, *Automotive News/New Zealand Herald*, 16 Apr, G-28.

Slater, S. F. and Narver, J. C. (2000) Intelligence generation and superior customer value, *Journal of the Academy of Marketing Science*, **28**(1): 120–127.

Sloan, A. P. (1963) *My Years with General Motors*, London: Sidgwick and Jackson.

Sloane, A. (2002) Big and bold, *New Zealand Herald*, 20 Feb, F-1.

Snyder, J. (1985) GM's visionary: Roger Smith steers drive to market-oriented future, *Advertising Age*, 30 Dec, **1**: 28–29.

Sorkin, A. R. (2003) McDonald's said to weigh an arches-only strategy,

*New York Times*, 28 Mar (http://nyTimes.com/2003/03/28/business/28BURG.html).

Sorkin, A. R. and Norris, F. (2001) Hewlett-Packard to acquire Compaq in 25 billion deal, *New York Times*, 4 Sep (http://www.nytimes.com/2001/09/04/technology/04DEAL.html).

Srivastava, R. K., Shervani, T. A. and Fahey, L. (1998) Market-based assets and shareholder value: a framework of analysis, *Journal of Marketing*, **62** (Jan): 2–18.

Stewart, T. (1998) Packaging what you know, *Fortune*, 9 Nov: 121–122.

Stires, D. (2002). Fallen arches, *Fortune*, **145**(9): 74–76.

Storbacka, K., Strandvik, T. and Gronroos, C. (1994) Managing customer relationships for profit: the dynamics of relationship quality, *International Journal of Service Industry Management*, **5**(5): 21–38.

*Sunday Star–Times* (2003) Big Mac running out of burger fuel, 19 Jan, E5.

Taher, A., Leigh, T. W. and French, W. A. (1996) Augmented retail services: the lifetime value of affection, *Journal of Business Research*, **35**: 217–228.

Tapscott, D. and Caston, A. (1993) *Paradigm Shift: The New Promise of Information Technology*, New York: McGraw-Hill.

Tax, S. S., and Brown, S. W. (1998) Recovering and learning from service failure, *Sloan Management Review*, Fall: 75–87.

Taylor, A. (1994) The golden age of autos, *Fortune*, 4 Apr: 40–50.

Taylor, A. (1997) GM: drive to get into gear, *Fortune*, 28 Apr: 76–84.

Taylor, A. (2003) Just another sexy sports car?, *Fortune*, 17 Mar: 66–69.

Tedlow, R. S. (1990) *New and Improved: The Story of Mass Marketing in America*, New York: Basic Books.

Tetenbaum, T. (1999). Beating the odds of merger and acquisition failure: seven key practices that improve the chance for expected integration and synergies, *Organisational Dynamics*, **28**(2): 22–36.

Tierney, C. (2003) Audi, Volvo, Acura...Chrysler, *Business Week*, 14 Apr: 66–67.

Tierney, C., Karnitschnig, M. and Muller, J. (2000) Defiant Daimler, *Business Week*, 7 Aug: 25–29.

*Time* (1980) Detroit's uphill battle, 8 Sep: 56–62.

*Time* (1984a) Mr Smith shakes up Detroit, 16 Jan: 53.

*Time* (1984b) Manufacturing is in flower, 26 Mar: 48–50.

*Time* (1985) GM picks the winner, 5 Aug.

*Time* (1998) Ray Kroc: Burger Meister, 7 Dec: 107–108.

Treacy, M. and Wiersema, F. (1993) Customer intimacy and other value disciplines, *Harvard Business Review*, Jan–Feb: 84–93

Treacy, M. and Wiersema, F. (1995a) *The Discipline of Market Leaders*, London: Harper Collins.

Treacy, M. and Wiersema, F. (1995b) How market leaders keep their edge, *Fortune*, 16 Feb: 62–67.

Tynan, C. (1999) Metaphor, marketing and marriage, *Irish Marketing Review*, **12**(1): 17–26.

Unilever (2003) *Fourth Quarter and Annual Results 2002*, RNS no. 4321H, Unilever plc, 13 Feb.

Varey, R. J. (1985) A model of internal marketing for building and sustaining a competitive service advantage, *Journal of Marketing Management*, **11**: 41–54.

Venkatraman, N. (1994) IT-enabled business transformation: from automation to business scope redefinition, *Sloan Management Review*, Winter: 73–87.

Venkatraman, N. (2000) Five steps to a dot-com strategy: how to find your footing on the web, *Sloan Management Review*, Spring: 15–28.

Vlasic, B. (1996) Can Chrysler keep it up?, *Business Week*, 25 Nov, 56–61.

Vlasic, B. and Stertz, B. (2001) *Taken For a Ride: How Daimler-Benz Drove Off With Chrysler,* New York: Harper Business.

von Krogh, G. and Cusumano, M. (2001). Three strategies for managing fast growth, *Sloan Management Review*, **42**(2): 53–61.

Voyle, S. (2000) Unilever puts faith in brands and partnership with retailers, *Financial Times*, 10–11 Jun: 10.

Waller, D. (2001) *Wheels on Fire: The Amazing Inside Story of the DaimlerChrysler Merger,* London: Hodder and Stoughton.

*Wall Street Journal*, 2003, Two shampoos lather up for duel, 28 Jan, B7.

Ward, J. and Peppard, J. (2002) *Strategic Planning for Information Systems*, Wiley: New York.

Warner, F. (2003) Auto sales are down, punish the parts makers, *New York Times*, 16 Mar (http://www.nytimes.com/2003/03/16/automobiles/16DELP).

Waters, R. (1999) Introduction: time for new trade-offs, in *FT Guide to Digital Business*, ed. R. Walters, Autumn, 1–29, London: FT Publishing.

Waters, R. and Kehoe, L. (2002) Merger most horrid, *Financial Times*, 21 Mar: 12.

Weber, M. (1964) *The Theory of Social and Economic Organization*, New York: Free Press.

Webster, F. E. (1981) Top management's concerns about marketing: issues for the 1980s, *Journal of Marketing*, **45**, Summer: 9–16.

Webster, F. E. (1988) Comment by Frederick E. Webster, *Journal of Marketing,* **52**(4): 48–51.

Webster, F. E. (1992) The changing role of marketing competition, *Journal of Marketing*, **56**, Oct: 1–17.

Welch, D. (2001) GM picks up speed, *Business Week*, 18 Jun: 36–38.

Welch, D. (2003) Rick Wagoner's game plan, *Business Week*, 10 Feb: 44–50.

Wensley, R. (1995) A critical review of research in marketing, *British Journal of Management*, **6**, Dec: 63–82.

Whetten, D. A. (1989) What constitutes a theoretical contribution, *Academy of Management Review*, **14**(4), 490–495.

Whittington, R. and Whipp, R. (1992) Professional ideology and marketing implementation, *European Journal of Marketing*, **26**(1): 52–63.

Whitwell, G., Lukas, B. A. and Doyle, P. (2003) *Marketing Management: A Strategic Value-Based Approach,* Australia: John Wiley.

Wilkinson, I. (2002) Discussion: studying what practitioners believe (http://www.columbia.edu/~pbp1/elmar/d933.txt).

Wilson, A. (2002) Suppliers cite a failed, broken business model, *Automotive News*, 14 Jan (http://www.autonews.com/printStory.cms?articleId =37812).

Wilson, A. and Sherefkin, R. (2002) More tremors in store for a shaken industry, *Automotive News*, 21 Jan (http://www.autonews.com/printStory.cms?articleId=37890).

Winchester, S. (2002) *The Map That Changed the World*, Penguin Books: London.

Wind, J. and Mahajan, V. (2000) Digital marketing, *European Business Forum*, 1, Spring: 20–27.

Wolfe, M. (2002) Media mergers: the wave rolls on, *McKinsey Quarterly*, 2 (http://www.mckinseyquarterly.com/article_page.asp?tk=317583: 1173:17&ar=1173&L2=17&L3= 104).

Womack, J. P., Jones, D. T. and Roos, D. (1990) *The Machine that Changed the World,* New York: Rawson Associates.

Wootten, G. (2003). Channel conflict and high involvement internet purchases – a qualitative cross-cultural perspective of policing parallel importing, *Qualitative Market Research an International Journal*, **6**(1): 48–57.

Wright, C. and Sparks, L. (1999) Loyalty saturation in retailing: exploring the end of retail loyalty cards, *International Journal of Retail and Distribution Management*, **27**(10): 429–440.

Zaltman, J. (2000) Consumer researchers: take a hike!, *Journal of Consumer Research*, **26**, Mar: 423–428.

Zingales, L. (2000) In search of new foundations, *Journal of Finance*, LV, **4**, Aug: 1623–1653.